Twain's Brand

TWAIN'S BRAND

Humor in Contemporary American Culture

JUDITH YAROSS LEE

University Press of Mississippi / Jackson

www.upress.state.ms.us

The University Press of Mississippi is a member
of the Association of American University Presses.

Copyright © 2012 by University Press of Mississippi
All rights reserved
Manufactured in the United States of America

First printing 2012

∞

Library of Congress Cataloging-in-Publication Data
Lee, Judith Yaross, 1949–
Twain's brand : humor in contemporary American
culture / Judith Yaross Lee.
p. cm.
Includes bibliographical references and index.
ISBN 978-1-61703-643-9 (cloth : alk. paper) —
ISBN 978-1-61703-644-6 (ebook) 1. American wit
and humor—History and criticism. I. Title.
PS430.L44 2012
817.009—dc23   2012013004

British Library Cataloging-in-Publication Data available

To my family—small recompense
for their humor, love, and joy

Contents

ix   Acknowledgments

xiii   Abbreviations

3   **CHAPTER ONE**
Twain's Brand and the Modern Mood

27   **CHAPTER TWO**
Standing Up: The Self-Made Comedian

71   **CHAPTER THREE**
Humor and Empire

107   **CHAPTER FOUR**
Kid Stuff: The Vernacular Vision and the Visual Vernacular

159   **CHAPTER FIVE**
Comic Brands: More than Funny Business

181   Notes

195   Bibliography

215   Index

Acknowledgments

I have racked up a pile of debts while writing this book and can only begin to repay them here. My greatest gratitude is to my husband, Joseph W. Slade, whose kindness and generosity are exceeded only by his patience; without his examples of scholarship and ambition I might not have pursued my own. Our children, Marya, Joe, and Alison, remind me often how much I still have to learn about humor, while my parents, Lillian and Irving Yaross, still practicing their professions well into their eighties, provide ongoing lessons about the value of humor, family, and work.

Seetha Srinivasan, director emerita of the University Press of Mississippi, understood and encouraged this project from the start, made key recommendations along the way, and did me yet another favor in passing me on to Walter Biggins after her retirement—one of many editorial gifts she has bestowed since acquiring *Garrison Keillor: A Voice of America* so long ago. Anne Stascavage and Carol Cox brought their keen eyes to the manuscript. Colleagues in the Mark Twain Circle and the American Humor Studies Association have taught me most of what I know about Samuel Clemens, Mark Twain, and American humor through their scholarly work and fellowship, both models for the profession. Their attention to early versions of my arguments at conferences challenged me to improve them. Robert Hirst of the Mark Twain Papers and Project at the University of California's Bancroft Library in Berkeley provided copies of unpublished letters and other help, not to mention leading his colleagues to prepare their wonderful scholarly editions of Twain's works. Kevin Mac Donnell provided information on Twain-branded goods during a very early phase of the project and supplied beautiful images of Mark Twain's Scrap Book and associated marketing materials at the end. Mark Woodhouse, archivist for the Elmira College Mark Twain Collection, helped me understand what I found on the shelves in the library at Quarry Farm. An Cardoen of Belgium's Royal Museum for Central Africa promptly secured scans and permissions for letters in the Henry M. Stanley Archives.

Acknowledgments

I could not have finished *Twain's Brand* without research support in many forms from Ohio University. I am grateful for travel funds, sabbatical leave, and other research assistance received from Claudia Hale, Scott Titsworth, and Jerry Miller, directors of the School of Communication Studies, and to former dean Gregory Shepherd of the Scripps College of Communication for securing resources for faculty despite tough times. For the production of color plates, I owe special thanks to Eric Rothenbuhler and Jerry Miller for their help in securing grants from Scripps College Faculty Development Fund and the School of Communication Studies to supplement funds from the Faculty Research Support Program of the Office of Research and Sponsored Programs. Lindsey Rose, Jeffrey Kuznekoff, and Efraim Kotey provided excellent bibliographic assistance. Communication bibliographers Jessica Hagman and her predecessor Char Booth at Alden Library tracked down and purchased much-needed materials, while the librarians and staff of Alden's Document Delivery Service kept the pdfs and ILLs coming as fast as my requests. I appreciated being able to share work in progress at a 2010 English Department event organized by Langston Hughes Professor Amrijit Singh and department chair Marsha Dutton to commemorate the centennial of Clemens's death and to discuss *Connecticut Yankee* with students in the Honors Tutorial College reading group led by Dean Jeremy Webster.

Broad public interest in Mark Twain inspired me to write this book for general readers intrigued by humor as well as for scholars of American culture, and I hope that the final result bears evidence of what I learned from audiences at Ohio University, the University of Helsinki, the Center for Mark Twain Studies at Elmira College, the West Virginia Humanities Council, Davis and Elkins College, West Virginia Wesleyan University, and the Mark Twain House and Museum. I am particularly grateful to Barbara Snedecor and the Center for Mark Twain Studies at Elmira College for the privilege of spending several nights in 2009 at Quarry Farm, where the Clemenses summered with Livy's sister and her husband, and to Kerry Driscoll for the wonderful invitation to join her and Craig Hotchkiss of the Mark Twain House and Museum as faculty for their 2011 NEH Summer Teachers' Institute, Mark Twain and the Culture of Progress.

Portions of chapters 2 and 3 appeared in the *Mark Twain Annual* as "Mark Twain as a Stand-up Comedian" (2006) and "The International Twain and American Nationalist Humor: Vernacular Humor as a Post-Colonial Rhetoric" (2008). Portions of chapter 5 were published as "Communities of Comedy and Commerce: More than Funny Business" in *Communities and Connections: Writings in North American Studies*, edited by Ari Helo (Helsinki, Finland: Renvall Institute and University of Helsinki Press, 2007). Both James Caron, who read an early draft of chapter 2, and Sharon McCoy, who critiqued my analysis of *Huckleberry Finn*, gave me splendid advice, not all of which I took. Those are the parts that are wrong.

Abbreviations

Works by Mark Twain, other humor under discussion, and frequently referenced scholarship are cited parenthetically in the text with the abbreviations below. Brief citations to other works are given in the notes to each chapter. Full citations to all works are in the bibliography.

AMT	Twain, *Autobiography of Mark Twain*
AR	McGruder, *All the Rage*
B	McGruder, *The Boondocks*
CI	Twain, *Mark Twain, the Complete Interviews*
CR	Budd, *Mark Twain: The Contemporary Reviews*
CTS	Twain, *Collected Tales, Sketches, Speeches, & Essays*
CY	Twain, *A Connecticut Yankee in King Arthur's Court*
HF	Twain, *Adventures of Huckleberry Finn*
Galaxy	Twain, *Contributions to* The Galaxy
GAN	Roth, *The Great American Novel*
MSM	Twain, *Mysterious Stranger Manuscripts*
MTB	Paine, *Mark Twain, a Biography*
MTBE	Twain, *Mark Twain at the* Buffalo Express
MTD	Fears, *Mark Twain Day by Day*
MTE	Twain, *Mark Twain in Eruption*
MTEncy	LeMaster and Wilson, *Mark Twain Encyclopedia*
MTH	Frear, *Mark Twain and Hawaii*
MTHL	Twain and Howells, *Mark Twain–Howells Letters*
MTJB	Baetzhold, *Mark Twain and John Bull*
MTL	Twain, *Mark Twain's Letters*
MTLib	Gribben, *Mark Twain's Library*
MTLC	Fatout, *Mark Twain on the Lecture Circuit*
MTBM	Webster, *Mark Twain, Business Man*
MTS	Twain, *Mark Twain Speaking*

NJ	Twain, *Mark Twain's Notebooks & Journals*
OHD	Barry, *One! Hundred! Demons!*
PAA	Roth, *The Plot Against America*
PE	McGruder, *Public Enemy #2*
RBH	McGruder, *A Right to Be Hostile*

Twain's Brand

CHAPTER ONE

Twain's Brand and the Modern Mood

Mark Twain tops most lists of great American humorists, yet analyses of his significance treat American culture as if humor were barely part of it. Among many likely reasons for this oversight, including resistance to studying humor as too recreational for research, is the belief that Twain's humor belongs to a trivial nineteenth-century popular culture of dialect writing, hoaxes, and tall yarns, while his themes, especially race and politics, belong to the twentieth-century canon of belle lettres. *Twain's Brand* approaches Twain's humor and its legacy differently. Here I show that Samuel L. Clemens adapted nineteenth-century comic traditions to burgeoning twentieth-century cultural trends in ways that won popular and economic success in his own time, expressed modern views of self and society, and anticipated contemporary American humor and culture in many ways. That is, Mark Twain's comic capital remains productive and profitable today.

Consider humor in the contemporary American scene. Comedy clubs run coast to coast. Sitcoms dominate television syndication. Multiplexes screen documentary political satires along with romantic and slapstick comedies. Jokes circulate by e-mail and Twitter. Television ads highlight absurd situtations. A clown greets customers at McDonald's restaurants, while cartoon characters signify products from Michelin tires to Microsoft Word. Humor tinges public affairs, from politicians' appearances on late-night television to stand-up comedians Marc Maron and Al Franken's installation as hosts on the short-lived liberal answer to conservative talk radio, *Air America* (2004–2010), and

> When I first began to lecture, and in my earlier writings, my sole idea was to make comic capital out of everything I saw and heard.
> —**Samuel L. Clemens**
> to Archibald Henderson[1]

satiric TV pundit Stephen Colbert's flirtation with the 2012 Republican presidential primary. Among the many comic news outlets ranging from print to podcasts, the nightly current events satire *The Daily Show* (1996–) has become a major news source for young adults on cable TV's Comedy Central since the humor channel debuted on April Fool's Day, 1991.[2] Humor has also penetrated more hallowed corners of American culture. The arrival of "The Funny Pages" in the *New York Times*'s magazine on September 18, 2005, signaled that the medium of comics had finally won respect—at least in the intellectually ambitious genre of the graphic novel, of which Art Spiegelman's Holocaust narrative *Maus* (1986) remains the breakthrough example; the mass genre of "the funnies" is still banned from the *Times*, which abandoned the experiment in 2009. More telling, novelist Philip Roth, once ostracized for the exhuberant sexual humor of *Portnoy's Complaint* (1969), now holds American hopes for the Nobel Prize in Literature.

The present explosion of humor reminds us what underlies Mark Twain's: humor is more than a playful mode for apprehending the world and expressing oneself in it. Through its orientation toward an audience, toward an intended effect, and toward a specific attitude or viewpoint, humor reveals itself as a comic rhetoric that articulates cultural politics. Indeed, despite its marginal status in recent scholarship, American humor has been understood as an index to the culture at least since 1838, when a British critic found inklings of cultural independence in the humor of Jack Downing and Davy Crockett. The critic's rationale remains useful despite his outmoded conception of humor as "the collective mind of the nation": a nation's humor is its "institutions, laws, customs, manners, habits, characters, convictions,—their scenery whether of the sea, the city, or the hills,—expressed in the language of the ludicrous."[3] Such a view recognizes ideology and the state as well as physical environment, social practices, and beliefs as forces shaping people's lives. Experiences and minds vary a great deal among American residents and sojourners of different eras, sexes, and ethnic, racial, economic, regional backgrounds (and among individuals within those categories), yet still we all share—if only contrapuntally, to use Edward Said's term for the distinct, often reciprocal effects felt by various social groups[4]—the public culture of national politics and mass media. In fact, popular print media helped construct the modern nation-state in post-Gutenberg Europe, as Benedict Anderson showed in *Imagined Communities*. Today American mass media likewise help constitute our national culture at home and abroad, with humor playing a special role. Television, for example, structures daily life in the homes where its programs are consumed as well as in the federal politics that seek to influence its messages even as politicians and policies themselves reflect media practices, audiences, and corporate sponsors. International trade extends mediated images and expressions of U.S. culture around the world, where audiences receive them with varying degrees of approval. Receive them they do, especially in comic form: box-office receipts show that comedy outpaces all other genres of film.[5] But humor complicates this rhetorical process. While humor can emerge unintentionally at an object's expense, as in the classic case when someone slips on a banana peel with no harm except to the ego, humor in popular culture is a rhetorical mode defined when audiences certify attempts to elicit ridicule, incongruity, or other comic amusement. Humor succeeds across media of all types from television and the Internet to newspaper comics and the novel when audiences validate those attempts through their own enjoyment.

As a rhetorical process, humor draws on intellect and social knowledge to translate social life into the language of the ludicrous, which varies like other languages from culture to culture and place to place. What counts as funny gets shaped by culture, especially in the ideologies behind what we call common sense, in much the same way that native speakers acquire their mother tongue: through trial and error early in life, when some sounds are affirmed and others dismissed (and may not be even pronounceable years later). Humorists and audiences collaborate in choosing what counts as ludicrous—that is, playful and amusing. On this point, if on nothing else, theorists both familiar and lesser known agree: Aristotle, Sigmund Freud, George Herbert Mead, Kenneth Burke, Johan Huizinga, Mikhail Bakhtin among the household names, Elliot Oring, Victor Raskin, and Simon Critchley among the specialists.[6] Tacitly the humorist and audience collude to suspend social rules for the shared thrill of violating them, if only symbolically through language, visual art, or other mode of representation, such as dress or mime—as in the hilarious travesties of classical dance, including *Swan Lake*, by the transvestite troupe Les Ballets Trockadero de Monte Carlo—even as the transgressions of joking implicitly reassert the very cultural codes that the humor rejects. And we recognize the translation of life to the ludicrous in a cognitive operation increasingly confirmed by neuroscience as what Nancy Walker called the capacity to "perceive irony and incongruity, . . . [and] hold two contradictory realities in suspension simultaneously."[7]

Yet humor operates covertly. That's why explaining a joke destroys its humor and why humor studies struggle for scholarly recognition: society protects the pleasures and subversions of humor by insisting that jokes don't matter. That's also why Mark Twain warned that "humor must not professedly teach, and it must not professedly preach." He saw that humorist and audience can enjoy humor's transgressive pleasures only by treating humor as play, as symbolic rather than instrumental activity. But when he added that "it must do both if it would live forever" and then defined *forever* as thirty years, he stressed the immediate social relevance of comic play (*MTE* 202). In that sense, whether ridiculous or sublime, American humor reveals the state of the nation.

Twain's Brand explores how, in ways that Mark Twain anticipated, contemporary humor encapsulates American culture today, especially elements related to our postindustrial economy based on global trade in electronic and print media, performances, and other forms of intellectual property. Of the many links among comedy, commerce, and culture, two stand out. First of all, humor can be understood, like all interpersonal communication, as an economic transaction in which the customer is always right. The humorist exchanges a comic gambit (an idea or representation in a joke, cartoon, or other form, including play with the rules or codes of language) with an audience whose laughter, applause, or other symbolic response specifies what's funny, how funny it is, and what's not funny at all. Second, the capitalism underlying American popular culture explicitly makes the humor audience a real rather than metaphorical customer and a commodity in its own right. That is, in today's marketing-driven economy, customers are not only an audience who purchase entertainment, often via mass media, but also a demographic commodity for sale to advertisers. For their part, advertisers aim for the audience of readers, viewers, and consumers to identify as a community and vote as a bloc—always with dollars, sometimes also with ballots. The language of the ludicrous inflects contemporary American culture from entertainment to business and politics as a result, because the postindustrial, information economy of today trades in ideas, attitudes, and audiences—the stuff of humor—instead of goods. As manner becomes matter, humor becomes the ideal commodity to be marketed and sold as a brand.

America acquired its most iconic comic brand, Mark Twain, because Samuel Clemens understood and exploited the new information economy as it emerged after the Civil War. America's transition from an industrial base of manufacturing to an information base of mass media, digital communications, and professional knowledge just recently reached maturity, but the process began in Twain's day, when allied industries such as public relations and advertising also acquired their modern forms.

Mark Twain's role in this process reflects an ability to seize the opportunities of his time. Mythologizing has made Twain a nineteenth-century icon, but the life of Samuel Clemens straddled two centuries, and his humor bridges their world views. Clemens was born in Florida, Missouri, in 1835, a time just two generations removed from the American Revolution and fourteen years after Missouri joined the union as a slave state; in 1839, when the family moved thirty miles to Hannibal, just across the Mississippi River from Quincy, Illinois, the area was still considered the West. Thus he grew up poised not only between the cultural forces of East and West, but also between the ideals of North and South—a position shaping his sense of comic incongruity as born of cultural contrasts. Clemens died in 1910, after American capitalism, communication, and consumerism had taken their modern forms, the Spanish-American War had placed the U.S. among the world's international powers, and imperialism set Europe on its course toward World War I.

The rhetoric, themes, and techniques of his humor pulsed to the beat of his changing world. His early fiction and platform lectures burlesqued conventional religious tracts, children's fables, and journalistic genres; the writing and performances of his middle years satirized America's struggles with racism, sectionalism, and romanticism; his late work—consistently modernist in its moral relativism and much of it too politically incorrect to be published in its day—blasts industrialization, imperialism, greed, and the entire human race, often in terms more despairing than in his letter to William Dean Howells on May 12–13, 1899: "Damn these human beings; if I had invented them I would go hide my head in a bag" (*MTHL*, 2:695).[8] Indeed, Twain's brand of humor increasingly reflected modern ideas and values as its nineteenth-century forms and settings acquired distinctly discordant, modern themes. The ironies of the so-called "evasion sequence" at the end of *Adventures of Huckleberry Finn*, for instance, inject post-Reconstruction despair into antebellum burlesque. More directly, the scathing sarcasm of his "Salutation-Speech from the Nineteenth Century to the Twentieth," published in the New York *Herald* December 30, 1900, sees the new era as cause for lament: "the stately matron named Christendom" has returned "bedraggled, besmirched, and dishonored from pirate-raids in Kia-Chow, Manchuria, South Africa, and the Philippines, her mouth full of pious hypocrisies" (*CTS* 2:456).

In fact, the years from 1875 to 1910, when the U.S. entered the world stage as a modern industrial nation with a burgeoning postindustrial information economy of publishing, electronic communication, advertising, and publicity, coincide with the years of Twain's most mature writing. His major novels begin with *The Adventures of Tom Sawyer* (1876) and *Adventures of Huckleberry Finn* (1884) and end with *A Connecticut Yankee in King Arthur's Court* (1889) and *The Tragedy of Pudd'nhead Wilson* (1894). Short works that speak profoundly to modern concerns, such as "What Is Man?" (1906), also date from this period. From 1897 to 1908 he worked on *The Mysterious Stranger* manuscripts, left unfinished along with other provocative late works at his death in 1910. By that year, as William Leach has described in *Land of Desire* (1993), American culture had abandoned a Calvinist spirit of work, sin, self-denial, and hope and reorganized aesthetically, socially, and politically around an economy based on "self- indulgence, self-gratification, and self-pleasure" through the consumption of mass-marketed goods and entertainments.[9] These developments remain significant today, when services have displaced goods as 55 percent of U.S. GDP, while advertising, publicity, and mass media alone total more than $1 trillion annually, nearly 30 percent that of manufacturing.[10] But a century ago, when these trends formed the backdrop for Thorstein Veblen's attack on conspicuous consumption in *The Theory of the Leisure Class* (1899), Twain had already sided with the masses. In "Edward Mills and George Benton: A Tale" (1880) he lampooned the virtues of self-denial. He brought a more rueful tone to humor about money following his mortifying bankruptcy amid the recession of 1893, with ironic explorations of "clean, imaginary cash" in "The $30,000 Bequest" (1904). Yet Clemens managed to leave his daughter an estate of more than $600,000 in 1910 ($14.2 million in 2011 dollars), despite setbacks and lavish spending,[11] because he understood how to exploit Mark Twain as a brand-name commodity of the information economy.

Clemens fed the expanding American media environment as a printer, journalist, literary author, performer, publisher, copyright owner, and celebrity. Newspapers more than tripled in number during his career, rising from 5,871 to 20,806 between 1870 and 1900 and to 22,603 in 1909; magazines grew even more dramatically.[12] He graduated from printer's apprentice to "unsanctified newspaper reporter" and popular author in time to feed these widening outlets.[13] With apparent prescience he began a monthly magazine column in 1868 and purchased a one-third interest in a newspaper in 1869 (*Galaxy*, *MTBE*). Periodicals flourished in part from advertising, which increased tenfold from 1867 to 1900 to become a $500 million business,[14] and Mark Twain participated in the new journalism as a subject of newspaper and magazine items as well as a writer of them. Advertising, fueled by post–Civil War booms in population and manufacturing, got an additional boost in 1870 from America's first trademark legislation, which in turn spurred brand-name marketing: the number of brand names and trademarks registered with the U.S. patent office swelled tenfold between 1871 and 1875 (from 121 to 1,138) and another tenfold following legislation in 1881 and 1883, yielding more than 10,000 registered trademarks by 1906[15]—the year in which Mark Twain adopted the white suit as his icon. (He declared the suit "the uniform of the American Association of Purity and Perfection, of which I am president, secretary and treasurer, and the only man in the United States eligible to membership."[16]) From 1884 to 1894 Clemens contributed to a national explosion in book publishing as the owner of Charles L. Webster and Company, which brought out *Huckleberry Finn*, Ulysses S. Grant's *Personal Memoirs* (1885–86), and *The Library of American Literature* (11 vols., 1889–91), among other works: the number of titles in the U.S. more than doubled between 1880 and 1890, then tripled by 1910, the year he died.[17] By that time many hundreds of newspaper and magazine items had reported his writings, remarks, and doings.

His career was spurred by major advancements in communication technology, including the typewriter and Linotype if not his beloved Paige Compositor. His experiments with new illustration technologies, in particular, as Bruce Michelson details in *Printer's Devil*, imbued narratives from *A Tramp Abroad* (1880) to *King Leopold's Soliloquy* (1905) with a modern complexity of media and standpoints. Such protomodernism is less surprising when we remember that Clemens saw the paradigm-shifting developments of modern science, intellectual displacements that validated social, psychological, and aesthetic relativism through such landmarks as Darwin's groundbreaking *On the Origin of Species* (1859), William James's *Principles of Psychology* (1890), Sigmund Freud's *Interpretation of Dreams* (1899), and the equations by which James Clerk Maxwell set forth the electromagnetic theory of electric waves and light (1855) and Albert Einstein established the relativity of time and space (1905). More prosaically, also in place in the U.S. by Clemens's death in 1910 were the more familiar electronic elements of today's information economy: the transatlantic telegraph network (1866), telephone (1876), radio (the "wireless telegraphy" of American Marconi, 1899, before voice and music broadcasting, 1906), and the Hollerith punch card calculation system (forerunner of programmable computers, devised for the 1890 census). The nineteenth century invented modern information technology, though its full cultural and economic impact took decades to mature into postindustrialism.

Brands and brand names drive the information economy worldwide. Brands serve three distinct but interrelated information functions:

denotation, to name a good or service; *differentiation*, to distinguish one from another; and *connotation*, to symbolize a set of associated ideas.[18] When durable goods take a backseat to the less tangible postindustrial commodities of media (information) and services (know-how), brands become crucial to denote, differentiate, and symbolize commodities. In fact, rhetoric itself becomes the product of the information economy as brands supply literal and metaphorical meaning for economic transactions by differentiating one brand from another.

This trend explains the recent rise in the value of organizations' so-called "brand equity." Material assets accounted for less than 30 percent of the total market value of top publicly traded companies in 2002, down from 60 percent in the late 1980s; the value of the brand name accounted for the rest.[19] As intangible but not immeasurable assets, brands have become so important that nonprofit philanthropic and educational organizations, athletes, and performers have joined the widget-makers in branding themselves.[20] In this way brands have moved beyond their original function to designate goods; now brands identify and even create communities of consumption and ideology. British branding consultant Steve Hilton put it this way: "Brands promote social cohesion, both nationally and globally, by enabling shared participation in aspirational and democratic narratives."[21]

Samuel Clemens seized upon branding along with the more tangible opportunities of this new, postindustrial capitalism. He drew on recent legislation in a November 1882 lawsuit claiming that a pirated edition of *Sketches New and Old* violated his exclusive right to use *Mark Twain* as a trademark. The judge in *Clemens v. Belford, Clarke Company* rejected this attempt to close loopholes in American copyright laws, which put uncopyrighted newspaper stories in the public domain while trademarks could be renewed forever, in a decision holding that "[t]rade marks only protect vendible merchandise, and can not be applied to or protect literary property."[22] But Clemens continued to conflate the two, establishing *Mark Twain* as a brand name commodity through mutually reinforcing comic journalism, performances, authorship, and entrepreneurship. (For evidence of his de facto success, note that some scholars cite *Mark Twain* as a trademark, despite the lawsuit's failure.)[23] Indeed, his creation of the Mark Twain Company to manage his copyrights in 1908 merely formalized the branding process that had united his pseudonymous writings, comic persona, and physical body for more than forty years. Friends already called him "Mark" as well as "Sam" when he became a comic performer in 1866, three years after adopting *Mark Twain* as his pen name

FIGURE 1 The absence of the name *Mark Twain* from this 1872 image testifies to his international stature as the embodiment of American humor. Pirated editions of his work sold so well that he traveled to England to arrange an authorized publication of *Roughing It*. (Etching by Frederick Waddy. "American Humour," *Once a Week* [London] n.s., 10 [14 December 1872]: 519.)

for the Virginia City, Nevada, *Territorial Enterprise*, in a letter published February 3, 1863.

Throughout his lifetime Clemens treated Mark Twain as a comic commodity to be marketed through modern media buzz. He exploited the links between publicity and profit and the synergy among various media as early as the summer of 1868, when he promoted an upcoming lecture by inventing scandals about himself and planting the hoax in San Francisco newspapers (*MTS*, 25). Like P. T. Barnum, whose appetite for publicity he burlesqued in "Barnum's First Speech in Congress" (1867), Mark Twain used newspaper humor to promote lectures, performances to subsidize book writing (*Innocents Abroad, Roughing It, Following the Equator*), books to sell magazine pieces, and fiction to supply lecture material. The process eventually moved from the stage to less overtly performative venues—including literary narration as well as after-dinner and occasional speaking—but it continued to trade, in the literal commercial sense, on Mark Twain's celebrity.

Twain's brand had already achieved such international recognition by December 14, 1872, when a caricature in the London periodical *Once a Week* depicted Samuel Clemens (who had visited England August 31–November 12 of that year) astride a frog leaping over a hedge[24] (figure 1). The image, labeled "AMERICAN HUMOUR," characterizes Mark Twain as the quintessential American and the embodiment of American humor, not simply the author of the "Jumping Frog" tale. The news item accompanying the cartoon likewise emphasized Twain's Americanness even though the artist dressed him like a British rider and imagined a tidy hedge for a frontier obstacle. "California has developed a literature of its own, and its proudest boast is the possession of Mark Twain," the author explained near the beginning of the article. His praise for "the peculiar humour invented by our American cousins" mixed imperial condescension with Anglo-American kinship amid promises of "a hearty welcome whenever he revisits the Old Country." Yet this early commentator did not hesitate to proclaim: "Mark Twain is altogether the best living exponent of American humour."[25] In commercial terms, Twain's significance as a humorist traded on his Americanness.

The image of an American writer in a British periodical highlighted in its own way the global dimensions of the growing information economy in the 1870s. Even in this early stage, international media trade had spawned at least seven pirated British editions of Twain's works (*MTJB*, 4–5), which (not at all coincidentally) added to his transatlantic honor and fame. In fact, the author of the *Once a Week* article accompanying the caricature seemed to know Twain's writing primarily through such pirated editions as John Camden Hotten's *Innocents Abroad* (2 vols., 1870), *Eye Openers* (1871), and *Screamers* (1871). Royalties lost from piracy had led Clemens earlier in 1872 to authorize a British edition of his newly published *Roughing It* by Routledge and Sons, who themselves had pirated *The Celebrated Jumping Frog* (1867) and *Burlesque Autobiography* (1871), as Howard Baetzhold has detailed (*MTJB*, 4–5). The deal had prompted the London visit and occasioned what Clemens described to his wife as a "blast at Hotten" in the September 21, 1872, London *Spectator* (*MTL* 5:169). There he asked the public to grant him the preference that the copyright laws did not:

My books are bad enough just as they are written; then what must they be after Mr. John Camden Hotten has composed half-a-dozen chapters & added the same to them? . . . . & then, on the strength of having evolved these marvels from his own consciousness, go & "copyright" the entire book, & put in the title-page a picture of a man with his hand in another man's pocket, & the legend "All Rights Reserved." (I only *suppose* the picture; still it would be a rather neat thing.)

. . . Mr. Hotten prints unrevised, uncorrected, & in some respects, spurious books, with my name to them as author, & thus embitters his customers against one of the most innocent of men. Messrs. George Routledge & Sons are the only English publishers who pay me any copyright, & therefore, if my books are to disseminate either suffering or crime among readers of our language, I would ever so much rather they did it through that house, & then I could contemplate the spectacle calmly as the dividends came in. (*MTL* 5:163-64)[26]

While these remarks anticipate his later crusade to tighten copyright protection, they also show that he saw his books as commodities in an economy that runs on intellectual property and brand image. He displaces outrage at piracy with jokes about branding: he imagines Hotten's colophon (a printer's trademark) as an image of a pickpocket, identifies the counterfeit product as dangerous, and declares its "customers" (not himself or his publisher) as Hotten's chief victims. He contrasts this caricature with the genuine article, the dignified businessman and brand-name product identified at the end of the letter, signed "Samuel L. Clemens ('Mark Twain')" (*MTL* 5:164). He clearly understood, along with Hotten and the Routledges, the significance and value of Twain's brand.

By depicting the American writer in English riding gear and the frog leaping a tidy English hedge, the *Once a Week* caricature also points to international exchange as a major theme, not just a backdrop, for Clemens's career. His writings and lectures imported people, places, and incidents from the Sandwich Islands (now Hawaii), Europe, and the Holy Land into the U.S. for audiences' pleasure. His 1872 visit to London reversed the process. Even as he sought material for a new book on England (replacing earlier plans to write about Cuba [*MTJB*, 3]), his presence, his speeches, and his writing exported the U.S—in the language of the ludicrous—back to England and from there to Australia, India, and other colonies around the world through exports of British journalism. Invidious cross-cultural

FIGURE 2 This image of Matthew Arnold faced an item declaring him "the great apostle to the Philistines of this later age" (320), showing the status that Mark Twain had reached in English cultural circles when his caricature ran two months later in the same weekly magazine. (Etching by Frederick Waddy. "Sweetness and Light," *Once a Week* [London] n.s., 10 [12 October 1872]: 321.)

contrasts nonetheless constituted a major comic trope of Twain's writings. Characterizations, dialects, plots, and other devices tweaked non-Americans (especially of high rank) as socially and morally inferior to their American counterparts not only in travel books such as *Innocents Abroad*, *Roughing It*, and *Following the Equator* (1897), but also in political fantasies such as *The Prince and the Pauper* (1882) and *Connecticut Yankee*, and in social novels such as *Huckleberry Finn* and *Pudd'nhead Wilson*. Mark Twain's humor and characters emerged in the same transatlantic context of pro-American difference that Waddy highlights from a British

SAMUEL LANGHORNE CLEMENS ("MARK TWAIN")   CHARLES GODFREY LELAND ("HANS BREITMANN")

FIGURE 3 The unsigned illustrations for "Two American Humorists," which appeared while Clemens visited England, indicate not only Britons' interest in Mark Twain and his peers, but also editors' desire to capitalize on the writers' popularity with their portraits. ("Two American Humorists," *Graphic* [London], 5 October 1872: 324.)

perspective with his image of Twain on frog-back: the American rider's incongruous mount ridicules his social savvy and, in light of the caption, his country.

Frederick Waddy specialized in irreverent caricatures of England's most notable figures for *Once a Week*. During Clemens's visit, Waddy depicted Matthew Arnold as a trapeze artist swinging from poetry to philosophy for an essay celebrating "the great apostle to the Philistines of this later age,"[27] so "American Humour" put Twain in high company (figure 2). More to the point, it also summed up Twain's brand, made his face increasingly recognizable on the international scene, and shows that editors found his reputation sufficiently marketable to warrant the expense of commissioning an image. In fact, a dignified quarter-page portrait appeared on October 5, midway through his visit, in a kindred periodical, the London *Graphic*, to illustrate an article less than half that size, "Two American Humorists—Hans Breitmann and Mark Twain" (figure 3).[28] But it could not compete in marketing value with Waddy's caricature, as an astute publicist saw. A few weeks after it ran in *Once a Week*, the image reappeared in an advertising poster for Twain's February 3, 1873, Brooklyn Academy of Music performance (*MTH*, 189, 173). Neither the English publication nor the Brooklyn reprint identified the figure as Mark Twain;

that his face and the frog were enough to identify him testifies to his brand recognition a dozen years before the publication of *Huckleberry Finn*.

Always Clemens sought to control the brand's identity. His complaint about Hotten's piracy in the 1872 London *Spectator* also gave him a platform to disclaim responsibility for five tales that critics had scorned. By 1880, he was bragging about his media savvy to his brother Orion. Sam confessed, "*I* take precaution against unnecessary publicity"—already defined as any interference with his ability to make a profit, such as verbatim newspaper reports of his lectures. And he boasted in 1887, "I have never yet allowed an interviewer or biography-sketcher to get out of me any circumstance of my history which I thought might be worth putting some day into my *auto*biography" (*MTBM*, 145–46, 389). (The surprising success of the first volume of his uncensored autobiography, with more than three hundred thousand copies rushed into print within weeks of its publication in 2010, validated this strategy.[29]) Similarly, he kept the name *Mark Twain* off writings that he considered inconsistent with his reputation as a humorist, such as the *Personal Recollections of Joan of Arc* serialized anonymously in *Harper's Magazine* (1895–96). And he protected both the social and commodity values of his brand name when he quietly transferred all real and intellectual property to his wife in 1894 before declaring his publishing house bankrupt and promising to pay all its debts with the worldwide tour that became *Following the Equator*.

With modern self-reflexivity, he used media as a topic as well as a tool. He lampooned the human interest news report and celebrity interview, two novelty journalistic genres of the post–Civil War period, most notably in "An Encounter with an Interviewer" (1874), while also exploiting them as publicity agents. Eventually, his more than three hundred interviews between 1879 and 1910 amounted to "more than any other human being except perhaps—but only perhaps—for a few statesmen or politicians," according to Louis J. Budd.[30] The earliest, "Mark Twain as a Pedestrian" and "Mark Twain: His Recent Walking Feat" (both 14 Nov. 1874) covered for the *Boston Evening Journal* and *Hartford Times*, respectively, what Daniel Boorstin in *The Image* termed a pseudoevent, an incident created for the purpose of attracting media reports. Clemens and his friend Joseph Twichell had planned to walk the hundred miles from Hartford to Boston, but gave up and took a train after about thirty-five miles in order to be on time for a dinner with *Atlantic* editor William Dean Howells. The Hartford story carried a verbatim transcript of the reporter's conversation with Clemens, who performed a little deadpan humor in denying that they had given up: "I didn't feel fatigued, and I had no desire to go to bed, but I had a pain through my left knee which interrupted my conversation with lockjaw every now and then" (*CI*, 3). The two interviews coincided with his debut in the distinguished *Atlantic* monthly magazine, which published "A True Story, Repeated Word for Word as I Heard It" in the November issue, as well as the successful New York City run of his play *Colonel Sellers*, thereby bringing him (by design?) to the attention of people who would not read "A True Story" or attend the theater. In this way, this early media coverage also certified Twain as a celebrity, a status conferred by mass media and famously defined by Boorstin as being "known for . . . well-knownness."[31] Clemens traded further on that publicity when he toured with George Washington Cable as the "Twins of Genius" for the 1884–85 lecture season with an eye to earning lecture fees and selling books, especially the newly published *Huckleberry Finn*, from which he read on stage. But pure pseudoevents burnished his fame throughout his career, as when his publisher, Harper and Brothers, sponsored his famous seventieth birthday dinner celebration at Delmonico's restaurant in 1905, then duly covered all the festivities, including toasts and speeches, in a special supplement to *Harper's Weekly*.[32]

Clemens's insights about marketing as a feature of modern life found their way into his writing as Mark Twain. One of the funniest moments in *A Connecticut Yankee in King Arthur's Court*, best known for its ambivalence about modern technology, gave marketing an international spin, as well. At a time when Pears' Soap was one of just four national brands other than patent medicines,[33] Twain parodied its marketing campaign by having protagonist Hank Morgan outfit wandering knights in sandwich boards to advertise the similarly named Persimmons Soap. The joke, enhanced by three illustrations that the author commissioned and chose, hinges on Hank's proclaimed "wholesome purposes in view toward the civilizing and uplifting" (*CY*, 190) of Arthurian Britain, to be achieved partly through promotion of regular bathing throughout the population but mostly (and more seriously) through commercial subversion and control of culture. Mocking an 1884 Pears' ad in which Henry Ward Beecher proclaimed, "If Cleanliness is next to Godliness, then Soap mst be considered as a Means of Grace," the climax of the joke conveys ambivalence about equating technical and moral progress: when a knight died after a bath, Hank changed the marketing slogan from the class-conscious "All the Prime-Donne Use It" to the religion-themed "Patronized by the Elect" (184–85, 188, figure 4). But the double entendre underlying the joke implies that Twain saw marketing's adaptability to new circumstances as

"THIS WOULD UNDERMINE THE CHURCH."

FIGURE 4 Jokes about Persimmons Soap in *A Connecticut Yankee in King Arthur's Court* show Mark Twain's interest in the new business of marketing and his ambivalence toward its rhetoric. (Illustrations by Daniel Beard, *CY*, 184–185.)

both its strength and its flaw. Only rhetoric committed to insincerity can so easily shift strategies.

Twain's response to the technical and economic changes of the 1880s also highlights his choice to set his major writings of the period in earlier days: *Huckleberry Finn* and *Pudd'nhead Wilson* in the antebellum era, *Connecticut Yankee*, *Joan of Arc*, and *The Mysterious Stranger* in the European Middle Ages, and *Extracts from Adam's Diary* and *Eve's Diary* in biblical times. Whatever its psychological significance, his choice of older settings seems canny as a marketing decision, given the nostalgia then feeding the local color movement and boy books, as does his decision not to publish his most avant-garde writing (such as the gender-bending "Wapping Alice" [comp. 1877–1907, pub. 1981]) while he lived.

Even as his imagination reached backward, however, his business practices looked ahead. As Louis Budd observed, Clemens treated Mark Twain "as a logo—a brand name, even—rather than a pen name" because he saw writing as a commercial project.[34] Over the years he attached the logo to "Mark Twain's Patent Scrap Book," which sold 26,310 copies by 1877 (*MTL* 5:145), and other products. He vigorously protected his copyrights by filing them first on British soil. He advocated for improved copyright protections for American authors for more than thirty years, as Siva Vaidhyanathan explains in *Copyrights and Copywrongs*,[35] and exploited his brand recognition as a celebrity humorist to do so. But he was not joking in December of 1881 when he told a Canadian audience (and, by extension the readers of his reprinted remarks in the Hartford *Courant* and *New York Times*) that "literary property . . . [should] be as sacred as whiskey":

> [I]f you steal another man's label to advertise your own brand of whiskey with, you will be heavily fined and otherwise punished for violating that trademark; if you steal the whiskey without the trademark, you go to jail; but if you could prove that the whiskey was literature, you can steal them both, and the law wouldn't say a word. It grieves me to think how far more profound and reverent a respect the law would have for literature if a body could only get drunk on it.[36]

He had gone to Canada to secure a British commonwealth copyright for *The Prince and the Pauper*, and his comments became part of a lifelong campaign to strengthen international copyright protection. But these efforts expose a modern understanding of the information economy along with personal economic interests. By insisting on the commodity value of his work, Twain led what Loren Glass calls "a fundamental transformation . . . in our basic understanding of literary property."[37] Indeed, Clemens called the lyceum performer himself "a piece of lecturing property."[38] And as Alan Gribben has pointed out, Twain claimed property value for his very life story, as well. One reason for his commercial orientation to authorship, Gribben has proposed, is that early jobs accustomed him to payment by the piece: by the em, as a printer; the voyage, as a river pilot; the ounce, as a miner; the column, as a journalist; the performance, as a lecturer.[39] But Clemens's claims of trademark status also have broader significance. All kidding aside, his equation of label, whiskey, and literature shows how well he understood that the emerging information economy trades more in intellectual property (copyrights and patents) and human knowledge (including comic skill and media know-how) than in goods (paper and ink). And he displayed this understanding in the multiple purposes of his Canadian visit, a combination of performance, copyright protection, and political advocacy that also provided marketing. Consumer marketing transformed pleasure itself into a commodity, one more mass-marketed good or service hawked (in a self-sustaining cycle) by commercial mass media, as William Leach has shown.[40] And it would be surprising, indeed, had the coauthor of the novel that named *The Gilded Age* (1873) failed to recognize that humor and its personification must also be commodified to function in a capitalist culture.

Though Twain pioneered comic branding, I do not claim in *Twain's Brand* that he begat all modern American humor. Whatever else one might say about Hemingway's extravagant 1935 dictum, "All modern American literature comes from one book by Mark Twain called *Huckleberry Finn*,"[41] it reflects the mood of his day but does not belong to ours. In the 1920s and '30s, worldwide nationalism spawned research in local and indigenous cultures (loosely defined) and the first scholarship in American folklore, humor, and literature—along with sentimental folklife organizations and fascist political groups. Humor based on regional settings and American colloquialisms had the political advantage of divergence from Anglo-European traditions of character and plot, but neither American humor nor modern American literature has ever been as monolithic as Hemingway asserts. The dramatic humor of stage and film, whether the slapstick of Jerry Lewis or the more cerebral conflicts of Woody Allen, belongs to international theatrical traditions, although it often draws characters and situations (its language of the ludicrous) from the same American folklife that feeds narrative humor. The wit of comic poetry, a staple from Ann Bradstreet through Robert Hollander, likewise participates in a transatlantic anglophone literary culture, as does a line of urbane literary prose running from Washington Irving of the early national period through the *New Yorker* writers of the 1920s and '30s to contemporary writers such as Thomas Pynchon and David Foster Wallace. The elevated language, respected literary forms (including verse), and intellectual assumptions of these and related writers evince origins distinct from the postcolonial mock-oral anecdotes of New England, Old Southwestern, and Sagebrush humor on which Mark Twain drew. Even today America's various geographical regions retain some distinctive comic traditions, such as the midwestern self-deprecation of Garrison Keillor and the southern class consciousness of Eudora Welty and Molly Ivins. Moreover, for all that pioneering humor scholars such as Walter Blair understood Twain's debts to New England comic moralists, tall talkers of the Old Southwest, and midcentury Literary Comedians to symbolize a triumphant amalgamation of regional traditions into a single national humor,[42] today we can just as easily see those relationships in other terms: as evidence of regional traditions' diffusion and interpenetration, of Clemens's own experience across the life and letters of the Midwest, Southwest, and West, and of Blair's ideological wish fulfillment amid the self-conscious, nationalist context of early scholarship on American culture.[43] (See chapter 3, "Humor and Empire," for more on this topic.) Though born in frontier Missouri, Clemens read and traveled widely: he had crossed the continent from New York to California and Iowa to New Orleans *and* visited colonial Hawaii by the time his first book appeared in 1867, a few weeks before he set off for Europe at the age of thirty-one. Just as he created his own brand of oral and literary humor from his imagination and from the journalistic, oral, and theatrical comic practices of his time (both homegrown and transatlantic), so many varied forms and genres of oral, print, and electronic media feed the creative expression of American humorists today.

Nor do I claim that all the graphic, oral, and literary humorists discussed here deliberately modeled their humor on Twain's. Biographical and critical details sometimes prove direct influence. For example, Bernard F. Rodgers, Jr., traced Philip Roth's comic experiments with the tall tale and vernacular narration, first noteworthy in the mock-oral monologue of *Portnoy's Complaint* (1969), to his studies at the University of Chicago with Napier Wilt and Walter Blair, two progenitors of American humor scholarship.[44] On the other hand, common interests and influences seem to have promoted mock-oral vernacular writing in nineteenth-century boy books. Written examples of local speech asserted regional identity in the years after the Civil War as mass literacy and national print media helped homogenize American English across politically reunified states. In this same period, children gained new social significance as independent moral agents (instead of parental property), as familial values associated with agricultural subsistence yielded to urban industrial imperatives; the urban U.S. population, 10.8 percent when Clemens was a boy in 1840, more than doubled to 25.7 percent by 1870 and reached 45.8 percent when he died in 1910 even as census totals over the same years rose from 17,063,353 to 35,558,371 and 92,228,496, respectively—an increase of 540 percent.[45] Together these two trends toward regional-national tension and children's autonomy shape the experiences of Horatio Alger's migrants to the city in *Ragged Dick* (1867) and its sequels along with the antics of rural rascals in Thomas Bailey Aldrich's *The Story of a Bad Boy* (1869) and Twain's *Adventures of Tom Sawyer* (1876). Popular tales of youthful escapades from many sources, not just Mark Twain's, also formed a backdrop for the graphic humor emerging from new print technologies at the end of the century, when the Yellow Kid debuted speaking an urban slang dialect in America's first newspaper comic strip, Richard Felton Outcault's *Hogan's Alley* (1895).

In fact, no American humorist working in any medium after 1880 could escape Twain's indirect influence, and his reputation remains as potent today as at his death in 1910. All his books remain in print, most in multiple editions and in many languages. Contemporary American high schools teach *Adventures of Huckleberry Finn* (1884) more often than any other novel or any other work of American literature, second only to Shakespeare's plays.[46] His witticisms (some spurious) average one quote every day of the year in some newspaper somewhere in the world.[47] Dozens of stage interpreters give voice to his words, while adaptations for stage, film, television, and comics continually bring his characters and plots to new audiences.[48] Biographers keep his own story alive on video and in print.[49] Clemens's image graces advertisements, and his imprimatur is invoked for praise or blame.[50] *Time* magazine put him on the cover of the July 14, 2008, issue headlining an essay on him as "America's Original Superstar" by Roy Blount, himself something of a vernacular oracle in the tradition of Twain's brand. Celebrations in 2010 of the centennial of his death led to public as well as academic celebrations across the U.S., culminating in the startling popular success of the first of three volumes in a scholarly edition of his unexpurgated, reconstructed autobiography. Comments on Amazon.com show that some readers had expected more vitriol and fewer footnotes, but more than a thousand users of the site approved the review by a reader who praised it as "Mark Twain's true speaking voice—he is doing a monologue in your presence, going wherever his memory takes him."[51] Cemented in these and other ways (and questions of merit aside), Twain's brand recognition means that audiences today, as in his own time, know his humor even without having opened any of his books.

Posthumous celebrity points to the continued relevance of Twain's brand in contemporary markets of American commerce and culture. As commercial brands succeed by providing practical and symbolic value to customers, so Twain's brand thrives by providing relevant comic entertainment to audiences—humor that doesn't *professedly* teach or preach, but nonetheless does both as its presence contributes to comic evaluation of the status quo. One sign of his brand's success is that royalties still flow from the copyrights he so carefully husbanded to the Mark Twain Company and its successor, the Mark Twain Foundation. Its funds got a huge boost late in 2010 as print runs on the new autobiography rose from an initial forty thousand copies to more than four hundred thousand while the book remained on the *New York Times* Best Sellers list for more than eight weeks during the Christmas shopping season.[52] Another sign is his stature as the personification of American humor in the Mark Twain Prize for American Humor, awarded annually since 1998 by the Kennedy Center for the Performing Arts. "American history is filled with countless comedians and writers of piercing wit who have left their mark on our ideas, attitudes, and language," went the announcement for the 2005 winner, Steve Martin. "The Kennedy Center Mark Twain Prize for American Humor was created to honor the brilliant minds that elbow American culture to see if it's still alive—and make us laugh about it." The history of the prize likewise sticks to the generic: "those who create humor from their uniquely American experiences."[53] Not that the recipients have been unworthy. Winners of the prize span a range of contemporary greats—Richard Pryor, Lily Tomlin, Bob Newhart, Whoopi Goldberg, Carl Reiner, Bill Cosby, Steve Martin, George Carlin, Tina Fey—who have mainly nationality and contemporaneity in common. Pryor, Reiner, and Martin all have substantial writing credits, especially in film and television; Neil Simon deserves recognition for theatrical comedy; and Cosby and Carlin share a literary bent in their storytelling. But not one winner to date is known mainly for fiction. The bias toward comic performance, though based in the Kennedy Center's mission, also suggests Twain's significance as a symbol—in this case, for leavening the elite aura of a national arts institution—of popular entertainment, democratic satire, and fun.

What I call Twain's brand, then, is more than a metaphor for the legacy of America's most famous humorist: rather, it highlights the interrelationship among culture and commerce in modern American humor, and Mark Twain's role in linking the three. The exchange of humor for laughter (and, from the audience's perspective, the exchange of money for humor) emphasizes that humor belongs to an economic system—and a global postindustrial economy in particular—as well as an aesthetic one. In arguing that Twain's brand defines an important trend in contemporary American culture, I show kinship between current practices and Twain's as evidence of their common origin in the modern, postindustrial condition. In this book I focus on four hallmarks of Twain's brand that have proven not only central to his own career and reputation, but also significant for contemporary American humorists across many media and comic practices, including stand-up comedy, prose fiction, comics, and the branding business itself. I concentrate on these hallmarks precisely because they range across media, genre, and social role in order to highlight their penetration in contemporary life. Humor has a place at the center of American culture, and Mark Twain's continued currency—as both a presence and a commodity—helps explain why.

One of these hallmarks is the *performed self*, a centerpiece of Mark Twain's early stage humor. Comic lectures brought him early visibility as a distinctive humorous personality as well as a writer, serving as entertainment (and a source of income) in their own right in addition to publicity for his books. In particular, his development of a stage persona at one barely visible fictive remove from his biographical self wrought comic confusion that also drives one strand of stand-up comedy today. Solo performances by humorists presenting fictional versions of themselves enact, as Mark Twain did, a modern conception of the self as born in social interaction, rather than existing prior to it. Not all stand-up comedy exploits this unstable self for humorous effect, because the genre ranges from solo joke telling to partner banter and physical clowning, but chapter 2, "Standing Up: The Self-Made Comedian," shows how performances that do privilege this comically unstable persona—including those by Jon Stewart, Garrison Keillor, Margaret Cho, and Jerry Seinfeld—update Twain's brand of humor for contemporary audiences.

A second hallmark of his brand, the *comic cross-cultural contrast*, lives on in American literary humor. Throughout his career, Mark Twain mined a nationalist strand of literary humor that celebrated American separation from imperial Britain through comically invidious contrasts of American values, language, characters, and experience with those of other cultures, especially the ostensibly more cultivated European aristocracies and their descendents among educated Americans. Regional and ethnic dialects joined other markers of democratic virtue, such as naïveté, as conventions of this postcolonial rhetoric, which was born soon after the American Revolution and remains influential in comic fiction today. But the most explicit forms of the contrast pitted Americans against Europeans on transatlantic visits, and as I detail in chapter 3, "Humor and Empire," in the hands of both Twain and Philip Roth the literary humor of the cross-cultural contrast finds cracks in democratic virtue from our own imperial sins.

A third hallmark, the *vernacular vision*, derives from the cross-cultural contrast, but goes to the heart of what so many readers love about Mark Twain's humor: the naïve ironies and antisocial antics of a young rascal like Huckleberry Finn. Astute readers see that Huck's semiliterate, colloquial writing wraps cultural critique in ostensibly innocent transgressions and misunderstanding; deadpan becomes humor as readers decode the irony of expressions that only seem inept. But while authors and scholars have extolled the literary impact of Twain's vernacular technique, its adaptation to other narrative media—especially the graphic humor of comics and animated cartoons—has gone unnoticed. Yet in the same way that Twain's rejection of a genteel literary style for Huck's vernacular narration enables satire that offers new ways of understanding our world, so vernacular graphic rhetoric—which replaces a professional aesthetic with an apparently naïve, untutored drawing style—critiques the status quo by offering new ways of seeing it. As I show in chapter 4, a visual vernacular strain of American graphic humor in the tradition of Twain's brand began soon after the publication of *Huckleberry Finn* and underlies contemporary graphic satire of American life. "Kid Stuff: The Vernacular Vision and the Visual Vernacular" explores how Twain's brand of vernacular rhetoric in *Huck* drives both its literary satire and a range of contemporary graphic counterparts from *The Simpsons* to Lynda Barry's memoir and Aaron McGruder's newspaper strip, *The Boondocks*.

A fourth hallmark of Twain's brand is *brand-name marketing* of humor itself. From books and magazines to cell phones and the Internet, the humor business of recent decades depends on the same brand-name promotion, cross-media synergy, and copyright practices that Samuel Clemens pioneered a century ago, when the information economy was young, as I show in chapter 5, "Comic Brands: More than Funny Business." Like any brand, the name *Mark Twain* associates certain traits and values with its signature product. These associations create financial worth for the brand as symbolic assets distinct from the use (functional) and exchange (material) values of a commodity itself. Branding experts contend that memorable "breakthrough performances" enable the greatest brands to capture the "collective imagination" of the culture,[54] yet still balance continuity and change over time. For instance, Coca-Cola became the world's leading brand (with symbolic equity valued at more than $70 million) through its promise to refresh body and body politic, although the terms of its commitment have changed over the years. The red italics that stood for "America, Democracy, and Coca-Cola" during World War II expanded their symbolic embrace to the globe in 1971, when the multiracial and multinational chorus of a television commercial proclaimed (in English!) "I'd like to teach the world to sing in perfect harmony"; the product also evolved by embracing sugar substitutes, aluminum cans, plastic bottles, and other innovations in order to stay current with consumers.[55]

So too with Twain's brand. Mark Twain's visual identity is, if not as ubiquitous as Coke's, certainly well established: the slender man in suit and bow tie has thick, wavy hair, bushy eyebrows, and an abundant, drooping mustache, and he typically has some emblematic prop—a white suit, a jumping frog, a steamboat steering wheel, a cigar or pipe, a boy with fishing rod or whitewash bucket and brush. And this image, like the name *Mark Twain*, aims to create an indelible impression that will sell something: lecture tickets, books and magazines, charitable causes, Mark Twain's Patent Scrap Book, the state of Missouri, American literature, American humor, American culture. Among scholars, "A True Story," *Tom Sawyer, Huckleberry Finn*, and the ironic late fiction have displaced 1860s favorites such as "The Celebrated Jumping Frog" and *Innocents Abroad* as breakthrough performances, but the persistence of Mark Twain's hallmark techniques in contemporary American oral, literary, and graphic humor, as well as in the international humor business, shows that now as in Sam Clemens's day, Twain's brand fits the modern mood.

CHAPTER TWO

Standing Up

The Self-Made Comedian

When Jon Stewart of Comedy Central's *The Daily Show* appeared on CNN's political talk show *Crossfire* on October 15, 2004, hosts Paul Begala and Tucker Carlson greeted him with praise for "his one-of-a-kind take on politics, the press and America." Begala and Carlson represented opposite poles on the political spectrum, but shared comic expectations for their guest, whom they described as "the most trusted name in fake news."[2] But Stewart, on a tour to publicize his recently published parody of a high school civics textbook, *America (The Book): A Citizen's Guide to Democracy Inaction*, had his own political agenda for this performance, and it did not include jokes. Instead of waiting for the liberal Begala or conservative Carlson to set him up for a punch line, Stewart seized the initiative and asked, "Why do we have to fight?" If the question at first seemed a disingenuous, deadpan gambit to mock the show's debate format, it soon proved serious as he implored his hosts to "[s]top, stop, stop, stop hurting America." Begala and Carlson quickly became defensive about their formula of polarized attacks; after Stewart, with a faux pause, accused them of being "partisan—what do you call it?—hacks," they criticized him as equally biased. Stewart sustained his critique with feigned surprise when Carlson scorned him for lobbing soft questions to Democratic presidential candidate John Kerry: "I didn't realize. . . . that the news organizations look to Comedy Central for their cues on integrity." But as the conflict devolved into vulgar insults,[3] it nonetheless played out the problem faced by any stand-up comedian who drops

> Stars can succeed by concealing who they are. Comedians can't.
> —**Jerry Seinfeld**[1]

the comic mask. Stewart insisted on separating his *Crossfire* appearance from his performances on *The Daily Show*, while the hosts—Stewart's audience, in the context of his own show—merged them. "The show that leads into me is puppets making crank phone calls," Stewart protested, emphasizing the difference between Comedy Central and CNN, while his hosts tried to gain control of the increasingly testy conversation. Begala took a subtle tack, asking, "Don't you have a stake in [the political process] . . . as not just a citizen, but as a professional comic?," but Carlson nailed the point with his question: "Is this really Jon Stewart?"

Although the most obvious effect of the hostilities between Stewart and his *Crossfire* hosts was that CNN cancelled the show soon afterwards, the display of assumptions about Stewart's comic persona remains important beyond that original context. Relations of a comic mask to the imagination behind it go to the essence of stand-up comedy, which equates performers' personas with their persons. Stewart understood his comic role on *The Daily Show* as expressing one persona among many, yet for Begala and Carlson it displaced all other manifestations of his self. In the process, their conflict illustrates what is at stake in one strand of stand-up comedy: confusion among performances of the self on stage, on the page or television, and in private life. Though not funny in the *Crossfire* incident, such confusion animates the brand of humor that links Mark Twain with contemporary performers as otherwise different from him and each other as Garrison Keillor and Margaret Cho, Jon Stewart and Jerry Seinfeld. All merge public and private personas to create an unstable comic self as a brand for professional and economic success.

Stand-up comedians perform oral narratives, usually monologues, in which they appear to express themselves rather than play a role. Lawrence E. Mintz claimed in an essay for *Comedy* (2005) that the genre of stand-up comedy actually encompasses a broad continuum of live performances ranging from solo and small-group verbal, musical, or physical clowning to direct joke telling and social commentary, but most scholars and audiences take the narrower view advocated by David Marc: "[T]he *absolute* 'directness of artist/audience communication' is the definitive feature of the art."[4] In fact, from its name to its stage conventions—typically a container of water, a microphone, and a stool or chair for the (apparently) uncostumed speaker—stand-up also clearly announces itself as a genre focused on the performance of an exposed individual, a performance that Marc described as "a naked self" who forgoes "the luxury of a clear-cut distinction between art and life."[5] The American fetish of the individual therefore finds an appropriate outlet in stand-up comedy even as it further pressures each comedian to cultivate a unique comic identity. Today, with thousands of would-be professionals jostling for attention on hundreds of stages, a comedian must cultivate and project a distinct and consistent brand of humor in order to move into the figurative and literal spotlight that means profit in the marketplace. In this way, stand-up comedy replicates and reinforces the overlap between self-presentation and public reputation, two elements of selfhood that media scholar Eric Rothenbuhler identified in another context as central to Americans' "cult of the individual." Indeed, comic confusion between self-presentation and public reputation in Twain's brand of stand-up demonstrates at a literal level Rothenbuhler's metaphorical claim that "reputation ... [is] a key currency in the cult of the individual."[6] A comedian's identity operates reciprocally to define a comedian's niche and reinforce his or her reputation and thereby secure commercial success.

Commodified as a brand, a comedian's distinctive identity helps the performer branch out and sell humor in various media and forms. Human and economic limits on live, unmediated performance drive comedians to seek the greater audiences and financial rewards of mass media. As Samuel Clemens gave comic lectures as Mark Twain to promote sales of current and recent books, so today most successful contemporary stand-up comedians extend their brands through situation comedies, late-night television, books, or films in a process that merges physical presence, professional imagination, and biographical identity with a comic persona. The process of brand definition and extension in stand-up comedy thus merges nineteenth-century American individualism and entrepreneurship with twentieth-century marketing and media to yield a comic and somewhat ironic variant of the self-made man. In fact, for all the consistency inherent in the concept of a comic brand—which depends after all on qualities that signify its difference from competitors—Twain's brand of solo performance humor hinges on a paradox: the creation of a durable persona who performs a comically unstable or unreliable self. Perhaps equally important, this brand of humor, with its (feigned) self-exposure, needs the audience to collaborate in sustaining the hoax.

The blend of commercial and interpersonal exchange in Twain's brand of stand-up comedy professionalizes ordinary social communication. Contemporary comedy venues reinforce the illusion of authentic rather than artful communication because nightclubs, home video screens, and audio technologies from radio to podcasts create (or simulate) intimate relations between storyteller and listener: one-on-one closeness reinforces illusions of authenticity by imitating naturally occurring conversation between friends. The nightclub remains the preferred venue to maintain that sense of intimacy. Large auditoriums use Jumbotron video screens to project facial expressions to the back row and capture some of that feeling, but even as the side-by-side contrast between live performer and magnified image underscores the distance between stage and audience, at some cost to illusions of authenticity, an established performer's reputation compensates for the distance and promotes willing suspension of disbelief. (Though Clemens performed in the days before microphones and often addressed small groups, his lectures drew large crowds from the time of his debut at the fifteen-hundred-to-two-thousand-seat San Francisco Academy of Music, which a reporter described as "stuffed to repletion" [MTLC, 38]). Stand-up's performance conventions remind us that, despite its commercial and environmental links to theater, these comedians purport to speak autobiographically and in their own voice. They engage in apparently authentic, if not convincingly spontaneous, communication with the audience. That's why their punch lines typically cap extended anecdotes and observations instead of one-line jokes. In this way their anecdotes resemble an individual's repertoire of life stories, the genre of anecdotes that folklorists call the personal experience narrative: firsthand accounts that illustrate some truth about human nature or society.[7] Although friends and family members may request the retelling of favorite tales, which get polished in form and style from repeated performance, personal experience narratives usually fit thematically within an ongoing conversation in which participants take turns speaking and listening. In stand-up, by contrast, the audience pays money to yield the floor to a performer and restricts its own communication to laughter, applause, boos, and so on. The stand-up comic creates popular culture by imitating folklore.

The license granted by the audience enables the comedian to perform the social functions of the Indian shaman, medieval carnival fool, or Renaissance jester, as observers from Mintz to Mikhail Bakhtin have explained.[8] For this reason, James Caron proposes that we understand the Mark Twain persona of the early newspaper sketches as a Citizen Clown, a figure who "dramatizes what ought to be done in his modern democratic society[,] . . . comically highlighting communal values by disrupting them." Caron argues that Clemens's most important transgressions "spelled out the genteel difference between the sanctified and the unsanctified,"[9] but the license granted by the audience also permits other transgressions. In live performance the audience sanctions the clown's transgressions to create an atmosphere of play, the spirit that includes what Johan Huizinga calls a "joyful mood" and "the consciousness . . . of 'only pretending'"[10]—that is, the pleasures of joking around. As the audience observes, applauds, and vicariously joins the clown in violating taboos, the performance both resists and reinforces the society's most salient rules. Among those is the authenticity of the self presented to others in interpersonal relationships.

The comic effect of this play, best described by Bakhtin in *Rabelais and His World* (1965/1984), seems to be what Louis J. Budd had in mind in 2002 when he compared Twain's after-dinner remarks to those of comedians today and claimed that his lectures "defied that genre [of the lecture] by approaching the stand-up comedy now common on cable TV."[11] As suggested by the list of stand-up comedians who have won the Mark Twain Prize for American Humor, Samuel Clemens gets credited as a pioneer of stand-up comedy, but exactly what he contributed to it as a genre of popular culture has been more assumed than defined.[12] Part of the problem in assessing his performances as stand-up reflects lack of scholarly consensus about how to think about modern comic genres and nineteenth-century antecedents. Most analyses of stand-up comedy treat it narrowly as a modern genre beginning with Lenny Bruce or Mort Sahl, although solo humorous performance in the United States dates back at least to the early nineteenth-century variety shows that Lawrence Levine describes in *Highbrow/Lowbrow*. No comprehensive history exists of stand-up in the United States, largely because the scope is daunting: a full account would incorporate theater history (including the minstrelsy, vaudeville, and British dance hall traditions) as well as folklore (storytelling), humor, and popular culture studies. The most recent edition of the *Greenwood Guide to American Popular Culture* (2002), for instance, has separate essays on comic books and comic strips, but none for stand-up comedy, and no one has attempted a major review of the scholarship on the subject since Stephanie Koziski Olson published a reference guide to stand-up for *Humor in America* (1988). Daniel Wickberg glosses over the comic lecture of the 1860s in tracing the stand-up monologue to vaudeville, which relied on professionals who sold jokes as a commodity; he argues that "the kind of humorous story advocated by Twain was increasingly marginal in the world of a market-oriented editor" of commercialized joke books.[13]

On the other hand, the spread of modern stand-up through HBO, Comedy Central, and franchised comedy clubs has prompted some useful recent theorizing about social relationships between the humorist and audience—an important development because stand-up is marked above all by face-to-face interaction that imitates a (mostly one-way) conversation. John Limon explains stand-up's profusion of sexual and scatological material in *Stand-up Comedy in Theory* (2000) through Freud's concept of jokework and Julie Kristeva's Freudian analysis of the abject, such as waste products that both do and do not belong to the body. Joanne Gilbert, who had a career in stand-up before becoming a communication professor, argues in *Performing Marginality* (2004) that stand-up comedy allows women and members of other marginalized groups to make mainstream audiences pay for the privilege of watching them perform the restrictions they face.[14] Despite their different goals, Limon and Gilbert agree that stand-up comedy relies on the transaction between performer and audience as the comedian humbles him- or herself in exchange for money and laughter. Mark Twain's self-deprecations belong to this category, and they characterize his stage performances more often than either the sharp satire of his late writings or the stand-up critiques of modern performers such as Richard Pryor or Chris Rock.

In my view, confessions of personal experience, anecdotes of opinion, and other narratives of individuality conveyed by one's choice of jokes and themes imply the comedian's unique character, but a comic must also appear unpredictable and even somewhat contradictory in order to maintain the element of surprise that prompts laughter. I distinguish Twain's brand of the observational or anecdotal stand-up comedy—with its ostensibly personal beliefs, insights, and experiences—from the more generic (folkloric, one might even say) stock of jokes and anecdotes on vaudeville or minstrel stages. Nonetheless, the two genres have obvious connections in solo performance and self-display, as does the variety of stand-up in which performers like Lily Tomlin inhabited explicitly fictitious personalities such as the antisocial toddler Edith Ann and the eavesdropping telephone operator Ernestine and, more recently, David Koechner sings off-color country music as Gerald "T-Bones" Tibbons, aka "The Naked Trucker." All varieties of stand-up display a comic self, but some rely on performance of a stable, even rigid, persona, whereas Twain's brand features an unstable self whose very slipperiness lies at the heart of its humor. This difference puts Mark Twain's comic stage lectures and occasional (e.g., after-dinner) speeches at or very near the start of observational and anecdotal stand-up.

Nineteenth-century reviewers declared Clemens's lecture style "peculiar and original"[15] because it diverged from familiar rhetorical practices, especially the reading of a prepared text. His innovations on the platform constituted performative breakthroughs that not only brought him popular and commercial success but also singled out his brand of performance from those of other comic and educational lecturers. His immediate predecessors on the comic lecture circuit included a number of so-called "Literary Comedians," writers who created comic personas for their pseudonymous writings. Notable contemporaries in this vein included John Phoenix (born George Horatio Derby), Artemus Ward (Charles Farrar Browne), and Petroleum Vesuvius Nasby (David Ross Locke). But in the course of his career Mark Twain developed the biggest comic reputation, which his stage performances enhanced, and eyewitness accounts indicate that his performances broke new ground in two main ways. (*MTH* has a sampling of reviews, 437–41.) First, unlike other comic lecturers, he did not read a text that portrayed him as an authority, albeit a defective one, but instead spoke with apparent spontaneity and deadpan naïveté. That is, he performed his comic persona without a script in evidence.In addition, through his performances he blurred the difference between his on-stage and off-stage personas, allowing the comic character represented by the pseudonym *Mark Twain* to merge with and eventually overtake the public physical and biographical person of Samuel Clemens. A report in the *New York Times* of an 1873 performance of his Sandwich Islands (Hawaii) lecture illustrates the effect: "Mr. Twain . . . interspersed his discourse with humorous sketches and witty allusions to the topics of the day, which kept his audience in a continuous roar of laughter. His attitudes, gestures, and looks, even his very silence were provocative of mirth."[16]

These breakthroughs run in a direct line to contemporary stand-up. Foremost is the performance of a modern sense of self constructed through performance. Unlike John Phoenix and Artemus Ward, Mark Twain invented several autobiographies for his comically created persona. Twain intensified the humor of this conceit, through which performer and audience played with ideas of authenticity and fictitiousness, by representing his ostensible experience as simultaneously a socially significant subject and a frivolous game. The persona of Mark Twain in the early lectures established his reputation as a popular performer whose brashness skated close to the edge of respectability (some claimed he crossed it), yet the techniques that proved controversial in the nineteenth century are so conventional today that John Limon's claim that stand-up concerns "the abject" applies precisely to the physiologically repulsive topics that Mark Twain described at the beginning of his Sandwich Islands lecture, a staple of his repertoire in a hundred performances between 1866 and 1873. In Twain's performance comic confusion between real and fictive, authentic and performed, matter and manner reflects a modern understanding of identity as unstable, fluid, and ultimately communicative: i.e., constructed through action and interaction. Clemens explored this confusion in fictions about twins and doubles well before it entered mainstream psychology in the 1890s, when it was a major plot device of *Pudd'nhead Wilson* and *Those Extraordinary Twins* (both 1894). It served as the foundation of *The Prince and the Pauper* (1881) and the comic conundrum of "Personal Habits of the Siamese Twins" (1869), and figured symbolically in many works as well. Gender and identity confusion features prominently in *Huckleberry Finn*, for instance, but also drives such pseudoautobiographical fictions as "The Facts Concerning the Recent Carnival of Crime in Connecticut" (1876), where "the facts" of the title turn out to be fiction as narrator Mark Twain, tormented by a stranger, "a caricature of me in little" identified as his conscience, frees himself from guilt and then slaughters the neighbors (*CTS* 1:645). In the context of comic stage performance, however, blurred distinctions between Samuel Clemens and Mark Twain also mocked the familiar Gilded Age mythos of the self-made man by taking it to a literal extreme. This joke struck a contemporary chord not only because Horatio Alger had begun publishing his tales of upward mobility in 1867,[17] but also because it drew upon a fundamental American tenet recently reinforced by the Civil War and the constitutional amendments that followed: that the democratic citizen was not constrained, like commoners in hereditary aristocracies, by "race, color, . . . previous condition of servitude," as the Fifteenth Amendment put it, or by any other circumstance beyond the individual's control. Rather, Americans made and remade themselves. In creating a comic self on the lecture platform for professional and financial success, Twain bequeathed to contemporary stand-up comedy a brand of humor that simultaneously fulfills and mocks the myth of the self-made American.

He understood that creation as his challenge and his achievement. "There is nothing that makes me prouder than to be regarded by intelligent people as 'authentic,'" Clemens wrote his early mentor Mary Mason Fairbanks in February 1868, acknowledging her praise of his first book, *The Celebrated Jumping Frog of Calaveras County*; "I don't care anything about being humorous, or poetical, or eloquent, or anything of that kind—the end & aim of my ambition is to be authentic—is to be considered authentic" (*MTL* 2:189). His clarification at the end of this statement reveals, as Everett Emerson observed, a hope "not so much to *be* authentic as to be *considered* authentic."[18] But the attitude is entirely appropriate for someone earning a living through oral comic performance and its print counterpart, the mock-oral narrative, in which authenticity is not a fact or state of being but the outcome of perception, a conclusion drawn by an audience. Indeed, Mark Twain's written and oral humor depends on the idea that individuals perform rather than express their characters. This conception underlies the stand-up comedy that Clemens performed from 1866 to 1874, but as late as his autobiographical dictation of July 31, 1906, he remained convinced the self was artificially constructed. "I think we never become really and genuinely our entire and honest selves until we are dead—and not then until we have been dead years and years," he mused, in a reminder that the autobiography was to be held until after his death. Then he added, performing the comedian for the stenographer, "People ought to start dead, and then they would be honest so much earlier" (*MTE*, 202–3). Stage performances by Mark Twain gave bodily form to a comic brand that easily moved from the stage and popular press to the market for books and other products, including American culture itself, in international trade. In this way, Samuel Clemens helped transform humor and humorist into commodities that could be branded, advertised, and sold—preferably in multiple media formats—in ways that now dominate the American entertainment business, and he could do so in part because his stand-up comedy as Mark Twain expressed a particularly modern sense of self and the world.

The genteel comic lectures offered by Mark Twain and his contemporaries rejected the lowbrow humor of the minstrel show and vaudeville but nonetheless edged close to the limits of respectability. (In all-male venues, he cheerfully went over the edge, most famously in "Some Thoughts on the Science of Onanism" [1879].) Clemens was highly skilled and successful in these productions, which he used throughout his career to drum up interest in his forthcoming books and to support an upper-middle-class lifestyle during tough economic times, both national and self-inflicted. But he also saw the platform as a money-making enterprise in its own right and as a means of supporting and marketing his work as a writer, and he humbled himself on stage (sometimes grudgingly) for the privilege. He toured his first lecture, "Our Fellow Savages of the Sandwich Islands," for a hundred performances beginning in 1866 in order to fund composition of a book on his Hawaiian experience.[19] He developed "The American Vandal Abroad" (1868–69) and "Roughing It on the Silver Frontier" (1871–73) to promote *Innocents Abroad* (1869) and *Roughing It* (1872), which became best sellers. He added readings when he returned to the platform in 1884–85 to market *Huckleberry Finn* (1884) on the "Twins of Genius" tour with George Washington Cable (1844–1925) and again in 1895–96 on the world tour that fed his last travel book, *Following the Equator* (1896). The incorporation of readings highlights the difference between these later tours and the stand-up comedy of his early platform career, which hinged on apparently spontaneous performance of an apparently authentic self.

Much of the humor of these early performances came from his platform presence as Mark Twain. He typically mocked himself even before starting to speak by entering in an awkward, physically clumsy, or bashful way; then he painstakingly drawled a combination of information, ridicule, jokes, purple prose, and self-deflation for the rest of the performance. In the early years he affected mental slowness through bewildered facial expressions, delight in his own jokes, and a tendency to drop punch lines (according to a reporter for the 1871 Chicago *Evening Post*) "as if he had just thought of them a minute before, and didn't perceive the point of them quite as soon as the audience" (*MTLC*, qtd. 91). Alternatively, he might applaud himself like a small child to comically undercut an eloquent description of the Kee-law-ay-oh volcano or Lake Tahoe. In addition, he spoke so slowly that a reporter for the Virginia City *Daily Trespass* quipped when reviewing his second western tour, "He still talks as rapidly as ever—gets out a word every three minutes" (*MTLC*, qtd. 93). (Recalling that drawl, his Nevada colleague William Wright, who wrote as Dan DeQuille, recollected that "this peculiarity is not natural but acquired. When he was a small boy he spoke so rapidly that his family constantly remonstrated with him"; the men were not childhood friends, but true or not, the effect confirms Jerry Seinfeld's insistence that "[c]omedy strength is slowness."[20]) Other reviewers noted that Mark Twain maintained a deadpan so intense that he actually seemed surprised and confused when people laughed at what he said. Enhancing all these effects was his simulation of spontaneous interpersonal remarks (conversation specialists call it "fresh talk") as he spoke from memory in a colloquial style, exhibiting "Mark Twain" as an authentic physical presence who seemed to express authentic ideas and emotions.

Among his anecdotes were personal experiences not too different from the ritual self-humiliations of recent stand-up comedians—for instance, Margaret Cho's description of kidney failure from excessive dieting in *I'm the One That I Want* (perf. 2000), or Richard Pryor's account of setting himself on fire in *Live on the Sunset Strip* (perf. 1982). A story told often recalled Mark Twain's terror as a boy camped out in his father's office overnight to avoid punishment after playing hooky from school. "The moon shed a ghastly light in the room, and presently I descried a long, dark, mysterious shape on the floor. . . . By and by when the moonlight fell upon it, I saw that it was a dead man lying there with his white face turned up in the moonlight. I never was so sick in all my life. I never wanted to take a walk so bad! I went away from there. I didn't hurry—simply went out the window—and took the sash along with me" (*MTS*, 5). Like his self-deprecation at the start of the "Roughing It" lecture—a recollection of the man who once introduced him by saying, "I don't know anything about this man; at least I know only two things: one is, that he has never been in the penitentiary; and the other is, I don't know why" (49)—this device serves the important comic function of giving the audience a socially superior position from which to look down and laugh at the performer, even if watching the stage from below.

Yet Twain's persona balanced comic self-deprecation with demonstrations of intellectual competence and rhetorical eloquence. He capped his jokes in the Sandwich Islands lecture—"There is not a spoonful of legitimate dirt in the whole group [of islands]" (*MTS*, 6)—with praise for Hawaii as the "almost soulless solitudes of the Pacific" (14), his hissing alliteration invoking quiet mood and island breeze. He extolled the Greek night in "The American Vandal" as "a spray of golden sparks that lost their brightness in the glory of the moon" (34) and maintained that awe to describe his forced march back to the ship after armed guards caught him and his friends stealing grapes: "Military escort—ah, I never traveled in so much state in all my life" (35). The "Roughing It" lecture likewise offset clowning with flourishes and facts.

Writing from a lecture tour on November 27, 1871, he confessed to his wife, Olivia, that he compared the juggling of jokes and seriousness in his lectures to "a running narrative-plank, with square holes in it, six inches apart, all the length of it" so that he might fill those holes with "plugs (half marked 'serious' & the others marked 'humorous') . . . according to the temper of the audience" (*MTL* 4, 498), and his construction metaphor points to the nature of the transaction between comedian and audience in both his day and ours. Definitions of stand-up as the performance of abjection or the performance of marginality cannot explain the inherent conflict between the "*absoluteness*" of direct artist-audience communication in stand-up and the artificiality of *any* artist-audience communication. That is, stand-up comedy's conflation of performed and authentic self relies on a modern idea of the self: a complex and unpredictable, apparently authentic persona socially constructed through human interaction. The stand-up comedian offers this self in deadpan earnest to the audience, who respond to its contradictions with the laughter of comic approval.

Samuel Clemens's success in sustaining Mark Twain as such a self distinguished him from comic contemporaries on the lecture circuit.[21] The stable ironies that made the character of Petroleum V. Nasby a good vehicle for anti-Confederate newspaper satire would have kept David Ross Locke (1833–1888) from disappearing behind his persona during lectures even if he had not kept his eyes glued to his manuscript in a manner that Twain found "destitute of art" (*AMT* 1:147). For a modern equivalent, imagine Stephen Colbert reading his mock-reactionary lines instead of speaking directly to the camera on *The Colbert Report* (Comedy Central, 2005–). Charles Dickens (1812–1870) no longer relied on his pseudonym "Boz" when he read in what Twain found a "rather monotonous" style that left him "a great deal disappointed" in an 1868 report for the *Alta California*.[22] By contrast, the persona of Artemus Ward, a spoof of P. T. Barnum, did displace Charles Farrar Browne (1834–1867) as the persona evolved from print into the more generic deadpan burlesque preacher of the lecture platform, but the humorist died too young to fully exploit it.

Mark Twain's deadpan self-deprecations, borrowed from Ward, burlesqued the conventional oratory of his day and showed that he wasn't a conventional lecturer, yet the real information he presented didn't reveal what he *was* instead. Randall Knoper argues in *Acting Naturally* that Twain's deadpan performances, however tame they seem by today's measure, skirted respectability by challenging the intellectual seriousness of not only the public lecture, but also contemporary ideas of manhood, gentility, and theatrical professionalism. I agree with Knoper that Clemens's body and voice unified the antics of the Wild Humorist of the Pacific Slope and gave coherence to the varied plugs along his "narrative-plank," to use his own metaphor, but as I read and try to hear the early lectures, his shifting comic postures add up to anything but what Knoper calls a "stable, continuous self." To the contrary, as Evan Carton has pointed out, the response of an 1869 Boston audience set the pattern for a long line of critics and scholars thereafter: "The audience gets into a queer state . . . . It knows not what to trust."[23]

In fact, compared to Ward's "The Babes in the Wood," the famous deadpan mock-sermon that inspired Clemens's earliest efforts on the platform, the Mark Twain persona was notable for its *in*stability and *in*consistency. Edgar M. Branch's reconstruction of "The Babes" shows that Ward kept listeners off guard as he set up each joke, but his pattern of anticlimax, diversion, and double entendre established a stable ironic persona appropriate to the overall pattern of his piece. His burlesque of a preacher's fulsome yet meaningless remarks projects one of those literary comedians whom Bernard DeVoto characterized as "Perfect Fools" for their "deliberate exploitation of psychological dissociation."[24] For example, in the third section of his lecture, Ward lauds French support for the American Revolution as he ticks off the various lecture topics he had rejected, then veers off on other tangents, warning France against a new American adventure and then concluding with a bad pun: "We want to do without Levi Napoleon. (I may have got his name wrong.) . . . We are very fond of music on this continent, but we can't stand French airs!"[25] Such high-toned nonsense reveals itself as a hoax, or practical joke, after Ward flits from joke to joke and introduces topic after topic without ever lighting on his title subject—the "babes in the wood" evidently referring to uninitiated listeners who expected him to discuss it.

Mark Twain owed huge debts to Artemus Ward's performance style, as Lawrence I. Berkove, Edgar Branch, and David E. E. Sloane have shown, but Clemens's innovations exchanged the literary comedian's stable persona for the stand-up comedian's comic confusion between art and life. Whereas Ward's solemn nonsense clearly lampooned famous contemporary preachers such as Henry Ward Beecher, Twain's burlesque of nineteenth-century oratory pointed only to the fictitious alter ego of Samuel L. Clemens. In this sense, the instability of Mark Twain as a comic persona expressed a modern view of reality as unknowable and of identity as socially constructed through communication—two ideas that continue to drive stand-up comedy today.

Almost from the start of his career Clemens comically blurred the difference between his on- and off-stage selves in the manner of today's stand-up comedians, who feign artless presentations of ostensibly authentic experiences in venues from *Late Show with David Letterman* to press club dinners. Clemens began performing his comic persona at public events like the Nevada mock legislature in mid-December of 1863, less than a year after his pseudonym first appeared in print and just before he first saw Ward perform on December 22.[26] In this regard, ceremonial speaking at banquets and other public events proved more significant to the development of the Mark Twain persona than platform lectures in theatrical settings, because nontheatrical stand-up moved comic play into everyday life. Indeed, nontheatrical performances moved it into daily life twice over. First, appearances at fund-raisers and club dinners gave the invented persona a social reality. Then Mark Twain's remarks became news when reported by journalists. By contrast, the comic lectures had tenuous links to reality, because they combined jokes and other fictions with facts and anecdotes (sometimes stretched) from his actual experiences in Hawaii, Europe, and Nevada. The "Vandal" and "Roughing It" lectures especially complicated the blurring of life and art because Clemens performed oral anecdotes based on his first two book-length written narratives. Things became more complicated still toward the end of his career, in the so-called "At Home" performances of the 1895–96 world tour, when he combined aloud readings from his books with apparently (but only apparently) unscripted oral anecdotes and personal narratives. Yet the blurring of art and life, humorist and persona, was already well developed in February 1873, when Frederick Waddy's caricature of Clemens astride the jumping frog (figure 1) announced Mark Twain's upcoming lecture at the Brooklyn Academy of Music. Less than ten years into the professional humor business, the caricature marked a milestone in what became a lifelong effort to equate the physical person of Samuel Clemens with the comic persona of Mark Twain and market them as America's premier comic brand.

Confusion between the authentic and performed selves also became an explicit part of the performances. He joked continuously, for example, about the fictitiousness of Mark Twain, even as he spoke in person about the actual experiences of Samuel Clemens in the Sandwich Islands or Europe. He also dispensed autobiographical fictions along with sundry facts. "One of my ancestors cut a conspicuous figure in the 'Boston massacre,'" he remarked in the Artemus Ward lecture (1871–72). "Why, to hear our family talk, you'd think that not a man named anything but Twain was in that massacre." The tale led up to a conventional joke about a purported ancestor killed at Bunker Hill: "He was everything, that ancestor of mine was—killed, wounded and missing. He was a prompt, businesslike fellow, and to make sure of being the last of the three he did it first of all—did it well, too—he was prompt that way—before a shot was fired" (*MTS*, 43). Jokes about ancestry appealed to democratic contempt for lineage, as Louis Budd has observed,[27] but challenges to authenticity were also in play. In the "Roughing It" lecture, Twain feigned inexperience to impress and amuse the audience with descriptions from apparently fresh eyes. Watching a storm in the valley from a western mountaintop became "a miracle of sublimity to a boy like me, who could hardly say that he had ever been away from home a single day in his life before" (51)—quite a stretcher from someone who had already seen Washington, D.C. (1854), Philadelphia (1854), New York City (1854), Cincinnati (1857), and New Orleans (1861), and had worked on and piloted riverboats (1857–1861) before he left Missouri for Nevada with his brother Orion on July 18, 1861.

Jokes about his authenticity continued throughout the humorist's career, particularly in after-dinner entertainment. The most notorious example comes from the Whittier Birthday Party speech (1877), which hinges on the difference between the Mark Twain character and the con men impersonating Emerson, Holmes, and Longfellow in order to wrangle hospitality from a miner while tramping through the Sierra Nevada: "Ah—imposters, were they?," scoffs the miner, confronted with yet another man claiming a famous literary name, "—are *you*?" (*MTS*, 4). The crowd apparently roared with laughter, but at least one participant and generations of scholars insisted that Clemens made a "hideous mistake" in telling a joke that poked fun at the day's leading poets in their presence.[28] Still, as late as his remarks at the Galveston Orphan Bazaar of 1900, Clemens put questions of authenticity at the core of a joke. After a fellow train passenger told him that "you look enough like Mark Twain to be his brother," Clemens admitted that he had always aspired to look like Twain and had in fact dressed for the role—only to be informed that "you look very well on the outside, but when it comes to the inside you are probably not in with the original" (346). Joking with the idea that Mark Twain himself is the real character and that Clemens's physical presence is something of a hoax shows how much fun he took with that confusion.

The Mark Twain persona's comic instability stemmed partly from burlesque of nineteenth-century oratorical conventions. Nineteenth-century American oratory followed a neoclassical model in which speakers carefully wrote and performed their remarks according to Cicero's five canons of rhetoric (invention, arrangement, style, memory, and delivery); the model also treated the speaker's character and knowledge (ethos) as important constituents of argument and rhetorical effect.[29] Twain already had strong ideas about rhetorical competence in February of 1867 when, fresh from his first lecture tour, he praised Rev. Henry Ward Beecher for his mastery of four of the five canons. In a March 1867, letter from New York to the readers of *Alta California*, Twain cited the excellent *invention* and *arrangement* of "mosaic work" in Beecher's sermon ("wherein poetry, pathos, humor, satire and eloquent declamation were happily blended upon a ground work of earnest exposition") as well as his *style* and *delivery*, omitting mention only of *memory*. (He particularly admired Beecher's ability to work an audience by "pausing impressively a second or two" before delivering a punch line at which "the congregation ... laughed like all possessed."[30] Twain likewise prepared his lectures following classical procedures even as his outcomes diverged from them. He meticulously drafted and revised his remarks, then rehearsed with painstaking attention to inflection, phrasing, timing, pauses, and physical mannerisms (*MTS*, xxii–iv; *MTLC*, 91), yet his alternation of clowning and competence debunked the classical ideal of a stable performance of ethos, a credible performance of self. Today's stand-up comedians rely on the same two-step rhetoric of inferiority and significance. Postures of inferiority support a comic mood by distinguishing the stand-up comedian from the preacher or teacher whose seriousness stand-up comedy rejects.

In the same vein, but more confounding to his persona, Twain made lying and falsehood the themes of his factual presentations. He often announced a loose affinity with truth. "I shall endeavor to tell the truth as nearly as a newspaper man can," he cautioned at the outset of the Sandwich Islands lecture (*MTS*, 4). Later he described the top of the mountain in Honolulu as "so cold that you can't speak the truth" (13) before ending the talk with an anecdote to illustrate that "these Sandwichers believe in a superstition that the biggest liars in the world have got to visit the islands some time before they die" (13). Similar admissions of lying frame the "Roughing It" lecture, where an ironic self-introduction launched the theme. "I ask leave to introduce to you the lecturer of the evening, Mr. Clemens, otherwise Mark Twain," he began, "a gentleman whose great learning, whose historical accuracy, whose devotion to science, and whose veneration for the truth, are only equaled by his high moral character and his majestic presence" (48). (The audience could see, as an Australian reporter noted in 1895, that "his figure is rather slight, not above middle height."[31]) The topic of lies returned toward the end, when Twain confessed, "A reporter has to lie a little, or they would discharge him. That is the only drawback to the profession. . . . Lying is bad—lying is very bad. . . . I think that for a man to tell a lie when he can't make anything by it, is wrong" (60). Then to prove that point, he dove into the story of a duel that he escaped only because a friend scared off the challengers with the lie that he had shot a sparrow through the head at thirty paces (61). And all this humor, based on the comic incongruity of informational lectures with lies as their theme, is of a piece with the live performance of an invented self.

With these two comic devices, truth about lies and performance of authenticity, Mark Twain brought a modern perspective to American humor's traditional contrast between characters and viewpoints, staples of the framed vernacular tale of Old Southwestern humor. This tradition capitalized on the idea that a single stable reality exists, although individuals may misinterpret or misrepresent it. A classic example is A. B. Longstreet's "Georgia Theatrics" (1835), whose narrator overhears a boy's imaginary fight and mistakes it for a "hellish deed."[32] *Huckleberry Finn* likewise incorporates divergent views into an otherwise stable reality: Tom's A-rabs *are* Huck's Sunday school, witches *are* hoaxes, and Twain helps readers see through the characters' various disguises and corruptions even though the so-called "evasion sequence" of the ending lacks a fixed moral standpoint that would end debate on its meaning. A less stable, more modernist view emerges in *Connecticut Yankee in King Arthur's Court* (1889), one of Twain's many dream works to portray reality as relative. Yet long before Hank Morgan saw pigs where Sandy saw princesses, Mark Twain's oral humor characterized reality and identity in the modern mode: as contingent on perception and constructed through rhetoric. Hence he reported that Sandwich Islanders "are very fond of dogs"—though he personally "would rather go hungry for two days than devour an old personal friend in that way" despite his recognition "after all it is only our cherished American sausage with the mystery removed" (*MTS,* 9–10). More emphatic was his declaration at the Washington Correspondents Club Banquet in 1868: "Look at the noble names of history! . . . look at Mother Eve! You need not look at her unless you want to, but Eve was ornamental, sir—particularly before the fashions changed!" (21). Indeed, relations of interior to exterior reality, comic in conception if not always in context, form a major theme as well as a device of Mark Twain's humor.[33] As early as 1866, he mined the conflict fully in "The American Vandal" lecture (oral precursor to *Innocents Abroad*), where romantic dreams of Venice, "the great city with its towers and steeples drowsing in a golden mist of sunset," gave way to the reality of "shadows among long rows of towering untenanted buildings" and the singing of "romantic gondoliers" turned into the "caterwauling" of a "ragged, barefooted guttersnipe" (30–31). And his portrait of himself as ridiculous sustains the paradox behind the contrast of perceptions by using literary skill to portray ineptitude.

The comic relativism of Twain's lectures parallels the hoaxes of his fiction. A hoax's humor reflects enjoyable friction between its credibility and its falsity. The hoaxer replaces facts with realistic details, understanding reality as a matter of rhetoric and perception. Unlike stable irony, which nudges an audience toward a text's opposite meaning, Twain's hoaxes tweak both "Mark Twain" and reality as comically indeterminate: performances of competent ineptitude, like truth about lies, are infinitely regressive. As we know from Lawrence Berkove's study of Nevada influences, Twain became immersed in the genre of the hoax during his years in the West, where the Sagebrush writers gave textual form to the highly competitive, aggressive economic, legal, and social environment of Nevada's silver rush. There he learned that success in all venues, from poker to politics (and journalism), involved bluffing and lying for money. Berkove sees the effects of this environment across Twain's fiction (164),[34] but it also marked his oral performances. For instance, a November 1863 comic speech in which he accepted a (fake) meerschaum pipe involved not one but two hoaxes: his friends' punning gift of a "mere-sham" meerschaum (get it?) and his own pretense of surprise and elaborate "impromptu" eloquence (*MTS,* 648). He recalled that the visiting Artemus Ward targeted him in a hoax again the next month by speaking jibberish but blaming the incoherence on a tipsy Clemens (*CTS* 1:231–234). The importance of the hoax as a comic mode for western humorists and their audiences may have paved the way for a comic persona who tells the truth about lies, and it surely explains why Clemens publicized his July 2, 1868, San Francisco lecture, a triumphant return to the scene of his debut, with a series of spurious handbills protesting his appearance (*MTB* 3: 1614). But exploiting hoaxes' humor about reality as a product of perception and viewpoint also gave Twain's stand-up comedy a distinctly modern and modernist twist.

In particular, Mark Twain's comic relativism corresponds to then-emerging concepts of modern psychology. Clemens had a lifelong interest in this science, which was then still accessible to amateurs.[35] He took verbatim notes from *Lectures on Mental Science According to the Philosophy of Phrenology* (1852) by George Sumner Weaver in 1855, when both men were living in St. Louis (*MTLib* 2:750). In 1884, Clemens joined the Society for Psychical Research (SPR), emphasizing in his membership letter his agreement with their conclusions about creative inspiration.[36] A decade earlier, he had speculated on psychological processes in an essay, "Mental Telegraphy" (comp. 1874), that attributed coincidences of thought, speech, and writing to communication between minds, but withheld the essay until 1891, when research by the SPR and William James (whose two-volume *Principles of Psychology* appeared that year) finally assured him that his musings would not be mistaken for humor (*CTS* 2:30). These interests make it not entirely surprising that Twain's humor expressed psychological ideas circulating in America at the time. But it is striking nonetheless that an 1878 essay by James presented one of the foundational claims of modern psychology in terms akin to ideas already in play for a decade in Mark Twain's oral and written humor: "The knower is an actor, and co-efficient of the truth. . . . Mental interests, hypotheses, postulates, so far as they are bases for human action—action which to a great extent transforms the world—help to *make* the truth which they declare . . . By its very essence, the reality of a thought is proportionate to the way it grasps us."[37] No evidence shows that Clemens read James's essay, which appeared in a scientific publication, yet here as in other instances, Clemens anticipated the key ideas of his time. But by joking with ideas that we now understand as the social construction of reality, Clemens positioned his humor as epistemologically modern—part of a world without stable values, knowledge, or viewpoint. His performance of an unstable, variable self belongs to that world.

Equally important, the comic self on display in Twain's performances anticipated James's contention in *Principles of Psychology* that personal identity represents a mere "perception of sameness among phenomena" because, far from existing within an individual, identity emerges from the individual's interactions with others. "A man has as many social selves as there are individuals who recognize him," James declared, because "he generally shows a different side of himself to . . . different groups." For James, identity results from attaching the various social selves to the human body they share. Personal identity, whether experienced as the agent-Ego or the subject-Me, results from social interaction rather than drives it; the sense of common ownership among one's selves derives from the same perception that leads a farmer to presume ownership of all cattle marked with his brand.[38] In this way, Samuel Clemens disappeared behind his comic performances as Mark Twain. James's conception of the self as variable, social, and enacted underlies the better-known writings of George Herbert Mead and Erving Goffman, most notably Goffman's argument in *The Presentation of Self in Everyday Life* (1959) that a self exists only because others have imputed it from the individual's performances in the dramas of daily life. As Goffman put it, "The self . . . is not an organic thing that has a specific location, whose fundamental fate is to be born, to mature, and to die; it is a dramatic effect arising diffusely from a scene that is presented, and the characteristic issue, the crucial concern, is whether it will be credited or discredited."[39] Goffman's line of thought remains so important today that it sustains Judith Butler's conception of gender as a performance, not a trait—an argument hailed as postmodern, despite its nineteenth-century origins, for emphasizing how social practices vary across time and peoples, and thus signify meanings as inherently unstable. By replacing an essential self with a performed one whose reality derives mainly from its persuasiveness in experiences shared by performer and audience, James and his intellectual heirs point to the modernity of Twain's oral humor. Links between the comic relativism of his persona and principles of modern thought likewise identify Twain's comic performances as precursors of contemporary stand-up comedy.

Clemens's worry that audiences would dismiss "Mental Telegraphy" as humor shows how clearly he understood, eight years after his 1866 debut as a comic platform performer, the socially constructed nature of his public persona as Mark Twain. This persona embodied the comic brand that he had meticulously crafted in collaboration with his audience through stagecraft, publicity, and rhetoric. I use the marketing term *brand* instead of the social term *reputation* not only to tie it to James's concept of the self, but also to take more literally Budd's point that Clemens treated Mark Twain "as a logo—a brand name" because he saw writing as a business.[40] The same can be said of his lecturing, only more so, because it brought more immediate profits along with the intangible rewards of applause. His success on tour in 1895 following the bankruptcy of his publishing house underlines the commercial appeal of his performances. But looking at *Mark Twain* as a brand also reveals how Clemens understood the modern brand-name economy emerging during his time. His ability to exploit it not only resulted in his becoming America's most famous humorist and first modern celebrity, as Budd has shown in *Our Mark Twain*, but also continues to define him, in the mode of modern stand-up comedians, as a distinctive brand of humor.

By emphasizing the performative accomplishment of stand-up comedy over the themes or psychological implications that have drawn most theoretical attention, I locate the contemporary relevance of Twain's brand of humor to its conception of the self as both the product of performance and a comic commodity on which to trade. In this genealogy, stand-up comedy depends far more on the development and display of a comic sensibility than on any particular topics and themes. And when performances of this sensibility or self are for sale, as in Twain's brand of stand-up comedy, so too the self becomes a commercial commodity to be branded and sold.

The idea of a humorist who plays a fictional version of him- or herself has enjoyed several variations in the twentieth century. One has been running for nearly thirty-five years in Garrison (née Gary) Keillor's mock-news reports from the fictitious Lake Wobegon, which he claims as "my hometown" on *A Prairie Home Companion* (1974-1987, 1993–present). Humor of identity is also a staple of celebrity situation comedy. This strand of performance humor underlay television adaptations of radio hits such as *The Jack Benny Program* (radio, 1932–55; TV 1950–65) and *The Burns and Allen Show* (radio, 1936–50; TV 1950–58) as well as situation comedies springing from nightclub routines, such as the one-sided telephone calls of *The Bob Newhart Show* (1972–78), and it has endured through the televised explorations of American diversity in *The [Bill] Cosby Show* (1969–71, 1984–92), *Ellen* [DeGeneres] (1994–98), Margaret Cho's *All-American Girl* (1994–95), *Everybody Hates Chris [Rock]* (2005–), and *The Sarah Silverman Program* (2007–10). The theatrical frame of celebrity situation comedy concedes that the comedian's character is invented, typically by giving the star a fictional surname, so that Mary Tyler Moore of the show bearing her name becomes *Mary Richards*, for instance. Closer to Twain's brand of stand-up, however, are the more playful, liminal distinctions between factual and fictitious representations of self that Garrison Keillor, Margaret Cho, and Jerry Seinfeld make central to their comic performances.

Though Keillor has described his monologues as sit-down rather than stand-up comedy, the weekly news from "Lake Wobegon, my hometown, out on the edge of the prairie" generates humor from the incongruity between the sincerity of Keillor's narration—full of realistic detail and sympathy for human foibles—and the virtuosity of the imagination displayed. With midwestern modesty, Keillor deflates such display with bits of self-deprecation, much as Twain deflated his virtuoso word paintings of Hawaii by applauding himself. Margaret Cho's stand-up routines play somewhat differently with the performance of the self as they proclaim and destabilize her identity. As she recounts experiences as the daughter of Korean immigrants, the target of racism, and a bisexual, she also shifts accents and allegiances in ways that resist her classification within any group. Keillor and Cho continue Twain's brand of humor by feigning artless presentations of purportedly authentic experiences, those evidently their own and those of obviously fictitious (or comically exaggerated) personas. But the alternation of stand-up and situation comedy in *Seinfeld* (1989–98) dramatized still more complexly the full dimensions of Twain's brand of comic performance. As Jerry Seinfeld performed stand-up riffs ostensibly based on the life experiences portrayed in the sitcom segments, questions of identity and reality arose from both sets of materials. By representing Jerry's direct communication to the audience, the stand-up segments conferred authenticity on the events dramatized in the sitcom segments even as the formulas of TV comedy implied the fictitiousness of the stand-up routines. Such mutually reinforcing performances imbue the celebrity comic's persona with faux authenticity.

Contemporary solo performance humor in the tradition of Twain's brand also points to Americans' continued obsession with the individual in the context of the contemporary American media environment, which privileges celebrity for its marketability as a name brand. If, as Rothenbuhler argues, Americans' fascination with celebrity represents worship in "The Church of the Cult of the Individual," which holds the self sacred as an ideological expression of individualism,[41] then we can understand why stand-up comedy, along with self-promotions through social media such as Facebook and Twitter, grows ever more important. At a time when technologies and corporations have dwarfed the individual human life, both live and mediated versions of stand-up comedy honor the individual as a social actor and a purveyor of unique insight.

Not every comedian who has toyed with the humor of identity has wholeheartedly enjoyed the comic confusion that results. Fans' intrusions into his daily life led Garrison Keillor to abandon *A Prairie Home Companion* at the height of its popularity in 1987 as a partly parodic, partly sincere reincarnation of old-time radio variety shows,[42] yet in 2012 he still mines humor born of ambiguity between his invented persona as Lake Wobegon's favorite son and his biography as Gary Edward Keillor of Anoka, Minnesota. He adopted the pseudonym in 1956, as an eighth grader, to bolster his ego in the face of a desire to write poetry. "I think I was trying to hide behind a name that meant strength and 'don't give me a hard time about this,'" he recalled years later.[43] He has played games with his identity since 1975, when he began mock-reports of visits to Lake Wobegon on *A Prairie Home Companion*, though the town dates back to his search for "a way of talking about my relatives" as host of Minnesota Educational Radio's *Morning Program* beginning in 1969.[44] Soon Lake Wobegon was an inside joke shared by Keillor and his local audience as home to an ever-growing list of absurd products and ironically downscale enterprises, all sold by or subsidiaries of the fictitious Jack's Auto Repair. On the *Morning Program* in 1971 he treated the place with delicious deadpan. "Lake Woebegone [sic] is guaranteed safe for children," he promised in a mock-commercial for wooded lots beside a large puddle near Jack's garage; "at no place is the water more than three feet deep."[45] By 1975, a year after *A Prairie Home Companion* went on the air as a live variety show, Keillor was inviting listeners to experience Lake Wobegon's eccentric local events at its weekly Visitors' Day. Invitations to the "Columbus Day Booya" evoked hoots of pleasure from the initiated in the theater on October 12, 1977, and surely puzzled newcomers who had not penetrated the hoax of an event held two weeks after Columbus Day (as one would expect from the inept) because the traditional "soup wasn't quite ready yet," though everyone surely got the joke by the time the host remarked, as an apparent afterthought, "A lot of people in Lake Wobegon claim that a few weeks before the Big Booya, all the stray dogs in town disappear, but—it'll be there anyway, if you want to take advantage of it." Over the next two years this kind of burlesque of local Minnesota customs turned into a mock–news report whose elaborate details rubbed incongruously against his opening announcement that "there isn't a great deal to report this week." But Keillor maintained his role as an insider reporting on "my hometown" even as he turned from deadpan ridicule of small-town commerce to more affectionate chronicles of his characters' lives, especially in the mature monologues after 1981.

In technique, inventing pseudoautobiographical stories to tell on radio did not differ very much from the first-person fiction he had written for many years, much of it published in *The New Yorker*, but the stories did not conflate Garrison Keillor with his narrators. By the early 1980s he had published stories in the voices of a baseball player ("How Are the Legs, Sam?," 1971), a country-western disc jockey ("On the Road, Almost," 1972), a newsletter writer ("Friendly Neighbor," 1973), a hard-boiled narrator ("Jack Schmidt, Arts Administrator," 1979), and Snow White ("My Stepmother, Myself," 1982). Moreover, by the time *A Prairie Home Companion* went national, he had written hundreds of hours of radio scripts that mimicked the voices of advertisers along with the various types who populated his parodies of radio dramas. In fact, the Lake Wobegon monologues developed partly out of a series of epistolary narratives that he wrote to read on the show, a feature inspired by stand-up comedian Jonathan Winters's letters from Mount Idy. This device allowed Keillor to experiment with varying degrees of irony and identification, and to merge literary and oral performance, as he imagined Barbara Ann Bunsen (named for the character of the Beach Boys' song) sometimes misrepresenting and sometimes misunderstanding her experiences in the Twin Cities as she wrote letters to her parents Clint and Arlene back in Lake Wobegon. The volume of material he wrote and presented for each show meant that he performed yet another variation on his persona with every new skit, mock-advertisement, and monologue. Though he began public radio work as a day job to provide income along with a diversion from freelancing as a poet and fiction writer, by the early 1990s he subordinated writing for the page to writing for performance, and Lake Wobegon displaced most other topics.

Counting himself among the often-retrograde members of the community where he grew up let Keillor sit on the fence between invented and actual autobiography, fictionalizing some experiences and fabricating others. The liminal position gave him the authority of a witness to absurdity yet tempered the ridicule by making it self-deflation as well. But the fuzzy line between imaginary and real seemed less funny to him after the success of *Lake Wobegon Days* (1985), when fans' interest in "the man from Lake Wobegon," as biographer Michael Fedo called him, extended to the radio host from Anoka. By 1986 he had tired sufficiently of the feigned authenticity of his role as witness to Lake Wobegon's comic realism that he agreed to televise some live broadcasts, exposing (and thereby, he hoped, dispelling) the powerful illlusions that radio inspires listeners to create from the disembodied voice. Reality proved insufficient, however. Fans staked out his home to watch him collect the newspaper from his front porch, Fedo began contacting Keillor's childhood friends and neighbors, and Keillor lost patience. He hired an attorney who warned the biographer and his potential sources that "Mr. Keillor's right to privacy, and the right to privacy of his family, will be protected by all appropriate means."[46] The next year Keillor interfered further with his fans' all-too-willing suspension of disbelief. A few months after leaving the U.S. to live in Denmark, he prefaced *Leaving Home* (1987), a collection of stories from the show's last season, with the claim "These stories are not about my family."[47]

Yet many purported to be. One of the televised monologues published in *Leaving Home*, "Aprille" (1986), masterfully argued to the contrary as it set Keillor's report of springtime rituals going on during his recent visit to Lake Wobegon against Chaucer's account of the onset of spring at the beginning of *The Canterbury Tales*, which gives the story its title.[48] Each "pilgrimage," as Keillor explicitly links them, forms a backdrop for the main stories, Lois Tollerud's crisis of faith during the weekend of her confirmation and Keillor's confession of his own dalliance with doubt. He wrings a lot of humor from these serious themes, not least because the whole narrative rests on a long-standing inside joke about the minute details of his visit to a town that everyone knows is made up. In this instance, however, humor also rests on the contrast between Chaucer's stately poetry of "Aprill, with his shoures soote"[49] and Keillor's colloquial tale of Lake Wobegon in springtime, with its "busloads of birds" and the Norwegian bachelor farmers' sheets, now getting their first wash since winter began. Comic details of Keillor's pilgrimage include his family's disappearance from the house just before he arrived, their hot coffee on the table evidence of flight, while those of Lois's weekend include television interference as signs of divine distance and a family's-worth of hot water on Sunday morning as evidence of benediction.

The three narratives entwine several times. Perhaps the most important and comic intersection occurs when Keillor, his pilgrimage diverted to a quest for a toilet, sees Lois in the road during a walk outside while her family eats her confirmation cake, with all thirty-one words of her confirmation verse inscribed on it in blue frosting. Keillor adopts Lois's point of view as she ponders questions of good and evil, and he continues to tell the story from her perspective as he describes her increasingly frantic efforts to escape the man standing nearby, a man whom "she knew . . . was put there by an evil force, . . . [and] was Evil roaming the world, and looking for whomever it may devour." Tension rises as he reports, voice dropping to a whisper, how she falls and begs for mercy: "'Please, please,' she said; 'don't do it.'" Then after a pause, he raises his pitch and his volume, and adds in a bewildered tone, "Which surprised me. . . ." The wrenching shift in perspective constitutes the punch line: the unexpected revelation that *he* was the man standing there, that Lois made a mistake, resolves the tension through anticlimax, rescuing the tale's humor as well as Lois herself. By turning the joke on himself—reframing a presumed embodiment of evil as a guy who drank too much coffee—Keillor characterizes himself as a bumbler whose veracity extends to exposing his own foolishness. This self-deprecation, in turn, keeps the story from devolving into pompous preaching on the problem of evil even as it expresses a sincere religious sensibility that sustains a joke about the imagination as a source of truth.

Two other anecdotes in "Aprille," also ostensible memories, likewise reinforce his performances of comic inferiority and pseudoveracity. One story, which he shares with Lois, sets him among a group of unruly Boy Scouts whose refusal to learn semaphore signals so infuriated their adult leader that he unthinkingly threw away his much-beloved binoculars in frustration. Lois responds to this tale of comic retribution, worth telling for the intergenerational conflict even apart from its analogy to throwing away one's religious values in the heat of the moment, with skepticism that undercuts the parable. "That's not true, is it?" she replies, and when he concedes, "No, it's not," his stature as a preacher suffers another blow, to the benefit of humor. The second anecdote has him riding a bus with his aunt Lois and playing a game in which each pretended not to know the other, an experience that he found scary even aside from the symbolism of imagining a life estranged from God. This anecdote he lets stand as autobiographical. All the narratives, and all the religious and secular pilgrimages, come together at the end when Keillor equates the eternal return of spring with the eternal potential for goodness, shifting smoothly from his own prose to Chaucer's verse. "Well, I'm transformed by this world, the one that I look at. It's so beautiful. I believe that it has the power to make us brave, and to make us good. . . . It has the power to give us faith, the sweet breath of the wind and 'the tendre croppes, and the smale fowles maken melodye, that slepen all the nycht with open eye.'" As joke and parable intertwine in performance, so humor slips in and out of seriousness, fiction affirms its value as a source of knowledge, and Keillor's self moves in and out of view.

Twenty-five years later Keillor continues to narrate parables, fictions, and lies about his Lake Wobegon relations. The monologue from February

4, 2010, for instance, follows a structure similar to "Aprille": it opens with comments about cold weather in Lake Wobegon, segues to a memorized text that he recites (this time, verses from 1 Corinthians 13, "Love is patient, love is kind . . ."), then describes a recent visit to "my cousin Barbara" en route to two related, ostensibly autobiographical anecdotes before returning to the love theme to close the monologue. He sustains the comic incongruity of Lake Wobegon as "the little town that time forgot"—one of the many jokes, along with its location in Mist (i.e., missed) County, about the town's fictitiousness—when he draws lessons for the audience about the backward way in which he and Barbara finally resolved the rift that had arisen between them after he loaned her money five years earlier: Barbara accepted his "peace offering" of home-baked banana bread and a quart of Bailey's Irish Cream and declared them good. "And so peace was made," he reports. "This is how we do this in Lake Wobegon, you see. This goes against psychology, which tells you that you should talk through these things, but we believe that if you talk through your problems, you find new ones, and you dig the hole deeper and you open a whole fresh can of worms. And so, the way that we solve problems is just to look at them and deny that they ever existed." His claim to a family connection with Barbara, however realistically detailed, seems unlikely if her "cream de cacao problem" were true, yet her drinking helps ward off sentimentality in the homely object lesson and links this anecdote to the next, Keillor's memory of the night her father, Drunk Uncle Jack, "saved my life this February night when I was thirteen." This tale recycles a number of favorite themes. One jokes about how Minnesotans kept warm before lightweight thermal wear "by the exertion of carrying heavy clothing," an update of his August 28, 1976, mock-ad for Jack's Warm Coat, "lined with over a hundred pounds of Jack's Hot Rocks." Another plays with comic euphemisms for bodily functions as he recounts the event that led to his rescue: his desperation to urinate in the middle of that subzero night during a Boy Scout camping trip and the modesty that led him deep into the woods for privacy, even though "when it's that cold there isn't much to see. The male organ sorta nestles up next to the pancreas"—an observation similar to his punning comment in "Guys on Ice," from January 15, 1983, that in the cold "all men are created equal." Both jokes violate taboos on public talk, but the recent one goes further, reinforcing a comic contrast between short size and extravagant details and recounting crude physical details in elegant words. He recalls how as a thirteen-year-old he produced a urinary "arc . . . twelve feet long," a physiological marvel that inspired further awe by changing from steaming liquid when it left the body to "ice chips when it hit the ground." And add to that feat how in those halcyon days his bladder held a volume so great that he could inscribe his name *and* the start of the Gettysburg Address in the snow before realizing that he was cold enough to die from exposure. The performance of authenticity generates humor as realism and stretchers conflict. Humor keeps sentimentality at bay leading into the conclusion, where we learn that Aunt Evelyn had exiled Jack for having taken up with a female trucker and that rescuing Keillor had also derailed Jack's plan to kill himself. Keeping the humor levels high through double entendres, Keillor counters Jack's claim that the woman was fixing his brake linings by noting that really "she was working on his transmission . . . [and] his universal joint," with the result that Jack and the boy both look a little foolish amid their mutual gratitude before Keillor yields to sentiment at the end, where he reinvokes the love theme from Corinthians to conclude by declaring, "Love never ends. . . . Faith, hope, and love: these abide, and the greatest of these is love." Even when he recycles jokes and preaches lessons, Keillor puts new spins on comic self-deflation.

In fact, the focus of the story, though not its comic rhetoric, changed a few months later in a live performance at Ohio University on April 13, 2010, part of his *Stories from Lake Wobegon* tour. Jack's complicated love life dropped out of the story, which now stressed the embarrassment his drinking caused the whole family. The new version had many of the same details, especially those related to the young man's modesty and urinary prowess, and some similar performance techniques, such as the euphemistic description of the effects of cold on the penis and his lyrical mimicry of Uncle Jack singing "Roll Me Over in the Clover." But this account did not report that Keillor and Uncle Jack saved each other's lives, nor imply that Uncle Jack had redeemed himself by saving his nephew. Rather, this telling illustrated that "nothing you ever do for children is forgotten" and showed how he learned generosity toward those whom others scorn. But even as he changed the tale from an exemplar of intergenerational dependence to proof that the least of us still has value in the eyes of a child, ridicule of his youthful foolishness remained intact. And he reinforced that self-deprecation in his report that he began telling Lake Wobegon stories as a kind of male Scheherazade, hoping to impress the young woman lying next to him in his tiny, run-down New York City room, though his "motives were not pure." The performance was more stand-up comedy—down to the stage set only with a four-legged wooden stool and a card table with a bottle of water—than radio monologue. Instead of delivering announcements, mock-ads, radio dramas, musical acts, and the fictitious "News from Lake Wobegon" of *A Prairie Home Companion*, Keillor engaged in a virtuoso demonstration of imagination, memory, and fortitude for nearly two hours without intermission as he wove together stories about himself, contemporary American life, and Lake Wobegon's values. In tribute to the effect that he has called a séance, the audience laughed but mostly withheld applause to avoid breaking the spell.

His strategy of self-mockery has grown in rhetorical significance since he began *A Prairie Home Companion*, sustaining his persona through comic clashes among the virtuosity of his storytelling, the realism of his fictions, and examples of his ineptitude. He performs this contradictory, unstable self by alternating professions of inferiority with demonstrations of narrative excellence, often through a comic pose that in the context of his radio persona I have called "the Amateur." Like Mark Twain, who juggled postures of mock-superiority such as the foolish Sentimentalist and the Instructor and postures of mock-inferiority such as the comic Sufferer and Simpleton, Keillor constantly shifts his self-characterization for comic effect.[50] He mocks himself as a radio professional through the inferior poses of the Amateur and the Shy Person as well as through the ironic superior poses of the Announcer and the Professional; and he keeps Lake Wobegon parables humorous by drawing oddball lessons in stories told from the standpoint of a Cracker-Barrel Philosopher, Preacher, or Witness. By adopting an inferior rhetorical stance, Keillor invites the audience to laugh *at* him through narrative details that illustrate his foolishness even as story structures and other large-scale elements, such as vocal modulations and themes, demonstrate his expertise and invite the audience to laugh *with* him as well. Likewise, a stance of undeserved superiority invites laughter *at* him for drawing an eccentric or foolish lesson from the case at hand. These performances of the self, theorized by Erving Goffman as impression management, extend from verbal techniques to physical presentation. For many years, Keillor's red socks have encouraged *A Prairie Home Companion*'s studio audiences not to take too seriously his authority as a broadcast host; his 2010 performance at Ohio University began without introduction as he walked slowly onstage wearing a black dinner jacket, ill-fitting tuxedo pants, an oversized long red tie in place of the usual black or white bowtie, and bright red suede rubber-soled shoes with matching socks. He costumed himself as a well-dressed clown. The combination of formality and dress-code violation evoked for me some of Mark Twain's feigned surprise at finding himself on stage.

Keillor's radio persona has relied on such comic instabilities of character for more than thirty-five years. Before an audience of twelve at the first live broadcast of *A Prairie Home Companion* on July 6, 1974, he paraded his incompetence with a long, deadpan riff about how he had originally planned to feature performances by a solo flutist and a Tibetan nose hummer, lectures on decorative knot-tying and the nuclear family, and a political speech about local charter reform, but ultimately decided to take the advice of the (fictitious) "chairman of our program committee, Sid Battista, who's had a lot of experience in the carnival business before he went into used cars" and so chose instead to bring on a guest "who's been in radio, and who knows how to do this"—as if Keillor had not himself "been in radio" for fifteen years already.[51] Similarly, on the show's tenth anniversary show in 1984, when he could no longer joke about the novelty of his format, he feigned frustration over both the show's growing popularity for "that, uh, kinda 'homespun quality'" and his audience's complaints about a growing tendency toward slickness. The latter he found particularly galling, he insisted, because "becoming slick is what I'd been trying to *do*— for *years* now! And it makes you feel bad, ya know, that people wouldn't notice.... kinda like getting dressed up for the dance and, uh, the lady tells you that, uh, she likes the way your hair sticks up in back, it reminds her of her brother, ya know."[52] He was still mining that vein four years later at the so-called "Farewell Performance" of June 13, 1987.[53] The printed program carried joking letters from his old imaginary advertiser Jack; one objected that "the show needs a professional emcee" and another that "thirty minutes of a man speaking in a flat Midwestern voice about guilt, death, the Christian faith, small town life—it isn't what people look for in a stage performance is it."[54] And on the live broadcast Keillor mocked himself as a humorist of very limited talent who would miss the audience more than they would miss him. "There's a lot of funnier people around, . . . and you're going to find another show. But you're my only audience.... I don't have any audience in Denmark. I'm not humorous there; I'm a very tall, quiet person who keeps saying the same things over and over again 'cause that's all I know."

He continues to find new ways to reprise that refrain, which rhetoricians call the modesty trope. As recently as February 27, 2010, he joked about why Minnesotans continue to endure their grimly cold, long winters despite aspirations to the good life. The Sioux and Ojibway, he claimed, "had ambitions to move off to the Southwest and become Navajo or Hopi, but they didn't have the job skills—they weren't able to make blankets . . . of the sort that would appeal to white consumers. . . . [So] they had to stay put. Which is my story as well." With this absurd account of the survival of the first Minnesotans and their link to present-day inhabitants, he went on, "I used to be fairly smart, and I knew something about electronics, and then I made the mistake of getting behind a microphone, and it's true what they say: you do not learn anything when you are talking. And so here I am. And this is, this is all that I, this is all that I know how to do—is just to, is just to talk." Whether intuitive or planned, the hesitations toward the end of this riff stylistically highlight his comic claims of failure. Minnesotans as a species, he implies, are just inept. And he follows with details apparently designed to prove that his success on *A Prairie Home Companion* is actually an illusion. His ratings are good only because they include "plants in greenhouses" ("my vocal range seems to be good for the production of certain kinds of flowers") and residents in nursing homes "who are unable to reach the radio dial." And to reinforce these claims to failure, he not only repeats "this is all I know how to do," but also shares details of "the distinguished career that I imagined for myself" as a glamorous singer who crooned about his "desire to be loved by one person and not by millions." So no matter what his radio audience or the world at large thinks of his success, he implies, he remains a failure in his own mind. And he performs his persona accordingly, both within the fictive world of the monologues and in his direct communication with the audience.

That is, like Mark Twain, the Garrison Keillor of *A Prairie Home Companion* makes his persona's authenticity the central joke of his comic performances and has carried it from radio into his humor in other media. He wrote the screenplay for the 2006 film *A Prairie Home Companion*, directed by Robert Altman, and starred in it playing a self-parodic character named Garrison Keillor, the has-been radio host of a soon-to-be cancelled show much like the one broadcast on Minnesota Public Radio. Thus the film further conflates the comic confusion in Keillor's radio performances between his authentic and represented selves, in addition to bringing to the big screen such long-standing jokes as his radio show's unviable premise and relations between radio and reality. In making backstage matters the front-stage subject of the film, Keillor also brought to it the same postmodern self-reflexivity about the interpenetration of performers' on-stage personas and off-stage lives that he had explored in two 1973 short stories, "The Slim Graves Show" and "Friendly Neighbors."

So central are jokes about Keillor's performance of identity and character that they run in and out of the main plot in his 2009 novel *Pilgrims: A Wobegon Romance*, the tale of a Lake Wobegon mission to honor a hometown hero's grave in a World War II cemetery outside Rome. The novel focuses mainly on Marjorie Krebsbach's quest for self-fulfillment, yet the woebegone figure of "Mr. Keillor" comes in for special ridicule befitting the punning subtitle. He puts himself at the bottom of the list of characters that prefaces the narrative. Identifying his character as "GARY KEILLOR, radio show host" restores his given name but treats *it* as the pseudonym with a winking reminder that the folks from Lake Wobegon knew him from childhood. And as soon as he appears, "Mr. Keillor" proves himself a woebegone figure, indeed, equally slow of step and mind, an improbable and undeserving celebrity. On the one hand, he doesn't understand when the group asks him to take their photo, because "he was accustomed to being the photographee" (6); on the other, he doesn't deserve what fame he's got. The tale of his comic suffering on the plane ride to Italy, a trip he funded in a moment of ineptitude, sums up his situation: "the radio man wound up sandwiched between a large embittered man and his angry wife with a fretful child on her lap," a couple who did not recognize him until most of the way from Minneapolis to Amsterdam, when the wife took the opportunity to say that she no longer listened to his show before offering "one word of advice.... Don't sing. Someone should've told you this years ago. You're not a singer. Don't sing" (7). Not a good omen for a journey that he hopes will yield a new book about an Italian trip featuring a passionate romantic fantasy with someone much like himself as the protagonist. But the incident and third-person representations of the humorist match the shifting self-presentations of his oral humor.

The success of *A Prairie Home Companion* has spawned a series of endeavors that have reinforced and extended Keillor's brand of humor. A mail order catalog and website hawk "Pretty Good Goods" (a name that carries the imaginary Ralph's Pretty Good Grocery of Lake Wobegon into the real world of American trade) as well as recordings and other spin-offs from Keillor's show, including its short-lived alternative, the *American Radio Company of the Air*, which broadcast mostly from New York City from the fall of 1989 to 1992. His weekly syndicated newspaper column alternates satirical analyses of current events with wry personal narratives that offer comic lessons. More seriously, he contributes a regular poetry spot to a series of public service announcements on public radio. And he publishes anthologies of poetry as well as radio monologues and novels featuring familiar and new eccentrics from Lake Wobegon. Each of these endeavors varies his persona slightly, making it harder for the audience to know him even as he presents himself ever more frequently to the public. Keillor's 1985 prediction that "a minimum of 15 reviews of this book [*Lake Wobegon Days*] will refer to me as 'a modern-day Mark Twain'" arose from his frustration that "anyone who writes anything humorous who comes from anywhere west of Eighth Avenue is 'another Mark Twain.'"[55]

But while Keillor and Twain do share a midwestern approach to writing, especially in their middle American vernacular and moral standpoints,[56] what unites their oral humor is their choice to put a comically unstable self at the center of their performances. And both found this self a platform for branding other, more lucrative writing and commercial activities.

At first glance, the stand-up routines of Margaret Cho (1968–) have little in common with the comic performances of Keillor and Twain. The reviewer for *Library Journal* who categorized her body of work as "ethnic/lifestyle humor" in "anecdotal stories about sex, race, body image, and self-esteem"[57] set Cho's jokes about Asian American identity and sexual orientation far apart from even the most ribald of Twain's comic lectures, not to mention Keillor's ironic sentimentality, though both men invoked sexuality through comic circumlocutions and double entendres. But focusing on the *themes* of Cho's five recorded concert performances—*I'm the One That I Want* (2000), *Notorious C.H.O* (2002), *Revolution* (2003), *Assassin* (2005), *Beautiful* (2009)—reduces her humor to the generic while ignoring the techniques that make her funny. Not that the themes fail to apply. Cho's political routines inspired the American Civil Liberties Union of Southern California to honor her with a First Amendment Award in 2004 "for making a significant difference in promoting equal rights for all, regardless of race, sexual orientation or gender identity," even as her trash talk about sex and attacks on Republican conservatism have led some observers to designate her an heir to Lenny Bruce.[58] Her emphasis on her experiences as a woman, a minority, and a supporter of gay rights clearly supports Joanne Gilbert's claim in *Performing Marginality* that women comics make audiences pay—literally—for the off-stage suffering that they perform on stage.[59] Likewise, Cho's running jokes about bladder and bowel accidents, colonic irrigation, sex acts, and the "exploding vagina" of childbirth clearly belong to the carnivalesque celebrations of the "lower stratum" that Mikhail Bakhtin described in *Rabelais and His World* and to the tradition of comic abjection that John Limon outlined in *Stand-Up Comedy in Theory*. Bakhtin's analysis of the carnivalesque also invites questions about why American stand-up comedy remains a largely male arena when "woman . . . is the incarnation of this stratum that degrades and regenerates simultaneously," because "she lifts her skirts and shows the parts through which every thing passes (the underworld, the grave) and from which everything issues forth."[60] Limon resolves that paradox by claiming that postwar urban America replaces the carnivalesque with comic abjection, a tradition consisting of one part public humiliation and one part anxiety over the abject (defined by Freudian theorist Julia

Kristeva as those components ambiguously both part of our bodies and separate from them, especially urine, feces, and blood). Limon recognizes something like the unstable persona I discuss here in identifying "a structure of abjection insofar as comedians are not allowed to be either natural or artificial. (Are they themselves or acting? Are they in costume?)," but traces the American tradition of comic abjection back only to Lenny Bruce. Still, in Limon's terms, Cho stands boldly in a line in which the abject not only provides the modern comedian's subject and a metaphor for stand-up's liminal zone between art and life, but also symbolizes the performer's anxious relationship with the audience, whose response can certify success or signify failure.[61] But emphasis on theme and psychology, for all their power to explain humor's centrality to culture, ignores how form and performance create humor, which is a rhetorical effect.

In any case Cho's humor goes beyond the "trash talking" that has made her, as she proudly claims, "notorious." Form and performance intersect as Cho's stand-up comedy imitates genres of ordinary conversation, especially the pointed anecdote and the personal experience narrative. Organized toward a dramatic climax, punch line, or moral, these structures help Cho generate humor through a series of performative incongruities across varied topics and tones. In particular, she shifts identities, acts out transgressions, and mimics opposing perspectives in order to convert outrage to ridicule. Together Cho's strategies illustrate how Twain's brand of stand-up comedy relies on performance of a distinctive, unstable comic self.

Indeed, Cho's humor, like Twain's and Keillor's, suggests that the main message that stand-up comedy communicates is that *the comedian is funny*. That implication makes performance the chief force behind stand-up's forms and themes. As Cho demonstrates, the stand-up comedian performs a character very like, but not actually, him- or herself—if only because a stage performance by definition exists apart from ordinary social life. Autobiographical stories, anecdotes, social commentary, and other genres of ordinary conversation already stand at one remove from reality because they report rather than enact events, and the imitations of these genres in stand-up comedy stand a step further removed because the comedian speaks in the artificial context of stage performance instead of in ordinary conversation. Rules of performance license the comedian to lie, yet limit the audience to a few ritualized behaviors, mainly listening and conventional signals of approval or dislike (laughter and groans) but not conversational exchange; the heckler who violates the rules and interrupts a comedian ends up the target of comic attacks, often from the audience as well as the comic. My point here is not simply that stand-up invites the audience to suspend disbelief in the fiction of the comedian's authenticity, in which the performer dresses as him- or herself and breaks the so-called fourth wall of the stage to speak apparently unstudied first-person remarks. Rather, I argue that even a stand-up comedian like Cho, who has not adopted a pseudonym nor written fiction through other voices, plays with authenticity, partly by imitating familiar conversational and narrative forms. In this sense, her humor exposes the "absolute directness" of communication in stand-up *as* a performance, by definition an artificial context. Indeed, the sensibility that she performs asserts humor in part by challenging the very idea at the heart of authenticity: a stable identity.

She does so by constructing her riffs around shifts in voice, facial expression, and posture—shifts that signify distinct characters, viewpoints, times, or contexts. For instance, sixteen shifts occur within a segment of about four and a half minutes in "Asian American" on the DVD of *I'm the One That I Want* (2000/2001). She begins speaking to her theatrical audience as the apparently intimate, off-stage (private, not-comic) Margaret with a complaint about white people's difficulty with "the concept Asian American," in order to introduce a series of anecdotes illustrating the problem. In the first story, she mimics a white male ABC television host asking her to speak to their viewers, then embeds her remarks to the camera as the professional off-stage (public, not-comic) Margaret within comments directed once again in this pseudointimate persona to her current theatrical audience. But these two shifts also stand in for the setup and punch line of the joke, because he asks her to speak to the audience "in her native language," to which she replies slowly and deliberately, as if *he* and his largely white American audience were foreigners who barely knew English: "We're changing to an ABC affiliate." In the process, she modulates from the past to the present, then back and forth again before shifting to yet a different past moment in the second anecdote, a time change signalled by her imitating the beep of an answering machine. That sound leads to a riff in which she channels her mother's strong Korean dialect of English—first in a cooing maternal voice, then in a threatening one—as her mother reverses the American racist rule: "Don't marry a white man!" A second beep returns us to the present of the live performance, for a total of eight shifts in the first two minutes alone, including representations of three different individuals and an answering machine in three different time periods. And still Cho has yet to get to the main part of her story, the visit to her white boyfriend's family, a report in which she mimics herself first as a model minority, the dialect-speaking submissive Asian ("sank you, Mistah Eddie's fasah"), and finally as an aggressive dialect-speaking

Asian trash talker who shouts to compatriots while turning the gaze of racial control onto the white man: "You eye so big... why you so tall? You so tall! Godzirra!" The multiple characters she invokes in less than five minutes define Cho as a comic master even as they complicate her identity as an American, an Asian American, and a unique individual.

Cho subjects race and ethnicity to similar instability. Instead of merely using race as a theme for jokes, she *enacts* a comic rhetoric of race through verbal and bodily performance. One series of jokes plays with the contrast between Asian appearance and American speech patterns, as in the excerpt I've detailed from *I'm the One That I Want*. The TV interviewer assumes that her Asian face signifies alien identity; but just as often, she reverses the variables, contrasting mock-Asian dialect with hegemonic American practices. In *Notorious*, for example, she recalls how her teenage fantasies about being an actress clashed with the reality of limited opportunities for Asian performers. "Maybe I could play a hooker in something," she muses, reenacting her adolescent self looking in the mirror, then trying it out with plaintive desperation: "Sucky, fucky, two dollar." She pauses, then raises her pitch to a whine and adds, "Me love you long *time*!" Or, as in the "Asian American" riff, she temporarily throws off the confident American identity she so articulately asserted just a few minutes before and instead enacts a racist stereotype of submissiveness, incoherence, and disfluency through physical and linguistic burlesque. She bows to her white prospective in-laws, recasting them as a "host famiry" to her own foreignness as she resorts to obsequious, singsong praise: "America numba one." She plays a similar joke on the audience in *Revolution* when she unexpectedly strips off her Asian-themed beaded headdress, then removes her Chinese-bob wig, and finally explains, in a heavy African American accent, "You know I would neva get dis chinky of a haircut, please—oh, please!" (See plate 1.) By channelling African American dialect here and imitating Valley Girl talk in *Assassin*, Cho complicates assumptions about voice and face as markers of identity. And her comment near the start of *Assassin*, "Sometimes I'm at odds with my own ethnic identity," indicates awareness that her humor tweaks racial and ethnic stereotypes by challenging the very idea of race as a category stable enough for stereotyping.

Categories of gender don't fare much better. Cho calls herself a "fag hag" and enjoys considerable affection from gay and lesbian fans. She grew up in San Francisco in the gay neighborhood on Polk Street, where according to her 2001 memoir she came to appreciate the sexual safety of gay men, compared to the threatening gropings she experienced from their straight counterparts.[62] She married another comic performance artist, Al Ridenour, in 2003 and refers to her heterosexual relationships in all her performances, but refuses to identify herself with a particular sexual orientation. Her black-dialect joke in *Assassin* about "mens [who] . . . have no idea what pussy tastes like" follows on her comic rejection of all sexual labels in *I'm the One*, where she reports that she briefly questioned whether she was gay during a gig on what she calls the "Lesbian Love Boat," but finally concluded, "I'm just slutty." Nor does she limit herself to female characterizations. In yet another joke predicated on reversing conventional standpoints, she mimics an inarticulate macho dude in a memorable if not profoundly original riff in *Notorious* called "Heavy Flow," a variation on Gloria Steinem's feminist classic "If Men Could Menstruate" (1978). Not only does Cho drop her voice and adopt an inarticulate monotone, lamenting, "Oh, fuck man, I can't believe I got my period again, dude. That's fucked up. I already got it last month," but she also alters her posture to match as she acts out his imagined frustrations in detail, down to his asking, "Dude . . . You got a tampon in your truck?" before reassuming the pseudointimate Margaret persona and breaking the fourth wall of the stage to editorialize, "You know, they would never have protection. They would be using old socks. Coffee filters. . . . Every bachelor apartment would look like a murder scene." Then, after a long, twelve-second pause for laughter and a drink of water, she shifts to yet another character and another variation on her theme by asking, "And if gay men had a period?" Unlike Whoopi Goldberg, who sustained each of her fictional characters through a lengthy monologue in *Direct from Broadway* (1985), Cho fragments herself to reveal her individuality through the prism of dozens of other voices and personas.

As Cho's persona emerges from the performance of multiethnic voices, ambiguously gendered behavior, volatile emotions, and ironic discourse, her performances join the tradition of Twain's brand of stand-up comedy: the display of an unstable, modern self in comic play with the world. Not surprisingly, in this context, her return to television in 2008 for *The Cho Show*, a seven-episode hybrid of sitcom and reality show on the VH1 cable channel, purported to show her on- and offstage in what a promotional article called "her favorite role, herself."[63] Her physical person and comic sensibility unify all her eclectic voices, moves, and moods. Each voice has its own exaggerated face and postures that contrast with the more conversational tones and expression of her apparently autobiographical self, resulting in a series of comically complex incongruities: between enacted imitations and direct address, herself and others, anger and ridicule, authenticity and pose. The anecdotes and personal narratives of Cho's stand-up comedy at once assert and undercut their claims to authority as spontaneous talk. By so skillfully imitating other characters, Cho paradoxically implies not only that her direct address expresses her authentic self, but also that this apparently authentic persona represents just another fictitious pose.

She creates this sense of authenticity by imitating naturally occurring conversational and narrative forms. For Cho, three forms predominate: the current events comment, anecdotal remark, and personal experience narrative. The current events comment and anecdotal remark, which both occur in ordinary conversation, easily serve as joke setups, as when Cho opened her *Notorious* performance by reporting her response to the 9/11 attacks: she went to Ground Zero "day after day, giving blow jobs to rescue workers. . . . yeah, because we all have to do our part." But like many stand-up comedians, Cho makes longer narratives of personal experience the centerpiece of her show. The "Asian American" excerpt has all four hallmarks of this genre as theorized by folklorist Sandra D. Stahl. Personal narratives claim to recount a true story with the narrator as the protagonist, as in Cho's examples of white and Asian racism in *I'm the One*. These tales also have a dramatic structure, often with a crisis and climax, as when Cho jokes about how the racist gaze converts her from Eddie's American girlfriend into a submissive alien who bows and speaks pidgen English to "Mistah Eddie's faddah." And finally, personal narratives illustrate some lesson or "covertly held value" that the teller seeks to share with the listener,[64] as when Cho shows how ethnic minorities can turn the tables on the majority by reversing—and thereby implicitly critiquing—hegemonic standards of normality. In *I'm the One*, the white view of Asians as short people with small eyes is displaced by an Asian gaze that reframes whites as big oafs with bug eyes ("You catch fly with your eye?"). But not all of Cho's personal narratives take this long form. For example, an extremely compressed story and lesson emerged from her comment in *Notorious* about giving blow jobs at Ground Zero, when she added, "You find out a lot about yourself during times of crisis. And I found out, I lost my gag reflex. I call that a triumph of the human spirit." She mocks herself along with postcrisis triumphalism in light ridicule of the American Christian tradition of seeking evidence of redemption in suffering. Generic conversational forms turn comic in Cho's performance precisely because, through a process that Victor Raskin calls "script opposition,"[65] a veneer of narrative authenticity hides the underlying joke structure and enables comic surprise. Naturally occurring talk may express any mood, follow any kind of structure, or ramble quite formlessly, whereas stand-up comedy creates the illusion of spontaneous talk to conceal its narrative movement toward a punch line.

The earnest themes of any personal narrative emerge as character, behavior, and attitude coalesce in performance,[66] and Cho's riffs follow that pattern. Sometimes she draws broad generalizations about human nature, such as the inevitability of one's own racial standpoint, and sometimes she draws incongruous conclusions about individuals or situations, such as the loss of her gag reflex or sphincter control. But all kidding aside, her chief lesson is acceptance of herself and others, especially those deviants from American cultural and mediated perfection: chubby women, gays and lesbians, nonwhites, political liberals in a time of social conservatism. Cho's surprisingly wholesome celebration of conventional deviance not only provides a humorous attitude and ironic tone that run through her filmed performances, but also organizes her comic rhetoric by embedding a potentially saccharine, conventional message within outrageous displays of social and sexual transgression. In *I'm the One That I Want*, it's the tale of her recovery from the humiliations of her failed television series. In *Notorious* and *Revolution*, it's the ungovernable body: horny, excreting, fat, gay, raced. In *Assassin*, filmed during the 2004 presidential race, it's the Republican right. Just as the personal narratives of daily life offer their themes in order to reveal and express the teller's identity by implying "a stable character or world view,"[67] so Cho keeps humor alive in her shows by subordinating her themes to her performance itself of a comic sensibility. But unlike her counterparts in naturally occurring conversation, she asserts this sensibility by playing with and challenging the very idea of the stable self and viewpoint.

And judging by the laughter in the theater and critics' reviews, she is at her funniest—that is, her most successful—in routines that contain the most instability, the most shifts. Her audience laughs much more intensely in *I'm the One That I Want*, which won awards from *New York* magazine and *Entertainment Weekly*,[68] than in *Assassin*, which most critics consider her least funny performance film and which records the least laughter from the audience. Not at all coincidentally, I think, Cho speaks more often in her usual conversational voice, and less often in the voices of other characters, in *Assassin* than in earlier shows. Likely for the same reason, the lines that her fans recite during pre- and postshow interviews to express their appreciation and approval of her humor come mainly from her earlier recordings, especially *I'm the One*. In fact, the lines they quote most often come not from the persona of Cho herself, but from her representations of other characters, especially her mother ("Don't marry a white man!") and the nurse's aide who introduces herself like a server in a restaurant: "My name is Gwen, and I'm here to wa-a-a-a-arsh your vagina!" These preferences point to the paradox at the heart of Twain's brand of stand-up: although Cho's films record her audiences praising how "real" she is, her stand-up comedy and its success clearly depend on her morphing from one artful presentation to another, some of them apparently Margaret Cho, a self implied in performance.

Equally noteworthy is Cho's success at extending her comic brand from the stage into commercial media. Her breakthrough performance constituted a branding feat in its own right: her stage show *I'm the One That I Want* became a video with the same name, which also became the title of her first book. Moreover, all this success built on a thirty-minute tale of failure broken into a series of comic riffs, the saga of her cancelled sitcom *All American Girl* (ABC, 1994–95). The show's premise drew loosely from her stage act's jokes about the conflicting values of a young Asian American woman and her immigrant parents. Doubtless the show's difficulties had many sources, including a premise of intercultural conflict already worn from use in *I Love Lucy* (1951–60) and *The Beverly Hillbillies* (1962–71) through *Mork and Mindy* (1978–82) and *The Fresh Prince of Bel-Air* (1990–96). But Cho claims in her act that the producers' racist Asian stereotypes crushed the humor, which was further doomed by the politics of her serving as a "Korean American role model," since "You know, I didn't play the violin" (*I'm the One*). These problems aside, the development of a sitcom vehicle for Cho in 1994 just as *Seinfeld* topped all records for TV ad sales[69] speaks to the importance of a stand-up comedian as a commodity suitable for marketing extensions in various media. In this context, Cho's return to television in 2008 proved both anticlimactic and validating. Her so-called "reality sitcom" on VH1 ran for just seven episodes from August 21 to September 25, 2008, but *The Cho Show* deliberately blurred the difference between her backstage and frontstage performances, further cementing her place, in the tradition of Twain's brand, as a comedian who trades on the confusion between her on- and offstage personas.

Critics such as David Marc treat situation and stand-up comedy as "aesthetically at odds," because stand-up privileges the individual while sitcoms depend on mass production techniques.[70] Sitcoms stress community over the individual, to be sure, especially the community symbolized by the family, although *Seinfeld*, *Friends* (NBC, 1994–2004), and other series about young, single urbanites replace the biological family with a peer-group equivalent. The celebrity sitcom unites the two genres, however. As they perform fictional versions of themselves in a sitcom, celebrity stand-up comedians unite life and art through their bodies and voices just as they do on stage. In the process they assert the authenticity of their performed selves even though any dramatic form casts the shadow of artifice on a representation. The comic gap between on- and offstage personas has always fueled the celebrity sitcom genre, but the show about the daily life of a comedian, *Seinfeld* (NBC 1989–98), turned the tradition on its head. *Seinfeld* revived George Burns and Gracie Allen's "mind-bending blurs of reality and fiction" (as David Bushman put it).[71] Taking the authenticity of the comedian's persona and materials as its premise exposed the open secret of Twain's brand of stand-up comedy: that comedians are actors who feign artless presentations of purportedly authentic identities and experiences.

Seinfeld grew famous as "a show about nothing," but it began as a sitcom that would explain "where comics get their material" by alternating scenes from Jerry Seinfeld's daily life with clips from his stand-up act.[72] The conceit emphasizes the origins of stand-up in autobiography, thereby branding the self twice over as a comic commodity, first to the network who bought the series and then to the advertisers who bought access to viewers through commercial time. But the conceit also confirms what Mark Twain's oral performances implied: that the art of stand-up rests on the comedian's ability to find and communicate humor, no matter what the topic. *Seinfeld*'s scripts further this implication by emphasizing conversation over plot and action. *Seinfeld*'s characters *discuss* madcap incidents, but seldom enact them; they perform their sensibilities as raconteurs, joke tellers, or straight men instead. The absence of action or familiar plot structures imitates—indeed, signifies—the formlessness and apparent meaninglessness of real life, but the show's monologues and dramatizations reinforce each other's claims to realism by exposing their artifice.

For instance, the episode "The Ex-Girlfriend," which led the second season, opens with Jerry's routine about drivers who obsess about changing lanes in order to escape heavy traffic, then cuts to a scene of George Costanza and Jerry sitting in a car as they talk about why George wants to break up with his girlfriend. Barely any physical movement and no plot-driven action occurs for the first five minutes of the episode: Jerry's arm motions as he imitates a driver trying to change lanes provide the liveliest physical action in the first three minutes, when Elaine walks up to the car and George gets out to let her in, a half-minute of movement followed by two more minutes of watching the two men in the front seat nod as Elaine, squeezed between them, tells a story about a man in her apartment building. But the episode does have a plot even in the absence of demonstrated action: in retrieving George's books from his girlfriend, Jerry becomes involved with her until she dumps *him* at the end of the sitcom segment because she saw and disliked his stand-up act. And that incident not only provides a tidy bit of symmetry by closing the sitcom segment where it began, in Jerry's car discussing a breakup with her, and not only gets him magically, painlessly, anticlimactically, and thus comically out of a relationship he did not want, but also triggers the insight of his closing monologue: "Women need to like the job of the guy they're with." The show's writers rejected sitcoms' conventional pratfalls, repartee, and plot structures, but the symmetry and reversals in the girlfriend plot reveal how form—any form—implies meanings and may imply a story as well. As in any other performance, in this slice of Jerry's life or this clip of his stand-up routine, authenticity is the rhetorical effect of artifice.

Production details of *Seinfeld* emphasize just how artificial the production of realism is. The need to have an appreciative audience for Jerry's stand-up led the producers to arrange for a warm-up act to precede him on the stage of the pretend comedy club that they created on the soundstage. Commentary on the first season DVD insists that the audience's "laughter . . . is genuine," but when Jerry performs for an audience of extras, cast for that role in a soundstage dressed to represent a club, his routine becomes an imitation of a stand-up act just as the sitcom segments already are imitations of life. Despite the show's premise that Jerry's stand-up routines came from the episodes dramatized by the sitcom, commentary on the first season DVD concedes that the reverse was true: first came Seinfeld's stand-up material ("The Stock Tip"), then an episode explaining its origin. The procedure makes comic sense: a good punch line needs just the right setup. It makes commercial sense, too. Seinfeld's branding cycle also originates in the comic's offstage and offscreen observations about life, moves to the stand-up performance and then to the sitcom screen (in imitations of both stage performance and life), and finally reenters offscreen life when recycled in the best-selling book *SeinLanguage* (1973). *Seinfeld's* tensions between authenticity and illusion, seriousness and joking, reality and play highlight the centrality of performed authenticity to Twain's brand of stand-up comedy.

An impression of authenticity supports extensions of the brand to new commercial contexts such as print and television, but comic branding itself depends on the achievement of apparent authenticity. *SeinLanguage's* publisher pointed to that effect when he crowed, "Would that all our authors had twenty-plus million people interested in them every week."[73] Indeed, *Seinfeld* lives on in syndication and DVD sales, its popularity so secure that in 2010, a decade after production ended, an adult-video catalogue featured a pornographic "XXX Parody" starring look-alikes of the cast.[74] Branding has fostered the expanded influence of stand-up comedy even as comedians have reinforced its importance.

In defining Twain's stand-up comedy as the performance of an apparently authentic yet unstable comic self, and identifying Garrison Keillor, Margaret Cho, Jon Stewart, and Jerry Seinfeld as contemporary heirs to this tradition, I privilege their common rhetorical practices over their very different topics, themes, and tones. That's because technique trumps topic in humor. Comedians aim above all to create humor, preferably by making the audience laugh aloud, and the social commentary or stories or jokes devised for this purpose are means to that end. Nonetheless, each comedian's signature humor relies on signature topics and themes as well as techniques. The comic sensibility communicated through a particular voice, face, and body inflects chosen topics with individual flavor in this most individualistic of social comic rituals. Keillor's autobiographical mock-mythology brings an insider's affection to critiques of American radio, commercial, and small-town traditions as well as to contemporary local, national, and cultural politics, while Cho's tales of abjection and sexual transgression scorn social conservatism from the sidelines, and Stewart's and Seinfeld's mock-naïveté challenges the status quo of contemporary American life. Yet all these contemporary comics, like Mark Twain, offer as their main humorous performance a particular kind of comic persona, an unstable self implied through representations that blend the invented and ironic with the authentic and reliable.

From the 1866 Sandwich Islands lecture to remarks at the 1909 graduation ceremonies of The Misses Tewksbury's School, where he told the girls, "I am seventy-three and one half years old, and have been smoking seventy-three of them" (*MTS*, 645), Twain's brand of solo performance broke with the stable comic persona of the clown, even the ironic variant pioneered by Artemus Ward and revived today by Steven Colbert, a figure whose right-wing politics endorse the left. (For that reason, not all the members of the immigration subcommittee of the House of Representatives enjoyed Colbert's in-character testimony on migrant farm labor on September 24, 2010.) If Ward and Colbert exemplify the figure that Bernard DeVoto called the Perfect Fool, comedians working within Twain's brand represent variations on the Imperfect Philosopher, a figure who subordinates all subjects to the rhetorical goal of laughter. The deepest observational insight of stand-up comedy will fail if it lacks humor, as we know from documentary footage of Lenny Bruce's last years, when he was too seriously political to be funny.[75] But the unpredictable, unstable persona commands attention that the accomplished humorist exploits, rewarding the attentive audience with insights worth laughter and thought. And audiences reciprocate with rewards of their own.

Each stand-up comedian faces the challenge of implying a unique persona—a distinctive brand of humor as comic identity—through direct address. As vehicles for expressing identity, ostensibly autobiographical tales hide the artifice of the comic's rhetoric. Concealment safeguards the punch line as it fosters comic incongruities by merging various feigned personas and comic poses with the stable body before us. And in the process of creating a comic self for professional and financial success, especially in the contemporary U.S., where politics still proclaim everyone's right to define her own identity and the information economy rewards brand extensions of media commodities, Twain's brand of stand-up comedy simultaneously fulfills and mocks the myth of the self-made American.

CHAPTER THREE

Humor and Empire

Matters of empire have inflected American literary humor for two hundred years because comic rhetoric carries ideological weight born of old colonial ties to Europe and elsewhere. A strand of humor expressing Anglo-American continuity runs through the present from eighteenth-century English wits like Alexander Pope, who displayed learned wit in essays and classical forms with an elevated literary style; American heirs range from poets such as John Woodworth (1768–1858), the "American Youth" who anonymously satirized Congress in *The Spunkiad* (1798), and the more famous James Russell Lowell (1819–1891) to contemporary epic novelists such as David Foster Wallace (1962–2008). Likewise, the colonization of African slaves in North America marks the voices and narratives of works as different as Zora Neale Hurston's *Jonah's Gourd Vine* (1934) and Ishmael Reed's *Flight to Canada* (1976) with African traditions of oral humor.[2] Humor also exposes disruption of imperial ties. The conflict between indigenous and colonizing sensibilities animates Junot Díaz's *Brief Wondrous Life of Oscar Wao* (2007), for instance, as tricksters evoke and avenge the *fukú americanus*, the original sin unleashed by Spain's invasion of the Americas.[3] But the best-known tradition of American literary humor, the British-American contrast, applauds America's divergence from European models of society and government. From its beginnings on the eighteenth-century New England stage, the British-American contrast flaunted America's regional and immigrant dialects, diverse population, and lack of cosmopolitan polish. Soon popular humorous writing of many types—New

> All our history, all our crimes, all the good things we've done are embedded in that thing, that fluid thing we call language.
>
> —Junot Díaz[1]

England cracker-barrel philosophy, tall and settlement tales from the Old Southwestern and western frontiers, newspaper hoaxes and local color fiction from all regions—likewise scorned gentility (of both foreign and domestic types) in favor of vulgar republican virtues that dramatized the superiority of the former colony and its homegrown political system to the imperial center and monarchy.

The British-American contrast tickled readers on both sides of the Atlantic in the nineteenth century because American claims to international superiority flew incongruously (not to say defensively) in the face of expanding European empires; reversed hierarchies of status and taste remained marketable here and abroad, confirming old patriotic prejudice on both sides, even after the U.S. became a world power in the mid-twentieth century. Colloquial American usage symbolized democratic ideology. What Leo Marx in 1958 called "The Vernacular Tradition" was canonized, in his famous formulation, as "a style with a politics in view . . . of an egalitarian faith . . . [that] sweeps aside received notions of class and status"; it originated, he argued, in "a drama of cultural contrast" between Americans and Europeans.[4] Twain made the point in "Concerning the American Language" (1882), a piece "crowded out" of his travel book *A Tramp Abroad* (1880), when he reminded the Englishman sharing his train compartment, "Your words 'gentleman' and 'lady' have a very restricted meaning; with us they include the bar-maid, butcher, burglar, harlot, and horse-thief" (*CTS*, 832). That is, both writers and theorists saw colonial and postcolonial relations in language politics. The cosmopolitan and imperial must always contend with the vernacular and local, according to Sheldon Pollock, who has studied how vernaculars relate to Sanscrit in southern Asia and to Latin in western Europe, and he concludes that "vernacular literary cultures were initiated by the conscious decisions of writers to reshape the boundaries of their cultural universe by renouncing the larger world for the smaller place."[5] In this vein, nineteenth-century American writers renounced political ties to empire through their preference for regional usage, which humorists took to extremes in capturing spoken local dialects, especially when set against British accents and forms. Jonathan Arac has objected to calling American colloquial English a vernacular, because only Indian languages are indigenous to North America.[6] Yet from today's standpoint we can see that the invidious U.S.–international contrast invested heavily not only in representing Americans on the world stage as politically innocent (and hence virtuous) victims of empire, but also in imagining U.S. history as a tale of Anglo-American family relations— as if European invasions, slaughter and dispossession of native peoples, enslavement of kidnapped Africans, and proxy wars with Spain, France, and the Netherlands played no part. Considering that policies of Manifest Destiny constituted the type of imperialism known as internal colonization, American humor's insistence on defining American virtue by contrast to imperial practice makes clear that suppressing our own imperialist acts was part of the point.

Twain's brand of humor reflects these trends. His explicit satires of what he euphemistically called "The Blessings of Civilization" (1901) date from the Spanish-American War of 1898, and his anti-imperialist politics go back at least to 1867, when he mocked U.S. plans to annex St. Thomas and Hawaii,[7] yet he also endorsed American continental expansion. He supported it outright in *Roughing It* (1872) and tacitly in other works by building upon antebellum comic traditions, especially the semiliterate letter and the mock–oral narrative. These forms personified the postcolonial values of the Anglo-American contrast in domestic terms through invidious contrasts between ostensibly superior easterners and unpolished westerners or between two other types contrasting high and low status, such as genteel and vulgar speakers. These variants shaped many of Twain's most famous works, including "Jim Smiley and His Jumping Frog" ("The Celebrated Jumping Frog of Calaveras County," 1865), "A True Story" (1874), *The Prince and the Pauper* (1882), *Huckleberry Finn* (1884), *A Connecticut Yankee in King Arthur's Court* (1889), and *Pudd'nhead Wilson* (1894). More to the point, their comic contrasts between vernacular and hegemonic—especially the American normality and foreign strangeness that Amy Kaplan cites to argue that Mark Twain's "famous 'homespun' qualities were . . . woven from the tangled threads of imperial travel," because they built on his early experiences in colonial Hawaii through his turn-of-the-century tour of the British Empire[8]—belong to a politicized tradition that antedates Clemens's childhood. He invokes the old postcolonial values in works that comically reverse the European invasion of North America by sending the American abroad, as in the big travel books that framed his career, *Innocents Abroad* (1868) and *Following the Equator* (1895), but *Connecticut Yankee* confronts the ideology of humor and empire head on. Here the Anglo-American contrast that structures the novel—set in a castle that Clemens visited as a Connecticut Yankee himself during his important London visit of 1872—also provides its plot and themes. And these latter seem finally to have given him some pause. As Mark Twain imagined Hank Morgan's efforts to colonize sixth-century Britain in the image of nineteenth-century America, the politics of Manifest Destiny finally caught up with the comic image of the virtuous democrat. Because Clemens could not rewrite European history and had to account for the bullet hole in Sir Sagramore's armor, plot problems he recognized early on (*N&J* 3:216–17), the close of Hank's story not only marks the failure of an American imperial adventure, but also concedes the failure of exceptionalist American ideals of national virtue. The impossibility of successful colonization of the sixth century by the nineteenth in *Connecticut Yankee* means that the same vernacular comic tradition that identifies Hank Morgan as a quintessentially American hero, "a Yankee of the Yankees" (*CY*, 50), and the same postcolonial plot that celebrates his triumph over British backwardness merge to make him a despot. Thus, the link between humor and empire in *Connecticut Yankee* exposes two frauds: defining U.S. democratic virtue in contrast to British aristocratic corruption and dismissing U.S. imperialism as delirium or a tall tale.

In this context, *Connecticut Yankee* represents a turning point in Twain's writing not simply because Hank's egalitarian rhetoric clashes with his imperialist enterprise, but also because the novel's humor grimly confirms imperialism and apocalypse as the fulfillment of American destiny. For all the patriotism of the international contrast, the rhetoric of humor and empire in *Connecticut Yankee* reveals American exceptionalism as a source of American corruption. And this element of Twain's late brand of humor, with its black-humorous implications of America's own European-style failings, lives on in twentieth-century literary humor, especially in the fiction of Philip Roth.

Indeed, if practices of empire include subordination of other nations and their values for purposes of self-aggrandizement and exploitation of extranational materials for domestic nation-building, then no contemporary American writer has addressed the imperialist assumptions of American literary humor more than Philip Roth. His experiences as a Jewish American child during the 1930s and '40s gave personal significance to the American exceptionalism underlying the British-American contrast even before he studied American humor as a graduate student at the University of Chicago in the 1950s. His autobiography recalls that "much of the exuberance with which I and others of my generation of Jewish children seized our opportunities after the war . . . came from our belief in the boundlessness of the democracy in which we lived and to which we belonged."[9] Nonetheless, in the early 1970s, a century after Twain's important first visit to England, Roth also found inspiration and opportunity in Europe. After the vernacular excesses of *Portnoy's Complaint* (1969) cost him the patronage of the American Jewish establishment and the political excesses of Watergate and Vietnam challenged his secular faith in the nation, Roth began to inject his American fictions with European contrasts. (Unlike Roth's obscene writings, Twain's circulated only in private editions, but both writers made literary breakthroughs through them.[10]) In *The Breast* (1972) and "I Always Wanted You to Admire My Fasting" (1973), Roth imports Kafka to the U.S., but two longer alternative histories make humor and empire central to their stories. The burlesque *Great American Novel* (1973), a tall tale in the classic antebellum tradition of Old Southwestern humor, challenges national myths of American innocence through a satire of Vietnam-era politics that retells the story of World War II by relocating it from the European theater to American baseball stadiums. More recently, the taller tale *The Plot Against America* (2004) satirizes George W. Bush's policies in the form of a mock-memoir that ostensibly recalls when the U.S. appeased Hitler and instituted campaigns against American Jews. Both of these counterhistories, like *Connecticut Yankee*, invoke the contrast's vernacular rhetoric of humor and empire to question exceptionalist American claims of virtue.

The ink on the Constitution had barely dried when Noah Webster exhorted Americans in 1789 to "establish a *national language*, as well as a national government" as "the means of commanding respect abroad"[11]— that is, from the imperial powers of Europe. A few years later, Royall Tyler's 1797 play *The Contrast* grafted republican politics onto English stage conventions in order to tout the superiority of the U.S. to Britain. The comic subplot of the play starred a young fellow called Jonathan, a New England bumpkin already known by that name in American folklore, who conveyed democratic ideology in the mode of the *eiron* of classical drama: a character whose outward simplicity and uncouthness belie his inner virtues. The American youth embodied the young nation who triumphed over its parent, the king of England. A key moment in the play involves Jonathan's performance of "Yankee Doodle," a revolutionary-era song originally spoofing New Englanders' rustic speech and manners but quickly turned by them into an affirmation of American distinction.[12] This and related appropriations converted contempt to pride and made British-American difference, especially language variation, a politically significant trope of American humor from an early point. Reversals of linguistic and political hierarchy served two political needs at once: they asserted the superiority of colony to imperial center; and they—*quite* conveniently— erased the difference between the colonized natives left out of this transatlantic family saga and the descendents of the English-speaking invaders who shaped it.

Within a generation Jonathan had left the subplot to become Jack Downing, the comic protagonist of Seba Smith's fictitious letters from a New England rube to his family. Downing's picturesque regionalisms and political naïveté exposed corruption in the capitols of Maine and Washington, appearing first in the Portland, Maine, *Daily Courier* in 1830 and newspapers across the country, and then, after spawning many imitations, in book collections published in the U.S. and England. The Downing letters shared their pride in American idiom, American character types, American settings, and American political ideology with the homespun tales of Thomas Chandler Haliburton's Yankee peddler Sam Slick and the memoir of tall-talking backwoodsman-turned-politician Colonel David Crockett. And in 1838 a reviewer for the *London and Westminster Review* seized on the nationalism common to the Downing, Slick, and Crockett books as evidence that "American literature has ceased to be exclusively imitative. A few writers have appeared in the United States, who, instead of being European and English in their styles of thought and diction, are American."[13] The phrase "styles of thought and diction" brings together the key elements of what became known as vernacular style—language and ideology, language *as* ideology, and a connotation of oral language—in perhaps the earliest claim of American humor's distinctiveness. Equally important, the standpoint of 1838 Britain characterized American humor ideologically in a transatlantic context as deviations from English customs, especially social refinement; deviations from English politics, especially the monarchy; distinctive American situations and setting, especially the so-called "wilderness"; and distinctive American language, especially by white English speakers who otherwise seemed to be kin. In fact, by 1838 the merger of American language, American behavior, and American ideology had already been cemented on both sides of the pond in the word *Americanism*.[14]

The same criteria gave international stature to Twain's humor thirty years later in the British marketplace, where attitudes of cultural superiority highlighted the Anglo-American divide. The 1870 *Saturday Review* loved Twain's satire of American boorishness and "the genuine unmistakable convictions of many of his countrymen" in *Innocents Abroad* (*CR*, 84). An 1872 review of *Roughing It* in the London *Examiner* scorned Twain's exuberance as the very opposite of English refinement, but conceded that it was only to be expected of life beyond the cosmopolitan center: "[T]he humour of strong, daring, adventurous spirits . . . [is] animated by wild, irregular passions, which may unfit them for settled life, but are among the very qualities required for semi-civilized regions, such as those that form the scene of Mr. Clemens's two books." As the English critic reframes lost colonial lands as "semi-civilized regions" and former British subjects as dehumanized "spirits ... animated by wild ... passions" (*CR*, 102–3), British amusement at Americanism translates the English dramatic tradition of the lower-class comic subplot to the political stage, where nation replaces class as the butt of the jokes. Reviews such as these illustrate how the British marketplace for books and ideas reinforced American postcolonial political inclinations into the 1870s and beyond, giving further resonance to the rhetoric of humor and empire.

As he described his new project to a friend in 1886, Twain envisioned *Connecticut Yankee* as "a *contrast*" between British and American "salients," including comic clashes between Malory's medieval literary English and Hank's nineteenth-century American urban slang.[15] Language differences mark Hank's arrival in sixth-century Britain, where his request to "see the head keeper a minute" fetches a "Prithee do not let me," and his introduction to Clarence, a court page, prompts him to the (stale) response, "Go 'long ... you ain't more than a paragraph" (*CY*, 61). His travels with Sandy revitalize worn jokes about talkative women by contrasting Hank's colloquial "somebody corners the market on *you*, and down goes your bucket-shop" with her "Whethersoever it be that my mind miscarrieth, bewraying simple language in such sort that the words do seem to come endlong and overthwart" (223). Representations of Malory's English in newspapers join verbal anachronisms like sixth-century marketing slogans to sustain the cultural contrast throughout the novel. In the final tournament, when Hank shows up wearing only a gymnast's leotard and tights to fight Sir Sagramour, decked out in full armor and lance as an "iron tower and gorgeous bed-quilt," the shocked queen shouts, "Alack, Sir Boss, wilt fight naked, and without lance or sword or—"; her remark adds to the contest between past and present, Yankee and England, in which Hank's lasso carries the day, culminating in his colloquial boast "the whole knight-errantry hive was just humming now" (432–33). Language also highlights Hank's effect on his Clarence, who became his lieutenant, in the Battle of the Sand Belt. As their dialogue about strategy omits all differences between sixth- and nineteenth-century English, so the last word from the action goes to Merlin, with his archaic "Ye were conquerors; ye are conquered! He sleepeth, now—and shall sleep thirteen centuries!" (489).

American readers seized on the conventional implications of the British-American contrast in approving the book's politics. When Edmund C. Stedman read the finished manuscript, he told Clemens that he loved its "magnificently riotous & rollicking imagination & humor" but found some of Hank's language "a trifle out of tone for a Brother Jonathan"(*CY*, qtd. 521). Like Stedman, twentieth-century scholars such as Henry Nash Smith and James Cox also saw the book within the vernacular tradition, and they lamented its failure to fulfill the American virtues that its conventions attached to Hank. But the ending did not trouble the august editor of the *Atlantic* (and Clemens's good friend), William Dean Howells, who lauded the novel's "delicious satire" and declared it "an object lesson in democracy."[16] Hank's knowledge of science, technology, history, and literature, his enthusiasm for challenge and democracy, his willingness to confront injustice, superstition, and ignorance—all cast him as the personification of what nineteenth-century Americans imagined as the U.S. at her best. British reviewers of Twain's day caught political implications that American readers missed. London's *Review of Reviews* concluded that the British lower classes, significantly empowered by American-style mass education, would likely side with the Yankee against the British, while the *New Review* sneered at the book's "patriotic prejudice" and asked, "Will the Connecticut Yankee take up his residence next at the Court of Kaiser William?" (*CR*, 308, 307). Yet Twain's own ambivalence toward Hank and his ambitions marked the project throughout and skewed his enterprise toward failure. The prime, rhetorical reason is that Twain built *Connecticut Yankee*'s humor on at least three ideological contradictions regarding American democratic values and empire, but a second, biographical reason is that the shadow of Henry Morton Stanley, seen in his day as a vernacular American hero and in ours as the quintessential European imperialist, fell over the book.

The most obvious contradiction underlying the novel concerns threats to Hank's moral authority from structural clashes among the comic contrast, the time-travel plot, and the tall tale. What good is the Yankee's democratic ideology if he's telling stretchers? He can't alter the course of history, so his chief success, like that of any tall talker, must be to dupe his audience into believing, if only briefly, that his tale is true. Twain signals the conventions of the tall tale from the opening narrative frame set in England's Warwick Castle. "I am an American," Hank begins, in an introduction that defines as well as describes: "a Yankee of the Yankees—and practical; yes, and nearly barren of sentiment, I suppose" (*CY*, 50). Thus the opening distinguishes the plain-speaking nineteenth-century New England mechanic, a man so hard-headed that even a "crusher" (51) from a crowbar fails to kill him, from two types of romantics: Mark Twain's version of the stereotypical gentleman narrator of a tall tale, in this case a gullible who dozes over his drink and dreams over his Malory; and the romantic characters of Arthurian literature, chivalric nobles with crude and violent lives. After the prefatory "Word of Explanation" casts Hank's tale as a series of stretchers, the product of many whiskeys on both sides, the inner narrative comically complicates the difference between the romantic and the real by insisting on his veracity. His prediction of the solar eclipse, his ability to smell pigs where Sandy sees princesses, and the hole in Sir Sagramour's armor all provide comic proof for his story, and he insists that "my situation was in the last degree serious, dream or no dream" (*CY*, 83). Yet for all the moral and political issues that Hank raises, the novel concludes with a "P.S. from M.T." that reinforces the opening frame's implications of Hank's instability as he continues confused over "dreams that were as real as reality—delirium, of course, but so real!" (492). Other details of the contrast, such as the affinities between Hank and Morgan le Fay and between Hank and Merlin, likewise diminish the moral superiority implied by the Yankee's democratic ideals and scientific know-how, as well as his greater sophistication than Sandy or Arthur. Twain reinforces these built-in contradictions when Hank draws on the long-established negative meaning of *Yankee*, "to defraud, cheat, or outsmart" (dating from 1801, according to Mathews's *Americanisms*), noting that the species has "a unique and shady reputation among all truly good and holy peoples" (286).

A second contradiction builds the postcolonial values of the comic contrast on the imperialist fantasy of Hank's modernization program. The contrast defines the Yankee's virtue in terms of his victimization by the British, while his importation of American-style democracy and technology hinges on his power as "The Boss." Even in the chapter entitled "The Boss," where he boasts that "in power I was equal to the king" he stresses the superior forces of church, aristocracy, and tradition that create his "anomalous position in King Arthur's kingdom" (*CY*, 109, 113). Likewise, the structure of the novel stresses his vulnerability by skewing the report of his experience: two chapters (X and XL) summarize the successes of ten years—"My works showed what a despot could do with the resources of a kingdom at his command," he boasts, hailing the advent of electricity and machinery, telephones and telegraphs, schools and a military academy, one thousand trained men and fifty "brilliant experts" (128)—while the other forty-one chapters detail the challenges of just a few months. Twain delivers these threats in a series of repeated episodes, some in pairs and others in series, that intensify the violence and raise the political stakes of Hank's continued presence in Britain as he falls from being "no shadow of a king; . . . [but] the very substance" (109) to a slave about to be hanged.

The two journeys that constitute the bulk of the novel chart this pattern: humorous events of the first tour reappear as serious threats in the second. The first journey ridicules danger, which Hank as a comic victim consistently fails to evaluate correctly. Expecting his pipe smoke to make attacking knights disappear as quickly as ignorant freemen, Sir Boss himself wants to vanish when it does not. To his surprise, that "perfect ass" Sandy deals easily with their uninjured attackers when he "would have considered ... [approaching them] a doubtful errand" (*CY*, 139, 169). And battling an ogre for hostages merely requires paying a swineherd for hogs because his successes on this mock quest depend less on demonstrations of strength than on illusions of peril. The journey with Arthur makes these real. Now death is everywhere: along the road, in a peasant's hut, in the manor house, even in children's play at hanging each other. Hank's comic sufferings in adapting to his new role as a knight in armor, unable to scratch an itch, give way to Arthur's difficulties adjusting to life as a peasant, with far more serious outcomes. For looking "about as humble as the leaning tower at Pisa," he earns a whipping (312). For insulting the knights who almost trample him, he and Hank are attacked. Although Hank and Sandy can buy freedom for a herd of pigs, he and Arthur are themselves "sold at auction, like swine" (392), because leaving the fantasy world of knights and castles for the realistic world of peasants and huts means that humor gives way to pain. Maintaining the novel's humor requires ever more extravagant demonstrations of nineteenth-century technology and ever more hyperbolic descriptions of its impact, with the result that the humor ever more emphatically equates Hank's success with American, and imperialist, violence.

The implication that Hank's victimization justifies increasing violence turns unwholesome, especially for modern readers, on two counts: Hank's imposition of American customs on a foreign people smacks of imperialism, and his firepower sets up an unfair fight. Howard Baetzhold objects to such readings as ahistorical,[17] yet both elements taint Hank's project from the start, and textual details suggest that at some level Mark Twain knew it. For example, when Hank saves himself by exploiting a solar eclipse, he compares himself to the original European invaders of North America, "Columbus, or Cortez, or one of those people" (*CY*, 86). In addition, he refers to his accomplishments as the beginnings of civilization in "a new country" and the "dark land" (120, 128), phrases that evoke the colonization of North America four centuries earlier and of Africa even as he was writing. As Kerry Driscoll has shown, Hank compares Arthur's subjects to "white Indians" and one of their magicians to an "Indian medicine man" (*CY*, 278); such details join others to invoke the ideology of progress underlying the forced "civilization" and assimilation of Native Americans in the nineteenth century.[18] Labeling Hank's battle with the knights the "last stand of the chivalry" (478), an allusion to General Custer at the Battle of the Little Bighorn (an event just a dozen years old when Twain wrote) likewise Americanizes the novel's conflict and aligns Hank with the forces of imperial conquest.

Moreover, the five skirmishes between Hank and knights that structure the novel chart a pattern of victimization from start to finish. The series varies Malory's account (quoted in the opening frame) of Sir Kay's heroic intervention in a fight of three knights against one. Hank mocks the absence of "those chivalrous magnanimities about which one reads so much" when "half a dozen knights and their squires" charge him and Sandy (*CY*, 167, 166), and the conflicts intensify as old and new world manners clash ever more violently with old and new world technologies. Hank can climb a tree to escape Sir Kay and puff on his pipe to halt the Duke and his sons (52, 167), but ongoing threats lead him to bomb the nobles who attack him and Arthur, shoot Sir Sagramour and ten other opponents in the tournament, and finally dynamite and electrocute twenty-five thousand knights in the Battle of the Sand Belt (317, 437, 476). Characterizing Hank as an embattled American underdog casts his aggression as self-defense; after Hank loses his lasso, Sir Sagramour defends his right to "kill a naked man" in the tournament (437), thereby justifying Hank's resort to the six-shooter, although he declared at the outset, "I was entering the lists to either destroy knight-errantry or be its victim" (430). As the British-American contrast implies that increasing danger and vulnerability call for increasing violence, a classic type of comic retribution, so the imperialist fantasy justifies the Old World pushback and expands both his arsenal and opportunities to use it. This set of contradictions means that Hank's vernacular values of egalitarianism, ingenuity, and practicality yield only ludicrous or lethal outcomes.

A third ideological contradiction emerges from Twain's comic language, especially the euphemisms and hyperbole of the novel's burlesque, which grows more extravagant even as the incidents Hank recounts grow morally and politically more serious. Despite the rising stakes, Morgan stresses his role as underdog by describing all his fights with the knights in similar terms, mocking their "bed-quilt" (*CY*, 51, 432) costumes, and admitting that they look "handsome" (167), or "gallant" (317), or "superb" (437), before dehumanizing them as "a whirr and a rush" (167), "a lightning express" (317), and "a moving black mass" (476, 485). Then, with violence downplayed, he implies that similar attackers receive similar punishments. His pipe smoke makes the "iron wave" of chivalry "go to pieces and scatter" (167); the dynamite bomb causes "a steady drizzle of microscopic fragments of hardware and horseflesh" (318); "the vast horseshoe wave" that reaches the mined Sand Belt becomes "a whirling tempest of rags and fragments" (476). Repetition treats mass murder as comic dehumanization, but his many details of the final battle turn the mood somber and dystopian. "Of course we could not *count* the dead," he concedes, "because they did not exist as individuals, but merely as homogenous protoplasm, with alloys of iron and buttons" (478). The victims of the minefield join those electrocuted as Hank's fence charges the armor of each knight and those who touch him to form "a solid wall of the dead—a bulwark, a breastwork, of corpses," and still Hank calls his troops to drown everyone and "vomit death into the fated ten thousand" (485–486). Burlesque violence requires fantasy, however, and here realism prevails as extravagant comic metaphor turns literal, satiric, and grim.

Overlap among these three sets of built-in contradictions shows how *Connecticut Yankee*'s humor rests on an ambivalent view of American imperial adventure. As Hank's tale veers from comic romp to dystopian catastrophe, vernacular ideology becomes imperialist rationale. But the novel's comic incongruities suggest that Twain did not so much lose control of his vernacular materials, as Smith and Cox have charged, as test and expose their limits. Indeed, the link between humor and empire in *Connecticut Yankee* presents the postcolonial comic rhetoric of American innocence as a mask for imperialism, American exceptionalism as a source of American corruption, Hank no better than Merlin—and indeed far worse, because the nineteenth-century American should know better.

Twain did not, of course, articulate this conclusion. The ideological investment of nineteenth-century readers *and* early American humor scholars in the virtuous vernacular speaker kept them all from seeing vernacular conventions as anything but positive, much less recognize their displacement of the U.S. imperialism of Manifest Destiny, as I have detailed elsewhere, but Howells summed up the consensus in defining *Connecticut Yankee*'s humor as "the American kind, the kind employed in the service of democracy."[19] Domestic imperialism hid in plain sight, however. While working on *Connecticut Yankee*, Clemens arranged for his firm Webster & Co. to publish books by the widows of two Civil War heroes whose postwar careers involved major military campaigns against native peoples. Almira Russell Hancock's *Reminiscences of Winfield Scott Hancock* (1887) and Elizabeth Bacon Custer's *Tenting on the Plains: or, General Custer in*

Kansas and Texas (1887) did not sell as well as Ulysses Grant's *Personal Memoirs* (2 vols., 1885–86), which Webster & Co. also published. But the firm took pride in having "cornered the market on war books"(as manager Charles Webster put it), and the volumes also served the charitable function of providing the widows with income (*MTD* 2:23, 116 [quote], 117). But the widows' books reinforced U.S. expansionist visions that General Custer himself described in *My Life on the Plains, Or, Personal Experiences with Indians* (1874), which opens by explaining that "civilization, propelled and directed by Yankee enterprise, adopted the motto, 'Westward the star of empire takes its way'" and implies that he merely did his part.[20] Clemens owned a copy of the book (originally serialized in *The Galaxy* in 1872, the year after Clemens left the magazine [*MTLib* 1:169, 250]), in which Custer reported an attack by Indians in terms very like Hank's description of the knights' charge, noting "the long glistening lance with its pennant of bright colors" and how "[s]uddenly, with wild ringing war-whoop, the entire band of warriors bore down upon the train and its little party of defenders."[21] Whatever their influence, these details highlight my main point here: that the international, postcolonial origins of the cultural distracted nineteenth-century Americans from the domestic implications of vernacular humor. The conventions of the framed vernacular tale used dialect humor to emphasize the triumphant (mostly white) western and southwestern lower-class Americans of their extended inner narratives, while the comically inept, barely described hegemons who narrated the slim outer frames colonized Indian lands.

Twain's use of the frame tale in *Connecticut Yankee* and elsewhere follows in this tradition, which further supports Kerry Driscoll's view that racism toward Native Americans shapes attitudes toward the preindustrial British in *Connecticut Yankee*. But I read *Connecticut Yankee*'s humor as deeply implicated in a critique of American imperialism also because recent scholarship by Stephen Sumida (on the *Yankee* as Twain's anti-imperialist novel of Hawaii), James Caron (on anti-imperialist satire in the Sandwich Islands [Hawaii] lectures of 1866–67), and John Carlos Rowe (on the novel's composition during European colonization of Africa)[22] have pointed me toward a possible model for Hank—an enthusiastic American tool of imperialism who served as a king's right-hand man while bringing modern technology and factories to a primitive culture like the place Hank called "this dark land" (*CY*, 128): Henry Morton Stanley.

Clemens's relationship with Stanley, whose explorations enabled European colonization of Africa, forms a backdrop for the composition of *Connecticut Yankee*. The men's paths crossed intermittently throughout Twain's career, often in contexts linked to *Connecticut Yankee* or imperialism, and Clemens recalled in a 1906 autobiographical dictation, "I knew Stanley well for thirty-seven years" (*MTL* 5: qtd. 201n.3). Their first encounter was in St. Louis on March 26, 1867, when, as a *Missouri Democrat* reporter, Stanley transcribed Twain's Sandwich Islands lecture in which he only half-joked that the native population "got consumptive when civilization got there, and they will shortly retire from business. When they pack up and leave, we will take possession as lawful heirs" (*MTL* 2:19).[23] The men met socially in London in the fall of 1872, as Stanley celebrated his success in finding Dr. David Livingstone in Africa and Clemens collected ideas for a book on England (including a visit to Warwick Castle, where *Connecticut Yankee* opens). Clemens sent Stanley a congratulatory letter signed "your fellow Missourian" on September 1, visited him on September 15, and sat facing him on October 21 across the narrow head table at the Royal Geographic Society banquet in Stanley's honor[24] (figure 5). Clemens left the dinner with admiration for Stanley's accomplishments and support for ending the African slave trade (as Hank would later advocate for Arthur's Britain)—along with contempt for the explorer's display of "wounded self-love" (reminiscent of Hank's rhetoric of victimization) over questions about the truth of his accomplishments and his "continued . . . snarling at England & the English" (just like Hank) even after the Society president apologized for having disbelieved Stanley's reported achievements. "[H]e will blacken his fair renown forever," Clemens wrote to Livy, aghast at Stanley's public lament at the banquet, "& come to be treated with contempt yet" (*MTL* 5:199–201). Fourteen years later, on December 8, 1886, barely a month after reading from an early draft of *Connecticut Yankee* at Governor's Island in New York City on November 11, Clemens hosted Stanley at a dinner party and overnight at home in conjunction with the explorer's lecture "Through the Dark Continent" in Hartford that evening (*MTHL* 576n.2). The next night in Boston Clemens heard the lecture a second time after he introduced Stanley to the audience with praise for his "indestructible Americanism" and superiority to Columbus. After all, Twain joked, Columbus "didn't need to do anything at all but sit in the cabin of his ship and hold his grip and sail straight on," whereas Stanley located Livingstone even after the man had made himself "as scarce as a teetotaler in a prohibition state" (*MTS*, 214–215).[25] (Twain also links Hank to Columbus, who "played an eclipse as a saving trump once, on some savages" [*CY*, 86].) Some time after this meeting, Sir Robert Smith became Hank Smith, and finally *Hank Morgan*,[26] a name suggestively close to *Henry Morton*.

FIGURE 5 During the explorer's visit to London in the fall of 1872, *Once a Week* honored Henry Morton Stanley for his success in finding Dr. David Livingstone in Africa after a two-year search. This caricature by Frederick Waddy appeared the week before the one of Samuel Clemens (figure 1), who sat across from Stanley at the Royal Geographic Society dinner in his honor. (Etching by Frederick Waddy. "He Found Livingstone," *Once a Week* [London] n.s., 10 [7 December 1872]: 497.)

Stanley had arrived in the U.S. on November 26, 1886, for fifty lectures based on his book *The Congo and the Founding of Its Free State* (1885), which touted commercial opportunities in central Africa.[27] He had dedicated the book to King Leopold II of Belgium after contracting with him in 1878 to survey the Congo River basin for international trade. By 1884, Stanley had helped Leopold establish sovereignty over the huge area known as the Congo Free State and supplied technical advice at the Berlin Conference of 1884–85, where thirteen nations including the U.S., Belgium, England,

and Germany organized the region's trade in the so-called "Scramble for Africa."²⁸ Footloose between expeditions, Stanley used his 1886 lecture tour to engage American support for a railway without which, he told reporters, "the Congo might as well be in the moon for all the benefit the white man will derive from it."²⁹ Two days after the Boston lecture, on December 11, Stanley was recalled to England for another African mission funded jointly by Leopold and English businessmen; the king sought to expand his Congo holdings, though the official goal was to rescue Emin Pasha, a provincial governor threatened by local Muslims who had isolated Emin as part of a jihad that three years before had cost twelve thousand Egyptian and colonial occupying forces.³⁰ (Rowe sees this religiously motivated conflict of November 1883 as a model for the novel's Battle of the Sand Belt, but Stanley's 1887 expedition included, in addition to 250,000 rounds of ammunition for repeating rifles, a Maxim Automatic Gun that fired 600 rounds per minute donated by the American inventor himself.³¹) Brief as it was, Stanley's American tour launched a four-year campaign by Clemens and business manager Webster to sign up the explorer either to write his autobiography for their publishing firm or to let them bring out the American edition of his next book of African adventures. One way to think about *Connecticut Yankee*'s humor of empire evolving in this context across three years of composition is that Mark Twain wrote the book that he couldn't get from Stanley. In any event, from July of 1885 through the end of 1889—throughout the composition of *Connecticut Yankee*—a series of letters and notebook entries shows that Stanley was on Twain's mind.³²

So were matters of empire. The patriotic defensiveness of the Anglo-American contrast found its way into the novel through a number of Clemens's activities during this period. Reading *The People's History of the English Aristocracy* (1887) by radical journalist George Standring along with critical writings by W. E. H. Lecky and Thomas Carlyle aroused Clemens's sense of justice and American superiority, as Howard Baetzhold has shown (*MTJB*, 110–11),³³ but other forces more closely linked to imperialism were also at play. He loudly resented elitists such as Matthew Arnold who condescended to Americans from the former imperial center. Twain sloughed off Arnold's 1882 attack on American literature, which cited Twain's humor as evidence of national inferiority, but gave an 1887 speech venting personal and patriotic offense after Arnold faulted the style of General Grant's *Personal Memoirs* (1885), Webster & Co.'s best seller, and unleashed long rants in his notebooks and the *Yankee* manuscript in response to Arnold's "Civilization in the United States" (1888), which expressed the imperialist's faith that *he* sets cultural standards.³⁴

Perhaps most stinging, Arnold disparaged the U.S. in words uncannily apt to Twain's project. "American civilisation . . . [has] little to nourish and delight the sense of beauty," Arnold declared, because the very landscape suffers from Americans' restlessness: "In the valley of the Connecticut you will find farm after farm which the Yankee settler has abandoned in order to go West." But the zinger of Arnold's attack came in his sneers at vernacular values and literature, especially as manifest in American humor. "In truth everything is against distinction in America," he scorned, "and against the sense of elevation to be gained through admiring and respecting it. The glorification of 'the average man,' who is quite a religion with statesmen and publicists there, is against it. The addiction to 'the funny man,' who is a national misfortune there, is against it."[35] Clemens took some comfort when Yale University awarded him an honorary master's degree the following June, providing an opportunity, as he thanked Yale president Timothy Dwight, to defend humor as "a useful trade, a worthy calling . . . [with] one serious purpose, one aim, one specialty, and it is constant to it—the deriding of shams, the exposure of pretentious falsities, the laughing of stupid superstitions out of existence," and to declare the humorist as a democrat to the core: "[W]hoso is by instinct engaged in this sort of warfare is the natural enemy of royalties, nobilities, privileges, and all kindred swindles, and the natural friend of human rights and human liberties" (*MTNJ* 3: qtd. 299). The postcolonial vernacular politics of *Connecticut Yankee*, with its insistence on modern America's superiority to stodgy, if genteel, Britain, could not want more fuel than Arnold's contempt, with its symbolic repetition of victimization at the unjust hand of the British empire.

We don't know what Stanley and Clemens covered in the late-night discussion that Joseph Twitchell recorded as having taken place over drinks in the Hartford house after the December 8, 1886, lecture, though we might imagine it to be like the fireside conversation between Hank and Twain at the start of the novel. Clemens was in the midst of contracting a book from the widow of General Winfield Scott Hancock, the Gettysburg hero whose 1867 military expedition to subdue the Plains Indians gave Stanley, then a *Missouri Democrat* reporter embedded with the troops, his first taste of conflicts between indigenous and industrial peoples, so perhaps the men reminisced about their first meeting at Twain's Sandwich Islands lecture in St. Louis just days before Stanley left for that job. We do know, however, that Stanley's identity as an American was on Twain's mind the next night in an explicit British-American contrast. He introduced the explorer's Boston lecture by extolling "his indestructible Americanism" and championing him as "a product of institutions which exist in no other country on earth—institutions that bring out all that is best and most heroic in a man"—sentiments that Hank Morgan would endorse. And, in remarks that link these patriotic allusions to Hank, Twain set Stanley against a British backdrop: "In this day and time, when it is the custom to ape and imitate English methods and fashions, it is like a breath of fresh air to stand in the presence of this untainted American citizen who has been caressed and complimented by half the crowned heads of Europe . . . And yet, when the untitled myriads of his own country put out their hands in welcome to greet him, 'Well done,' through the Congress of the United States, that is the crown that is worth all the rest to him" (*MTS*, 215). All the hallmarks of vernacular humor come together in this formulation: Jonathan's youth framed as New World "fresh"-ness in contrast to European staleness, American democracy as "untainted" natural goodness in contrast to corrupt monarchies, and the underdog's triumph as a comeuppance for those imperial snobs.

This praise for Stanley as a representative American comes as something of a surprise in light of the 1872 London letter from Clemens to his wife. There he bristled at Stanley's claims to American identity not only for their dishonesty, since Stanley's accent betrayed him as a foreigner to Twain's sharp ear, but also for the embarrassment to other Americans, because Stanley spoke so rudely in public. His "continued . . . snarling at England & the English" was all the more deplorable, Sam told Livy, because the English had treated the two of them so well. "Men are seated at table strictly according to their *rank*," he reported, sounding rather like Hank, "—so the idiot son of an earl would sit above the Speaker of the House of Commons—& so on. But as Americans have *no* rank, it is proper to place us either above or below the nobles. Courtesy rather forbids the latter, & so we get good seats" (*MTL* 5:199, 200). Ultimately, he concluded, for all Stanley's accomplishments, "I am really & truly glad this fellow is *not* American—though indeed he must have learned his puppyism with us." Fourteen years later, Twain's admiration for Stanley's accomplishments in Africa had pushed aside his earlier disgust at the explorer's deportment, or at least mention of it, but the Anglo-American contrast in the Boston introduction shows that Stanley's American identity and his embodiment of intrepidness remained fixed within a British context in Twain's mind. More important, he framed Stanley's triumph in the terms of the same Anglo-American vernacular context he was developing for *Connecticut Yankee*, a sign of its importance to him and his sense of its meanings for an audience.

No letter or notebook documents Clemens's thoughts on Stanley's lectures or African experiences, nor do marginal notes specify which of Stanley's books Clemens read by 1889, although he probably read *How I Found Livingstone* (1872) no later than the summer of 1887, because someone inscribed a copy to his nephew in Elmira, New York, where the Clemenses spent each summer, the previous January, a month after Stanley left Boston.[36] But newspaper accounts of the 1886 lectures offer tantalizing suggestions. All reported Stanley's lingering hurt that the Royal Geographic Society had dismissed him as "a sensational story-teller" fourteen years before,[37] casting him as a tall-talker like Hank. All reported threats to him and his entourage by spear-carrying natives whom he dispersed by discharging a revolver,[38] much as Hank puffs on his pipe, explodes the bomb, and shoots the knights. And the lecture series itself prompted other reports on U.S. involvement in the Congo. One newspaper declared the U.S. role in helping Leopold organize the Congo Free State "a matter of pride to every American," because as the first nation to recognize the state in April 1884 we "set the ball rolling" for the Berlin conference that would enable "Almost Unheard of Facilities for Fortune Making," as the headline put it, as well as end the slave trade and barriers to commerce.[39] By contrast with this upbeat assessment, U.S. business dealings abroad concerned Clemens as early as 1867, when he satirized the prospect of America's annexing the Sandwich Islands by predicting that it would backfire: "[T]hese people . . . will do everything wrong end first. Instead of fostering and encouraging a judicious system of railway speculation and all that sort of thing, they will elect the most incorruptible men to Congress" (*MTS*, 10). Thus it seems likely that American partnership with Europe in constituting the Congo Free State did not sit well with him in 1886, though he did not give full vent to the irony of U.S. support for its misleading name (being free only in trade, not politically) until 1905, when he published *King Leopold's Soliloquy*, a text that relegates Stanley (who had died the year before) to brief mention in an appendix about the Berlin Conference. In the context of *Connecticut Yankee*, however, Stanley's prediction that Congo's development would parallel the American West's might have started for Twain an unwelcome train of thought about Yankee imperialism at home and abroad: shortly before visiting the Clemenses in Hartford, Stanley told the *New York Times* that the proposed Congo railroad would attract a white population in the manner of the transcontinental railroad in the U.S. and that American officials were already scouting possibilities on the scene. His insistence that "[w]e don't want colonists. We want the trader" also follows the American pattern. But he drew an important distinction: "The negroes don't resent the invasion of civilization. They like it," he claimed, and sounding rather like Hank, Stanley gave an example: "At table . . . the negroes have adopted spoons and knives. I introduced some cheap Birmingham knives made with one rivet. They wouldn't have them. They said the iron wasn't good enough. Now they use knives made with three rivets. I introduced one-dollar knives, and I have sold at least 1,000 in one day."[40] Stanley's command of American idiom in this passage explains why Queen Victoria scorned him for his "strong American twang" even though he had emigrated to New Orleans from Wales at the age of sixteen and did not formalize his American citizenship until 1885, when he needed it to protect the American copyright of a new book.[41] Ever the opportunist, he changed citizenship again in 1892 in order to run for Parliament after he resettled in England. Hank Morgan shares more than a little of Henry Morgan Stanley's blend of the American and un-American.

I don't intend this circumstantial evidence to clinch a case for Stanley as the model for Hank. No evidence shows, for example, whether Clemens knew or Stanley repeated in Hartford the recipe for American involvement that he gave the *New York Herald* in April of 1875 during his second trip to Africa: that what central Africa needed from the U.S. instead of preachers was "the practical Christian tutor, who can teach people how to become Christians, cure their diseases, construct dwellings, understands agriculture and can turn his hand to anything . . . [and] be inspired by liberal principles, charity to all men,"[42]—a blueprint for Hank. But I do want to stress that Stanley's Hartford visit occurred during a critical period of the novel's composition, between November 1886 and the summer of 1887, when (as Howard Baetzhold put it) "Clemens' concept of the story of the Yankee's role seems to have changed drastically. . . . [from] profit for himself and for the king's treasury . . . [to] total reform of political and social evils in Arthur's kingdom,"[43] a shift toward Stanley's views of African colonialism. And I do claim that Stanley combines many of the contradictions we see in Hank—a vernacular American imperialist who works alongside a king to bring what he calls civilization and freedom to the people of an undeveloped land, yet always whines that he's an innocent victim—and that the example of Henry Morton Stanley means that these contradictions in Hank Morgan are neither signs of authorial confusion nor very far-fetched, and that Clemens may not have invented them out of whole cloth. Whatever the nature or degree of influence, Stanley embodies the link between vernacular humor and empire in *Connecticut Yankee*.

Lawrence Buell cites the reversal of American and British superiority in *Connecticut Yankee* as evidence that "the American post-colonial moment was over, or at least evanescent" from a cultural standpoint, and the plot by which Hank remakes sixth-century England in the American mold does suggest Twain's willingness to imagine America's international hegemony at the very time, as Buell reminds us, that "what is now called American imperialism" began its rise.[44] Yet the novel's comic tone and reliance on historically sincere postcolonial comic conventions complicate Mark Twain's representation of American imperial endeavors. Indeed, James Caron has recently shown how consistently Twain scorned imperialism using the same sarcastic locutions in his Sandwich Islands lectures of the late 1860s and his anti-imperialist essay of 1901, "To the Person Sitting in Darkness."[45] This consistency, along with the other links between humor and empire that I have detailed here, suggests that in *Connecticut Yankee* Twain implicitly acknowledged the ways in which the comic boosterism of the British-American contrast and American vernacular exceptionalism joined to repress the imperialist transgressions associated with Manifest Destiny in North America, if not yet in the so-called dark land of the Congo. We cannot know how consciously he alludes to American territorial ambitions when Hank longs to expand Britain, complaining that its small size required residents "to sleep with their knees pulled up because they couldn't stretch out without a passport" [*CY*, 187]). But in giving Hank's tale an ironic inflection akin to the burlesque of the evasion sequence in *Huckleberry Finn*, I am also suggesting that *Connecticut Yankee* anticipates Twain's later satires of imperialism, especially *King Leopold's Soliloquy* (1905), another monologue in which a bombastic speaker condemns himself. And whatever else they suggest, *Connecticut Yankee*'s links between humor and empire show Twain comically reframing American imperialism, both at home and abroad, at an earlier period than commonly thought.

Twentieth-century politics kept the vernacular European-American contrast salient even though America's international stature grew ever more secure in the twentieth century, bolstered by our role in two world wars and a technological leadership more advanced than Mark Twain had flaunted in *Connecticut Yankee*. As U.S. nationalism and nativism rose in tandem with their international counterparts during the 1920s and '30s, scholars in the nascent field of American studies emphasized the postcolonial biases of vernacular humor—especially the superiority of virtuous, untutored, but pragmatic American innocents to their learned, genteel, or otherwise elite antagonists. Jennette Tandy's dissertation, "Crackerbox Philosophers in American Humor and Satire" (1925), paved the way. In 1931, Constance Rourke theorized in *American Humor* that the "national character" consisted of the Yankee trader, the black minstrel, and the backwoodsman—three postcolonial regional folk types easily conflated into one. (Rourke's cast of quintessential Americans excluded Indians and women, not to mention the many immigrant groups and other regional figures, such as the German Hans and Norwegian Lena, whose folk identities entered popular culture during the antebellum period Rourke covered.[46]) A few years later Walter Blair likewise equated American comic conventions with a patriotic ideology of American democracy and Manifest Destiny in his (now embarrassingly named) *Native American Humor* (1937), which treated postcolonial and frontier concerns as the fulfillment of nationalist sensibilities expressed by vernacular voices. Over the next four decades, landmark scholarship by R. W. B. Lewis, Henry Nash Smith, Leo Marx, and others stressed postcolonial myths of America's domestic innocence over twentieth-century realities of rising international hegemony, setting vernacular humor firmly in the context now called American exceptionalism. Jewish-American humor in popular media—the vaudeville stage, the radio sitcom *The Goldbergs* (1929–46) and Leo Rosten's *The Education of H*Y*M*A*N K*A*P*L*A*N* (1937)—found the vernacular tradition especially useful, partly because comic rhetoric celebrating the triumph of a dialect-speaking underdog suits a historically persecuted people, partly because American mythology draws from congenial Old Testament concepts of redemption in the promised land, and (after World War II) partly because the U.S. role in opposing Hitler and ending the Holocaust renewed the contrast between European imperial corruption and American democratic virtue. By the 1970s, in works such as *Gravity's Rainbow* (1973), Thomas Pynchon and other novelists with a comic sensibility saw how conveniently vernacular ideology clothed American empire in an underdog's well-worn dress, and they upended the old conventions for purposes of contemporary satire. Recent comic novels of American life in Jewish and international contexts include Michael Chabon's *The Amazing Adventures of Kavalier and Clay* (2000) and Jonathan Safran Foer's *Everything Is Illuminated* (2002), but no contemporary writer has played with or thought about the imperialist assumptions of American vernacular humor more than Philip Roth.

"I find the kind of humor I admire in Mark Twain," Roth announced at a symposium early in his career. He was referring to "a kind of desperate humor" common to Twain, Dostoyevsky, and Jewish humorists, not the cracker-barrel philosophy often attributed to Twain,[47] and in two early satires Roth combined that humor with his University of Chicago professors' lessons on American humor. He dedicated the volume of anti-Nixon sketches *Our Gang* (1971) to Napier Wilt, who edited the important anthology *Some American Humorists* (1929), and inscribed a copy of *The Great American Novel* (1973) "To Walter Blair, who introduced me to the tall story."[48] Blair considered Alexander Portnoy one of those mock-oral narrators "too educated or too hard-boiled" for the vernacular tradition, but most of Roth's novels rely on the essential trait of vernacular humor—the colloquial narration that Blair called "a man's voice, speaking."[49] Equally important, the nineteenth-century ideology of American exceptionalism had already inflected Roth's perspective as a Jewish child growing up in Newark, New Jersey, during the 1930s and '40s. He wrote in *The Facts* that "growing up Jewish . . . and growing up American seemed to me indistinguishable" (122), and the effect was an "unambiguous sense, . . . immediately after the victory over Nazi fascism and Japanese militarism, of belonging to the greatest nation on earth." By contrast, he noted, the Europe of his ancestors and his wartime childhood was a place where "life was so awful, . . . so menacing or impoverished or hopelessly obstructed, that it was best forgotten" (123). Not surprisingly, therefore, when Roth reversed the invidious European-American contrast for comic effect, he not only sent Americans abroad, as Twain did, but also brought Europe to America in counterhistorical revisions of imperial invasion built on Twain's brand of humor and empire.

As the British-American contrast reversed nineteenth-century hierarchies, so Roth's fiction imagines the modern world with a vulnerable U.S. at its core. He imports international figures (dead and alive) and international incidents (real and imagined) into his American stories, and he condemns American protagonists to failure abroad. That's why all of world literature (plus a little world history) becomes the basis for the slapstick alternative history of *The Great American Novel* (1973), which locates the main events of World War II in American baseball stadiums. That's why Kafka turns up as Roth's New Jersey Hebrew school teacher in "I Always Wanted You to Admire My Fasting" (1973) and Anne Frank surfaces in contemporary Massachusetts in *The Ghost Writer* (1979). Reverse migrations likewise expose European corruption. The fictitious account of Roth's visit to Israel in *Operation Shylock* (1993) turns on what Michael Rothberg has called the "contrast between American normality and European extremity"[50]—terms surprisingly close to Amy Kaplan's view of Twain's imperialism, noted earlier. Whatever else Roth may have had in mind, vernacular convention dictates the failure of Nathan Zuckerman's marriage to an Englishwoman at the end of *The Counterlife* (1986) as he discovers that London, anti-Semitic to the core, embodies "Christendom." And the same rhetoric underlies Roth's recent allegorical satire of post–9/11 politics, *The Plot Against America* (2004), which reimagines World War II fascism as American jingoism in a tall story of how the U.S., with the charismatic anti-Semite Charles A. Lindbergh as president, fulfilled its patriotic ideals as Hitler's ally. Indeed, Roth's rhetoric of humor and empire remains consistent across the thirty-plus years between the extravagant burlesque of *The Great American Novel* and mock-autobiographical realism of *The Plot Against America*, although the two novels differ in materials, mood, and craftsmanship. Their twists on the conventional contrast between European corruption and American virtue, their use of history to ground a counterfactual memoir of conspiracy at high levels of American government, their displacement of World War II struggles onto the American scene, and their parodies of familiar rhetoric—all unite two otherwise disparate comic fictions through Twain's brand of humor and empire.

Roth spoke openly in a 1973 self-interview about his interest in using his baseball novel to explore "the *struggle* between the benign national myth of itself that a great power prefers to perpetuate and the relentlessly insidious, very nearly demonic reality (like the kind we had known in the sixties) that will not give an inch in behalf of that idealized mythology,"[51] and a similar struggle underlies *The Plot Against America*. Yet Roth's confession has led the few critics who've paid attention to the early novel to focus exclusively on its representation of domestic politics, as if the fear of communism in the 1950s and American exceptionalism itself had no international context, a myopia repeated in the post–9/11 allegorical readings of the later novel.[52] In contrast to Twain's problem of time travel in *Connecticut Yankee*, the historical settings of *The Great American Novel* and *The Plot Against America* let Roth end these books by affirming the triumph of American ideals, yet links between humor and empire in Roth's works—as in Twain's—identify the apparently democratic vernacular tradition as a self-serving mask for American corruption in the imperial European mold.

The delusions of grandeur expressed by the title *The Great American Novel* extend to the novel as a whole. Like *Connecticut Yankee*, *The Great American Novel* uses the traditional form of a mock-oral tall yarn to recount American national failure on the international stage. The ballplayers, fans, and managers of the Ruppert Mundys baseball team may look like homespun heroes, but they demonstrate mainly that the common man lacks common sense. The Mundys' ineptitude, instead of demonstrating earthiness, allows their exploitation by the brothers who own the team, the pitcher who turns Soviet spy, and the congressmen who aid him. As the loose conspiracy evolves into a firm plot, the U.S. emerges as a totalitarian state. Uncle Sam, the tale implies, differs little from Mother Russia, because the novel's conventional comic devices undercut its conventional nationalist ideology. From a formalist standpoint, the novel bears the hallmarks of tall tales—a box-like structure of inner and outer narratives, mock-oral narration filled with colloquialisms, a protagonist making outrageous claims—yet it not only spins comic lies about an apocryphal third major American baseball league, the Patriot League, and not only tells a shaggy dog story in which a U.S. conspiracy to hide the successful communist infiltration of the league leads paradoxically to the Soviet-style erasure of history, but also burlesques American literature from Hawthorne to Hemingway and satirizes Cold War domestic politics from McCarthy to Nixon; the Watergate investigation by the Senate Select Committee on Presidential Campaign Activities opened hearings just as Roth's book was published. By the end, however, history and fiction get so entangled in displays of political ineptitude that the mock-epic of World War II becomes also an indictment of contemporary American politics. Twain's brand of humor and empire in this tall tale, as in *Connecticut Yankee*, condemns vernacular values.

To convey his dark message about American government, Roth turns his reporter-narrator into a novelist, truth into fiction, and a conventional liar into an unconventional truth-teller: the extravagantly colloquial narrator Word Smith (get it?), a former sportswriter, claims that his version of the Mundys' wartime activities represents the great American novel—and the truth. Or, as he tells the chairman of the House Un-American Activities Committee (HUAC) before being carted off to jail for contempt of Congress, insisting that the charges of subversion against the Ruppert Mundys are absurd, "Truth is stranger than fiction, but stranger still are lies" (*GAN*, 372). Roth jokes about all three categories. Truth, fiction, and lies get hopelessly tangled in the literary and historical allusions running from the first sentence—"Call me Smitty" (1), with its allusion to *Moby-Dick*—to the last, an echo of Huck's sign-off, "Respectfully yours, Word Smith (Author of 'One Man's Opinion')" (382). Like Twain in *Connecticut Yankee*, Roth in *The Great American Novel* replaces faith in democratic man with contempt for the political animal. As Twain's novel ends in an endless loop of dreams and stories as the dying Yankee deliriously announces the king's arrival after chattering to his sixth-century wife, Sandy, about "Dreams that were as real as reality" (493), so too Roth's madman narrator ends a story that opened with contempt for the HUAC chairman by beseeching his communist counterpart, Chairman Mao, to publish the spiral of fictions and truths of his suppressed history as "art that reclaims what is and what was from those whose every word is a falsification and a betrayal of the truth" (382). The absurdity of Roth's novel offers traditional vernacular optimism only through the power of storytelling to delight and instruct.

The Great American Novel's exuberant humor frames America as the benevolent imperial center of the world. Worldwide conflicts of 1943 are reduced to squabbles occuring on American baseball fields. This comic of reversal of foreground and background puts American territory at the center of a war actually fought on the continents to our east and west. Considering the centrality of anti-Semitism to Hitler's imperial ambitions, it's not surprising that Papa Ellis, the immigrant owner of the Tri-City Greenbacks, tells his son, "[F]or a Jewish pois'n dis is de greatest country vat ever vas, in the history of de *voild*" (*GAN*, 272), but Roth emphasizes American dominance by relocating foreign people and places to the USA. He puts "the world-renowned 'Cradle of Civilization'" at "the corner of Tigris and Euphrates in Kakoola, Wisconsin" (150). Patriot League players include such international mythic greats as Jean-Paul "Frenchy" Astarte; John Baal, grandson of the legendary "Base" Baal and son of the infamous pitcher "Spit" Baal (104–105); Roland Agni, a magnificent athlete sacrificed (like the lamb for which he is named) to the Ruppert Mundys; and the notorious Gil Gamesh, pitcher extraordinaire of Babylonian extraction who was rumored to have taken "the Lord's name in vain, blaming Him" when his seventh major league start was rained out (56). And the plot turns on HUAC's self-centered conclusion about the real purposes of the U.S.-Soviet alliance during World War II: "[T]he war against the Germans and the Japanese has been used by the Communists to mask their subversive activities here in the United States" (336).

Here and elsewhere Roth comically blends history and fiction to create what he elsewhere called "a kind of passageway from the imaginary that comes to seem real to the real that comes to seem imaginary."[53] Smitty challenges an official at the Hall of Fame, "Just go down where you have buried the Patriot League records and you can look it up," alluding to James Thurber's mock-oral tall tale "You Could Look It Up" (1941), a direct influence on *The Great American Novel*, while issuing a similar challenge to Roth's readers. But in fact, Roth draws many of the novel's goofy details from historical fact. Isaac Ellis experiments with nuclear fission in his workshop under Greenback Stadium just as Enrico Fermi split the atom beneath the bleachers at the University of Chicago's Stagg Field (located, as Roth's allusion slyly reminds us, on *Ellis* Avenue). Congress holds hearings on the communist leanings of baseball players just as it once investigated those of Hollywood actors, and the novel's Red hunt has a fervent leader in the historical Congressman Martin Dies of Texas. Roth's fictional America enjoys three major baseball leagues just as it did during the brief life of the Federal League (1914–15). Ruppert Stadium houses the Ruppert Mundys instead of the Newark Bears of Roth's childhood, but the Mundys' left fielder Mike Rama quite literally follows in the footsteps of the historical "Pistol" Pete Reiser, who regularly hurled himself against the outfield wall, and their outfielder Bud Parusha carries on the tradition of the St. Louis Browns' Pete Gray, the first professional one-armed ballplayer.[54] The Mundys' Bob Yamm generates many kinds of humor: the tiny strike zone between the knees and shoulders of this midget batter belongs to the world of practical jokes, but Yamm is a descendent of both the fictional Pearl du Monville of Thurber's tall tale and his historical counterpart, the Browns' Eddie Gaedel. Together, they all prove that life sometimes imitates art.

The novel's central joke concerns baseball's identity as the American pastime and a game of records, and thus as a metaphor for American history as well as a governing principle for Roth's text. Its nine sections parallel the number of innings in a standard game (the two parts of "The Temptation of Roland Agni" suggest a seventh-inning stretch), while the seven inner chapters correspond to the maximum number of games in a world series. All these structural details suit a story that relates the game to major world issues, but this playful framework (like *Connecticut Yankee*'s) belies the novel's increasing seriousness. The first three chapters stand on myth and fantasy, focusing on the feud between pitcher Gil Gamesh and umpire Mike the Mouth, stories of the Mundys' players, and exhibition games against the Lunatics and Keepers in Asylum, Ohio. The last three chapters, by contrast, draw on history, recounting conferences in Angela Trust's underground bunker, experiments in Ellis's physics laboratory, and hearings by the House Un-American Activities Committee. In the center, the story of Bob Yamm, drawn from history and art, pivots between the poles of myth and fact.

Roth extends the extravagant claims of greatness with parodies of literary texts. These range from the opening allusion to *Moby-Dick* to an extended riff on *The Old Man and the Sea*, but for the topic of imperialism, the parody of Conrad's "Heart of Darkness" toward the end of the book is particularly significant. The episode recounts the experiences of Samuel Fairsmith, manager of the 1943 Mundys, a team so bad that its pitchers constituted a "council of elders . . . every last one of them flabby in the middle, arthritic in the shoulder, bald on the top" (*GAN*, 127). The Mundys' players upset him even more than the Africans to whom he benevolently brought the sport twenty years earlier on a worldwide proselytizing mission culminating in Japan. The Congolese took brilliantly to baseball, hitting the balls long, following through on the swing, and sliding fearlessly into base despite wearing only the briefest of loincloths. In fact, the players so loved this display of manhood that they insisted on sliding into first base, even on a walk, at which point Fairsmith felt he had to put his foot down. (In typically imperial rhetoric, Roth describes the scene generically as "the jungle" melodramatically located "a thousand miles into the primitive interior of Africa" [292] and maintains the ambiguity of the specific location until the anecdote's punch line, when he finally fixes the site as "the Congo" [304]). But the natives objected to their so-called Uncle Sam's adding this rule of his own devising, and they rebelled. Preparing to cannibalize him, they began a ritual of boiled baseballs and gloves, batting exhibitions, defloration of virgins with baseball bats, and other rites accompanied by chants "*Omoo! Omoo! Omoo!*" and "*Typee! Typee! Typee!*" (300–301)—allusions to Melville's novels of the South Seas, themselves exemplars of what David Spurr calls "the rhetoric of empire."[55] Finally, like Conrad's Marlow, Fairsmith "cried out twice, a cry that was no more than a breath: 'The horror! The horror!'" (304). Soon after, one of the village boys declared, "Mistah Baseball—he dead," although reports of his death turned out to be premature, and Fairsmith was rescued from a canoe found twenty miles from Stanleyville.

This parody and the novel's others, especially of canonical American fiction, also underscore Edward Said's argument in *Culture and Imperialism* (1993), published twenty years after *The Great American Novel*, about the role of national literary canons in sustaining imperialism.[56] Parallels between Said's analysis of Conrad's story and Roth's parody of it also suggest Roth's acknowledgment of the fragility—and price—of the imperial enterprise even when it succeeds.[57] The baseball-playing natives do not escape colonization, yet upholding their cultural rights in this case both strengthens and threatens imperial ties: sliding on a walk means upholding the primacy of western rules and regulations, an ideal of fairness that Fairsmith is finally forced to concede. In this context, for Fairsmith to say that the 1943 Mundys are "the most unprofessional, undignified, *immoral* athletes he had ever seen" (*GAN*, 292) is saying quite a lot—about not only their ethical failures but also the comic instabilities of the team and the American empire.

In the end, the novel's extravagant language and plot imply that even if all the world's gods converged on the U.S. in wartime in order to anoint the nation as divinely ordained, America is too corrupt for them to succeed. Nor can the traditionally heroic vernacular narrator. But even though *The Great American Novel* overflows with a silliness that softens these themes, they meant enough to Roth that he returned to them thirty years later, when he traded burlesque for understatement in *The Plot Against America*. The later novel builds its fantasy on historical fact rather than grafting history onto fantasy, and realistic details of family and national life replace one-liners such as "Sturgeon with Stalin, Cocktails with Molotov" (*GAN*, 334). Roth distanced himself from the narrative of the earlier book by attributing it to Smitty, a crackpot whose proof of conspiracy is the disappearance of evidence, a circularity of high foolishness even more absurd than Hank's claim that the bullet hole in Sir Sagramour's armor proves that he had travelled back to Arthurian Britain. By contrast, *The Plot Against America* is a mock-memoir by a mature narrator named Philip Roth on the turning point of his childhood, the election as president of the isolationist Charles A. Lindbergh, who appeased and supported Hitler, hosted von Ribbentrop at the White House, and instituted anti-Semitic measures against American Jews. In both novels, irony reveals the limits of American empire as a bulwark against the spread of communism, because American democracy's superiority to European oppression coexists with our failure to realize our ideals. But the vernacular humor of empire in *The Great American Novel*, where only history is at stake (and only baseball history, at that), turns deadly serious in *The Plot Against America*, where the republic is more than metaphorically threatened as Nazism infects domestic and foreign policy and anti-Semitic pogroms erupt across the states.

The Plot Against America not only imperially displaces wartime attention from Europe to the U.S., focusing instead on whether Lindbergh "is leaving the door open for a German conquest of America," as T. Austin Graham put it,[58] but also links the U.S. present to its imperialist past. Implicit contrasts between Europe and the U.S. drive the plot while details turn difference into likeness. Throughout the narrative, faith in America as an exceptional state, a benevolent democracy—the patriotic myths on which the narrator's father Herman Roth stakes his family's life—clashes with details of the nation's practices of internal colonization, present and past. Near the beginning Philip describes American Christians as "the great overpowering majority that fought the Revolution and founded the nation and conquered the wilderness and subjugated the Indian and enslaved the Negro and emancipated the Negro and segregated the Negro, ... settled the frontier, built the cities, governed the states, ... [etc.] who laid down the law and called the shots and read the riot act when they chose to" (*PAA*, 94). The description characterizes Manifest Destiny as an American version of *lebensraum*, the Nazi doctrine of expanded "living space" (the literal meaning of the term) for the Aryan people, achieved by conquering nearby states and exterminating Jews. Near the end of the novel, when his brother and father stop briefly in West Virginia after rescuing their ten-year-old former neighbor orphaned in a Kentucky pogrom, Philip compares their condition to earlier instances of colonial conquest. "An analogy could be made," he observes, "to the uninvited white settlers who first poured through the Appalachian barrier into the favorite hunting grounds of the Delaware and Algonquin tribes, except that instead of alien, strange-looking whites affronting the local inhabitants with their rapaciousness, these were alien, strange-looking Jews provocative merely by their presence. This time around, though, those violently defending their lands from usurpation and their way of life weren't Indians led by the great Tecumseh but upright American Christians unleashed by the acting president of the United States" (357). Subjugation and assimilation in this American tradition—that is, internal colonization—are the open purpose of President Lindbergh's Office of American Absorption (OAA), conveniently run by the collaborationist Rabbi Bengelsdorf of Newark. The OAA's "Just Folks" program is modeled on the anti-Semitic policies of the imperial Russian army, which drafted Jews in early adolescence in order to limit familial influence and assimilate them into the national culture. The OAA's "Homestead 42" initiative, on the other hand, updates imperial U.S. Indian policies now proudly described in bureaucratic euphemisms as "famous legislation, unique to America, which granted 160 acres of unoccupied public land vitually free to . . . provide adventurous Americans with exciting opportunities to expand their horizons and to strengthen their country" at the expense of the native peoples already in residence. Homestead 42, the OAA boasts, will "give emerging American families a once-in-a-lifetime opportunity to move their households, at government expense" and "provide a challenging environment steeped in our country's oldest traditions where parents and children can enrich their Americanness over the generations"—a modern-day Indian Removal Act that also, not coincidentally, cleanses American cities of Jewish presence (204–5). When narrator Philip Roth concludes that "our disgrace and our glory were one and the same" in the Lindbergh era

(107–8), the author sums up the contradictions of the American continental empire, where past is prologue.

Here international and domestic imperialism run in sync. Repeatedly Lindbergh praises Hitler for advancing American goals of "an independent destiny" (*PAA*, 84). The invasion of Poland? "With this act . . . Adolf Hitler has established himself as the world's greatest safeguard against the spread of Communism and its evils" (83). His attack on the Soviet Union? "Everyone in America knew that it was an unshakable conviction of the president's, as it was of his party's dominant right wing, that the best protection against the spread of Communism across Europe, into Asia and the Middle East, and as far as to our own hemisphere, was the total destruction of Stalin's Soviet Union by the military might of the Third Reich" (179). A so-called "Jewish conspiratorial plot against America"? (316). Lindbergh readies the nation "in the event of a surprise Canadian attack" from the north as German forces prepare to invade Mexico "to protect America's southern flank of the United States," and pogroms erupt in Nazi sympathy from coast to coast (317). The war typically understood to contrast Europe and the U.S., stressing "the result of the worldly ambitions of the European peoples and their effort to reach goals of military greatness, power, and wealth" (35), as the collaborationist Rabbi Bengelsdorf put it, instead reveals distinctions without a difference. American exceptionalism threatens to dissolve in similarity between the Nazi and American empires as the Roth family says goodbye to "exiled friends" (255) who have accepted relocation and as Herman Roth insists to his wife that Lindbergh, not Jews, represents the alien other: "The one who looks most American—and he's the one who is least American!" (256).

Lampoons of public rhetoric underline this point. Whereas parody in *The Great American Novel* debunked literary culture, parody in *Plot Against America* skewers governmental abuse. As the OAA examples show, Roth has mastered satiric bureaucratese, a rhetoric at least as old as Swift's "Modest Proposal" although the details in *The Plot Against America* are closer to Orwell's *1984*. The Good Neighbor project, for instance, expanded the homesteading plan through subsidies to encourage other groups to move into newly vacated apartments in Jewish neighborhoods and thereby "'enrich' the 'Americanness' of everyone involved" (*PAA*, 280). The parodies suggest that, despite their historical settings, both of Roth's novels allegorize contemporary politics. Roth's screed against the Nixon presidency, *Our Gang*, which likewise merges parody and satire, appeared just two years before *The Great American Novel*, with its echoes of the Pentagon Papers and Vietnam-era abuses such as the destruction of villages in order to save them. *The Plot Against America*, published shortly before the 2004 presidential election, satirizes George W. Bush's White House, which cozied up to the Saudis while abhorring Islamic fundamentalists, devised Clear Skies initiatives that increased pollution and invoked a Patriot Act that constrained civil liberties. Two passages from the novel speak directly to this point. Disgusted that the president would entertain Nazis at the White House, Philip's father, Herman, asks what Democrats across the country wondered during the Bush years: "How can this be happening in America? How can people like these be in charge of our country?" (196). Roth sides with his mother, who dismisses Herman's hopes that the next election will bring change: "The American people will vote and the Republicans will be even *stronger*" (198). The remark seems almost prescient in light of the 2004 presidential election, when John Kerry's defeat by thirty-four electoral votes and less than 3 percent of the popular vote emboldened the Republicans to declare a mandate. Even apart from the contemporary political parallels, however, Roth's parodies highlight the cynicism behind his satire of American democracy as hardly distinguishable from totalitarianism.

Both *The Great American Novel* and *The Plot Against America* reach crises in which domestic politics are driven by absurd claims of conspiracy that Roth, like Twain in *Connecticut Yankee*, must resolve while squaring his narratives with historical fact. Given the similarities between Roth's two novels despite the thirty years between them, it is less surprising that both dismiss their conspiracies in nearly identical language than that their rejections serve common themes of humor and empire, despite the books' different forms. Roth inverts the conventions of the tall tale when he undercuts his vernacular narrator Smitty as a crackpot who decries "this lunatic comedy in which American baseball players . . . denounce themselves and their teammates as Communist spies out of fear and intimidation and howling ignorance or . . . incorrigible human perversity and curdled genes" (*GAN*, 371). As Smitty dismisses the ballplayers' conspiracy to destroy baseball only to declare another conspiracy instead—this one a governmental cover-up of HUAC's gullibility—his obviously fictitious story becomes a double joke for readers who can identify its true precedents in baseball and political history. By contrast, in *The Plot Against America*, Roth bounces the conspiracy charge back from the Jews to the government by a very sane Fiorello LaGuardia, who insists (in a voice reminscent of Smitty's), "There's a plot afoot all right, and I'll gladly name the forces propelling it—hysteria, ignorance, malice, stupidity, hatred, and fear. What a repugnant spectacle our country has become!" (315). Thus the pugnacious LaGuardia, who with Herman Roth comes as close to a vernacular hero as this novel provides, especially in contrast to the high-toned rabbi and politicians who appease the Nazis, helps bring down Lindbergh's regime and replaces it with a third Roosevelt administration. For Hana Wirth-Nesher, this happy restoration of democracy marks the novel's "Americanness" in the same way that "its emphasis on communal rather than individual" trauma reveals its Jewish heritage.[59] The resolution makes good use of Lindbergh's disappearance to close the historical gap and provides an unequivocally comic conclusion to the chief complication of the novel's plot, but such a simplistic denouement is hardly satisfying: the spunk evinced by LaGuardia and the First Lady—like the comic machinery it resembles—slights the political and moral stakes set by the novel's exploration of imperial practices at home and abroad. Nonetheless, in both novels, Roth's humor of American empire decries the U.S. government as corrupt and American exceptionalism as a myth.

Humor and empire figure similarly across Roth's political fiction, which typically has a first-person narrator whose mock-oral voice, though not marked by regional or ethnic dialect, still invokes the implied contrasts of humor and empire. More than half a dozen novels, including late personal narratives, tie the individual to domestic and global affairs, as when the randy narrator of *The Dying Animal* (2001) declares himself the heir of the infamous Thomas Morton of Merry-Mount, whom William Bradford excoriated for "great licentiousness."[60] Likewise, the major novels constituting Roth's American trilogy represent historical movements through individuals' tragedies: the fall of a Vietnam-era family in *American Pastoral* (1997), the ruin of a World War II veteran in *I Married a Communist* (1998), the destruction of a Clinton-era African American professor passing for Jew in *The Human Stain* (2000). *The Plot Against America*'s satirical counterhistory extends this line of thought. Together with *The Great American Novel* and the (still more trivial) satire of Nixon, these works articulate Roth's dismay that the U.S. has squandered the prestige it garnered in World War II through the ill-conceived adventure of Vietnam, the witch hunts of the Cold War and the Clinton years, and the neoexceptionalism of post–9/11 Republican rule. Experiments with comic narration in these novels shape their political representations. Roth has played with the limits of realism and of narrative reliability throughout his fiction, most notably in the (pseudo)autobiographical fantasies *The Counterlife* (1986) and *Operation Shylock* (1993), but also in works as far back as *Portnoy's Complaint* (1969) and *The Breast* (1972), whose controversial sexual themes obscured his techniques. But Roth explicitly linked such narrative experimentation with political themes in a self-interview about *The Great American Novel*, where he described his desire to use Smitty's narration to create "a kind of passageway from the imaginary that comes to seem real to the real that comes to seem imaginary, a continuum between the credible incredible and the incredible credible."[61] The passageway, as evident in *The Great American Novel* and *The Plot Against America*, supports Roth's humor of empire.

Critics have tended to ignore *The Great American Novel* because its manic playfulness sets it apart from Roth's more serious work. Ross Posnock called it Roth's "weakest book" for its "foregrounding of linguistic exuberance at the expense of representation."[62] Yet as Derek Parker Royal points out, "Roth's first sustained critique of postwar America" appeared in *The Great American Novel*, where he also introduced the themes of his later political fiction, especially the exposure of what Royal calls the "reactionary foundations . . . of contemporary American politics."[63] But even more remarkable than the parallels between the burlesque of empire in *The Great American Novel* and the satire of empire in *The Plot Against America* is the continuity between the political outrage channelled through these works and his critique of America near the start of his career in 1961. In an essay published in *Commentary* not long after the Army-McCarthy hearings, but before the assassinations, riots, and protests shaping the Vietnam era's political divide, Roth lamented the absurdity of American culture:

> [T]he American writer in the middle of the 20th century has his hands full in trying to understand, and then describe, and then make *credible* much of the American reality. It stupefies, it sickens, it infuriates, and finally it is even a kind of embarrassment to one's own meager imagination. The actuality is continually outdoing our talents, and the culture tosses up figures almost daily that are the envy of any novelist. . . . What can the writer do with so much of the American reality as it is? . . . The attitude of the Beats (if such a phrase has meaning) is not in certain ways without appeal. The whole thing is a kind of joke. America, ha-ha. The only trouble is that such a position doesn't put very much distance between Beatdom and its sworn enemy, bestsellerdom—not much more, at any rate, than what it takes to get from one side of a nickel to the other: for what is America, ha-ha, but the simple reverse of America, hoo-ray?[64]

Continuity between these early ideas and those of 1973 and 2004 suggests that Roth's humor of empire presents solutions to the dilemma of

American myth and reality symbolized through the European-American contrast. Rather than choosing a position between inside and outside American exceptionalist ideology—between celebration and critique—Roth's humor of empire unites them in satire.

Roth's humor of empire also points to a signal way in which Mark Twain's brand remains relevant today. Cracks had appeared in vernacular humor's version of American exceptionalism by the time of *Connecticut Yankee*, a decade before the Spanish-American War openly manifested U.S. imperialism. Whereas Twain's pauper only clumsily played prince in 1882, in 1889 Hank's colonization of Britain as its Boss succeeds too well. Its hubris exposed, his protege, Clarence, describes their electrified defenses as "a trap of our own making"(*CY*, 489), poisoning them from the decaying bodies around them while protecting them from their military opponents. Twain's allegiance to the democratic ideology of vernacular humor made Hank a virtuous representative of American inventiveness, materialism, egalitarianism, and anticlericalism while setting him up as a victim of the British traditions of aristocracy and the established church, yet these commitments clashed hyperbolically—comically at the beginning, apocalyptically at the end—as the imperialist implications of Hank's nation-building emerged across three years of writing. The violent end of the inner tale, like Hank's delerium and death in the outer frame, shows how unpalatable Twain found those implications, despite their coherence in theme and language with earlier parts of the tale. If patriotic investment in vernacular ideology kept Twain's critique ambiguous for readers and scholars who accepted the postcolonial premises of its vernacular conventions, today his critique has a contemporary ring. Indeed, Philip Roth's examples of humor and empire make clear that the international context always implicit in American vernacular writing, born in nationalist defensiveness, contains the seeds of its own critique, a theme that also inspires a younger generation of writers working in the vernacular tradition. In sending his own young Jonathan abroad on a quest to find the woman who saved his grandfather from the Holocaust, Jonathan Safran Foer gives the role of dialect clown in his novel to a young Ukranian, but when, as the title puts it, "everything is illuminated," they learn that everyone is culpable. Likewise, in Junot Diaz's novel, when the *fukú* takes vengeance on young Oscar in the jungle, scene of the original imperialist crime, just after he discovers (contra Conrad) "The beauty! The beauty!" of sexual love, the lessons of his investigations are lost forever.[65] To imagine plainspeaking Americans conquering the world requires less invention today than in Mark Twain's day, given how small the world has grown through globalization, based on technologies of transport and communication beyond Hank Morgan's dreams of time travel, printing presses, and copyright. But this international context also explains why Twain's brand of humor and empire endures: the global information economy that Mark Twain helped build (and that Hank imported to Arthurian Britain through his printing press and copyright laws) challenges the exceptionalist national ideologies on which imperialism depends.

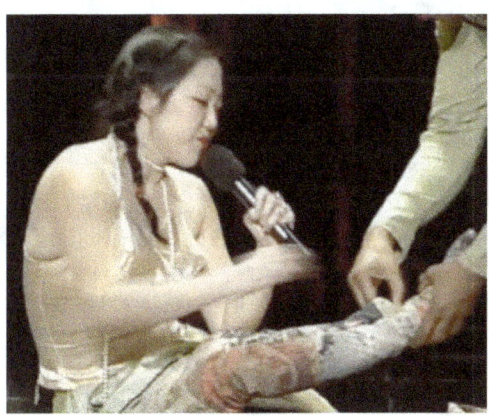

PLATE 1 Margaret Cho performs an unstable self in this sequence from *Revolution* (2004) as she peels away the outward signifiers of Asian American identity with which she began the show.

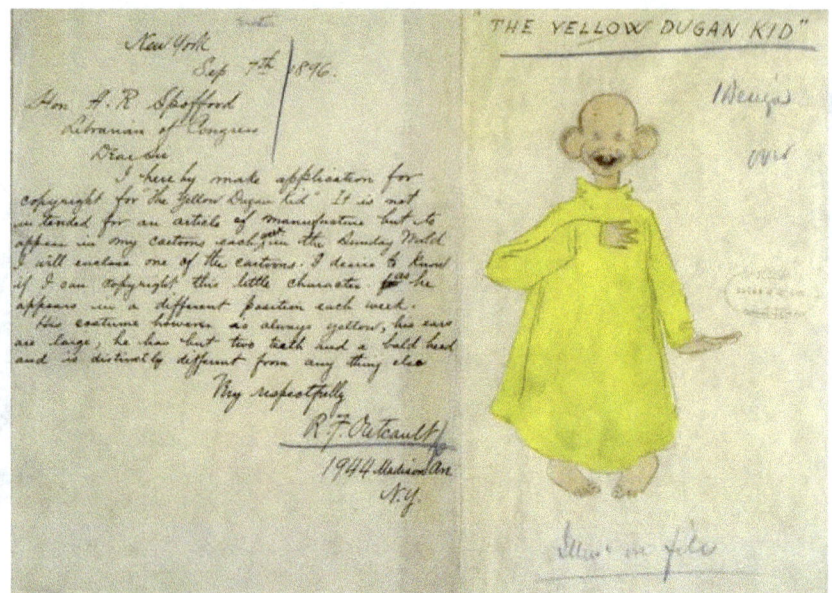

PLATE 2 R. F. Outcault's application to copyright the design of the Yellow Kid shows the oversized ears, misshapen feet, and crude form of the vernacular or amateur aesthetic. (Copyright registration of the "Yellow Dugan Kid," 7 September 1896. Library of Congress.)
<http://www.loc.gov/exhibits/treasures/images/vc192a.3.jpg>

PLATE 3 As the Yellow Kid confronts the reader with his naïve eyes and urban dialect, the caption calls attention to the vernacular satiric impulse of the image, with its scorn for what Huck calls "sivilization," as the antics in Hogan's Alley show that the residents have turned their own gaze upon the behavior of their so-called betters uptown. (Cartoon by R. F. Outcault. "A Secret Society Initiation in Hogan's Alley," *New York World*, 13 September 1896. Rpt. *R. F. Outcault's the Yellow Kid: A Centennial Celebration of the Kid Who Started the Comics* (Northampton, MA: Kitchen Sink Press, 1995), plate 36.

PLATE 4 Groening's early drawings of the Simpson family for the *Tracey Ullman Show* comically exaggerate their deviations from norms of propriety, including realism and physical attractiveness—features that carried over into the commercial animation produced for the Fox sitcom. (The Simpsons, Wikipedia; "The War of the Simpsons," season 2, episode 20, 5/2/1991.)

PLATE 5 With its crude forms, deformed limbs, bright colors, and two-dimensional representation, the vernacular amateur aesthetic of *The Simpsons* repudiates the realistic, professional beauty aesthetic of Disney animation, notable for its rich and nuanced colors, detailed scenes, realistic anatomy, and three-dimensional linear perspective. ("Last Exit to Springfield," season 4, episode 17, 3/11/1993; *The Lion King*, Walt Disney Studios, 1994.)

PLATE 6 Visual humor from peculiar, impossible, or significant points of view calls attention to animation's ability to create the scenes being shown. (Clockwise, from upper left, "Bart Gets Hit By a Car," season 2, episode 10, 1/10/1991; "Blood Feud," season 2, episode 22, 7/11/1991; "Bart's Dog Gets an F," season 2, episode 16, 3/7/1991; "One Enchanted Evening," season 1, episode 2, 5/13/1990.)

PLATE 7 Allusions to paintings, films, and other media create visual jokes by pointing to animation's distance from reality. A two-step sequence imitates the setup and punch line of an oral joke. ("Old Money," season 2, episode 17, 3/28/1991.)

PLATE 8 The similarity gestalt suggests that a relationship exists among like images, linking the criminal, business, and health enterprises of "Last Exit to Springfield" and equating Homer and Bart's self-indulgence in "Mr. Lisa Goes to Washington." ("Last Exit"; "Mr. Lisa," season 3, episode 2, 9/26/1991.)

PLATE 9 Lynda Barry's version of the vernacular aesthetic combines elaborate multimedia collages with glitter and flowers, doodles on lined yellow legal paper, and lettering with a brush; she invokes the intensity of children's crafts while giving feminist pride of place to women's tradition of textile art. (Lynda Barry, *One! Hundred! Demons!*, 14.)

PLATE 10 Scary, out-of-control adults populate the world of Barry's childhood, yet the humor of her amateur aesthetic tempers the mood. (Lynda Barry, *One! Hundred! Demons!*, 31.)

PLATE 11 Lynda's mention of democracy and a multiracial cast of characters expand the significance of this panel from childhood conflict to American racism. The image reinforces Lynda's status as an outsider by pushing her to the edge of the drawing. The rubber joints of the figures, like Lynda's excessive number of freckles and the irregular contours of the lettering and other lines, are hallmarks of Barry's vernacular style. (Lynda Barry, *One! Hundred! Demons!*, 17.)

PLATE 12 Arrows, labels, and comments within images raise questions of class status and materialism as they inject humor into otherwise sentimental or bathetic scenes. Barry invokes a sense of longing through contrasts between the urban industrial street behind Lynda and the bucolic landscape behind the "girlish girl." (Lynda Barry, *One! Hundred! Demons!*, 185.)

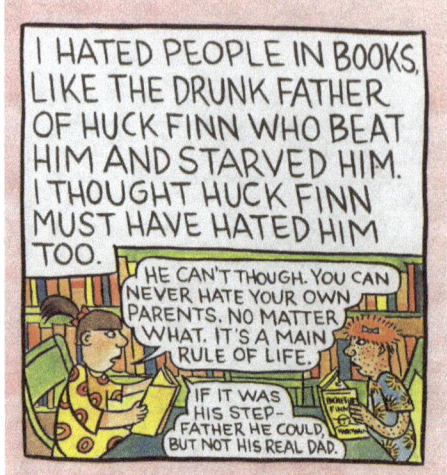 

PLATE 13 Lynda struggles with the taboo on hatred, especially hatred toward parents, even when they are abusive, as in *Huckleberry Finn* (left) and her own case: her mother's rage looms so large that it pushes Lynda's head half out of the picture. Barry separates this pair of related panels by many pages, part of a pattern that sprinkles details of trauma across the memoir and thus avoids a triumphant structure moving from misery to success. (Lynda Barry, *One! Hundred! Demons!*, 79, 95.)

PLATE 14 Verbal and visual details weave together three narrative strands on the closing page of "The Election": the movie myth of vernacular triumph in *It's a Wonderful Life*, the political reality of the Supreme Court's undemocratic end to the 2000 presidential vote count, and Barry's longing for justice in stories and life. The final panel merges cheery Christmas wishes to all with Barry's retreat from citizenship into private life and fantasy, as her planned escape to the movies implies the failure of democratic ideals to play out in American democracy. The couple's embrace expresses not only the power of love and art to counter despair, but also the limits of love or art to affect public life. (Lynda Barry, *One! Hundred! Demons!*, 204.)

PLATE 15 Barry emphasizes the shocking source of Lynda's depression and suffering in the pair of panels closing the ironically titled chapter "Resilience," where a structure from effect to cause contrasts the terrible fallout from her implied rape with the bucolic period beforehand, when colors were brighter and even her hair was perky. Everything is wrong in the last panel, where the narrator's thoughts about her experience press against the memories in the image of a man important only below the waist. (Lynda Barry, *One! Hundred! Demons!*, 72.)

PLATE 16 The cover of McGruder's *Boondocks* collection *Public Enemy #2* comically compares Huey Freeman to Angela Davis in a double visual joke: if he is really an outlaw like Davis, then his paranoia regarding the U.S. government is justified.

PLATE 17 Jazmine's frizzy, oversize pony tail contributes a running visual joke in *The Boondocks* about biracial vs. black identity. This Sunday color panel from December 5, 2004, setting the two kids against a spare background, highlights McGruder's vernacular aesthetic as it contrasts their small size and major concerns. (Aaron McGruder, *All the Rage*, 21.)

CHAPTER FOUR

Kid Stuff

The Vernacular Vision and the Visual Vernacular

Vernacular humor depends on a carefully constructed rhetoric of artlessness—it is a species of incongruity humor—but owes its cultural import to political meanings that led Leo Marx to call it "a style with a politics in view."[2] As detailed in chapter 3, these meanings gained traction after the American Revolution as American language and literature self-consciously diverged from British models: comic incongruities celebrated American distinction, which assigned political values to local colloquial styles and other deviations from social and literary norms. In its classic form, the vernacular style frames lack of linguistic and educational polish as political virtue, evidence of a figure's distance from—and ultimate unwillingness to be socialized into—corrupt social practices. Mark Twain played with vernaculars ranging from the colloquialisms of *Innocents Abroad* and urban slang of *Connecticut Yankee* to African American and Elizabethan dialects in "A True Story" and *1601*, respectively, but his most influential use, in *Adventures of Huckleberry Finn*, built on the vernacular style's heritage of political satire. Huck's naïve colloquial narrative fuses technique and theme into a "vernacular vision": a comic and ironic rhetoric of deep moral significance for "the fate of the republic and the moral constitution of its citizens," in Tom Quirk's words.[3] At its most penetrating—"more than décor," as James Cox put it—the vernacular vision conveys character and experience and critiques social values and norms as it mocks conventional modes of expression and representation.[4] Rejection of conventional (and conventionally romantic) literary language, characters, and plots

> It is half the art of storytelling to keep a story free from explanation as one reproduces it.
> —**Walter Benjamin,** "The Storyteller"[1]

gives ironic significance and status to their vulgar, comparatively realistic counterparts. Huck's semiliterate writing and naïve standpoint challenge the status quo when readers can see, as Huck and Jim cannot, how the subliterary expression and limited understanding that reflect the pair's inadequacies create ironies that also expose corruption in their so-called superiors and society at large. The satire turns sharp when readers find that their amusement at Huck and Jim's inferiority aligns themselves with the greatest threats to the pair's freedom, Miss Watson and Jim's captors, the real sinners in the ironic reversals that result when Huck decides to risk hell for Jim. Satire turns sharper still as saint and sinner, freeman and slave, civilized and not get hopelessly burlesqued when Huck masquerades as Tom Sawyer, who "took all that trouble and bother" (358) to free Jim although his owner Miss Watson had already done so, leading Huck to conclude that he must "light out for the Territory . . . because Aunt Sally she's going to adopt me and sivilize me" (362). Categories blur because the ironies of a vernacular vision offer new ways to see and know our world.

For all the celebration of Mark Twain's vernacular achievement and its influence on later American fiction, however, its parallel development in graphic humor has gone largely unnoticed. Yet some of today's most important graphic humor shows the vitality of Twain's brand of vernacular vision in contemporary American culture.[5] Translated into the graphic humor of cartoons and comics, the vernacular vision matches characters' colloquial or defective language with equally colloquial or defective visual representations. The explicitly naïve or amateurish images of vernacular graphic art joke about ways of seeing through faulty anatomy and perspective, childish forms and composition, unnatural colors, and other deliberate artistic defects in the same way that the mock-oral or dialect narration of vernacular writing jokes about ways of knowing through slang, misspellings, literalisms, and other deliberate linguistic defects. Correspondences between literary and graphic humor derive from the selection and organization of details within forms that have both visual and verbal dimensions. Print comics obviously mix representations of speech and action, which animated cartoons enact, but writing is also visual: it moves language from sound to space. Mock-oral texts, including Huck's narrative, often feature the variant and deliberately deviant spellings known as eye dialect, which not only denotes the sounds of oral language but also marks them visually as *sub*standard. As Mark Twain's vernacular vision gives new, ironic significance to Huck's deviant words and standpoints, so Twain's brand of the visual vernacular turns crude, unprofessional graphic art into satire of conventional representation, meaning, and values. Like the verbal vernacular, the visual vernacular turns style into content, and it too is a style with a politics in view. But the visual vernacular makes clear what the verbal vernacular has become too familiar to show: that vernacular humor revises our ways of seeing and knowing the world.

Through the visual vernacular, Twain's brand inflects some of the most popular and innovative contemporary graphic humor. The crudely shaped bodies and physical antics of Bart Simpson and his family help lampoon middle-class verities on the animated television series *The Simpsons* (1989–), a comic phenomenon whose significance can hardly be overstated: TV's longest-running situation comedy also parodies the genre's conventions and satirizes the ideologies of the American naïf and the American family as representatives of the nation—all at several visual removes from the typical sitcom's realistic live action. In print comics, pint-sized pundit and provocateur Huey Freeman so potently critiqued contemporary race relations, popular culture, and post–9/11 politics in Aaron McGruder's daily newspaper strip *The Boondocks* (1999–2006) that nervous editors cancelled it or moved it to the editorial page. Perhaps most poignantly, the young protagonists of Lynda Barry's alternative comics, especially her alter ego in her full-length graphic "autobifictionalography" *One! Hundred! Demons!* (2002), skewer the status quo through contrasts between the world of adult values and the inner lives of the children who endure them. Comic emblems of the American in a state of becoming, these youthful protagonists—like their kin populating dozens of other examples from *Hogan's Alley* (1895) to *South Park* (1997–)—extend and update vernacular tradition for contemporary popular culture by blending colloquial, unsentimental representations of children's mental and social lives with both a romantic sense of their potential for good and a jaundiced view of adult society. Their stories sustain Twain's brand of the vernacular vision by mocking how adults see and present the world. And what better way to emphasize the child's satiric viewpoint than through childlike pictures?

Behind the verbal and graphic distortions of the vernacular, however, and beyond its conventional associations with democratic liberation lies a paradox that vernacular ironies only intermittently bring into focus. Ambiguity and instability follow—along with co-option and awareness of failure—when the vernacular "sweeps away received notions of class and status—and of literature," as Marx put it.[6] That's partly because his 1958 claim that the vernacular style "is a vehicle for the affirmation of an egalitarian faith so radical that we can scarcely credit it today" reflects a rosy post–World War II optimism that ignores enduring American racial stratification and indulges in nationalist self-congratulation. But distortions of received notions at the heart of the vernacular tradition provide another reason, because they invoke the very strictures under critique. The ambiguities and ironies of the vernacular vision at its best let us glimpse this disappointment: they insist on the promise of democracy yet amuse and disturb us with its failure. As vernacular writing augured the modernist epistemology of varied viewpoints and truths, and their attendant ironies, vernacular drawing invokes postmodern anxiety that knowledge may not be power.

Verbal vernacular humor has thrived in American popular culture for more than two centuries because dialects mark a speaker's place, heritage, status, and education and thereby offer prime material and techniques for social satire. (Linguists commonly point out that while some dialects of a language have more status than others, *all* commonly used variants have equal validity as language.) American writers reversed English class politics, as explained in chapter 3, and colloquial American dialects, known collectively as "the vernacular," signified American identity and democratic virtue in American folklore and popular writing from the revolutionary era. Eighteenth-century New England humor mined a comic type known as "the vernacular oracle" or "cracker-barrel philosopher," an adult who cloaks social observations in pithy, colloquial speech as in the adages of Benjamin Franklin's *Poor Richard's Almanac* (1732–1758); Mark Twain tweaked that convention in the sardonic chapter epigraphs to *Following the Equator* (1897), purportedly drawn from *Pudd'nhead Wilson's Calendar*. A more important vernacular figure advanced a distinctly nationalist ideology by Americanizing a stock *eiron* character of classical drama: a youth (symbol of the New World) of outward simplicity (signaled by ignorant acts, rustic accent, and uncouth expressions) who triumphs through his inner virtues (as the former colony's democratic right trounced imperial might). Language politics thus had both national and international significance. They not only motivated Noah Webster's 1789 call for Americans to "establish a *national language*, as well as a national government" as "the means of commanding respect abroad,"[7] but also animated the key moment of Royall Tyler's play *The Contrast* (1797) when Jonathan, an already-classic New England bumpkin, performed "Yankee Doodle." As locals affirmed American distinction through the same song by which British soldiers had mocked New Englanders' regional speech and overall lack of polish,[8] so vernacular humor upended British prejudices about language as a marker of merit.

Naïve political commentary became a cultural staple after 1830, when Seba Smith's fictitious young New England peddler, Jack Downing, began reporting on state and national politics in letters home to his family. Descended from early British epistolary novels such as Samuel Richardson's *Pamela* (1740), Jack and other naïve American commentators acquired an American nationalist inflection from the political angle of the Downing letters, still hailed a generation later for "their true and genuine spirit of Yankeedom and . . . the real vernacular of the land" when they were collected and republished as *My Thirty Years Out of the Senate* (1859).[9] What Leo Marx in 1958 canonized as "The Vernacular Tradition" of colloquial American writing by Walt Whitman, Mark Twain, and others lauded the first-person, colloquial style as a "view of experience" grounded in a "radical program of freedom": "freedom *from* the oppression of society, and freedom *to* establish the egalitarian community."[10] Mark Twain's nineteenth-century audiences recognized the pro-American, pro-democratic, antiliterary, anti-elite, and anti-European implications of vernacular humor, whose politics echo today in the folksy speech of American candidates for public office.

Comic reversals of supposedly inferior young vernacular American speakers and supposedly superior representatives of the king's English were so popular that even some early nineteenth-century authors considered them clichés. For instance, "My Kinsman, Major Molineux" (1832), Nathaniel Hawthorne's ironic tale of American revolutionary politics, lampooned sentimental portraits of virtuous New England youth nearly forty years before Thomas Bailey Aldrich launched the spate of "bad boy books" in *The Story of a Bad Boy* (1870).[11] By that time, American humorists had long since appropriated as their special purview linguistic contrasts of many kinds: regional vs. national, raced vs. white, immigrant vs. domestic, mock-oral vs. literary, as well as American vs. British and European. Ambitious postbellum authors adapted dialect writing for writing now associated with the realism and local color movements, but the vernacular dialogue of bad boy books, including Mark Twain's *The Adventures of Tom Sawyer* (1876) and George W. Peck's *Peck's Bad Boy and His Pa* (1883), paved the way for *Huckleberry Finn*'s breakthrough use of a child's vernacular narration for social satire.

A stylistic rather than a scientific linguistic category,[12] the vernacular serves satire by countering hegemony in two ways. First of all, the choice to write in a vernacular implicitly acknowledges yet explicitly rejects nationally and internationally homogenized, politically powerful standards of language in favor of the colloquial speech of ordinary people and local places. In this way, varieties of vernacular American English behave like the more distinct and famous vernaculars from Italian to Hindi. As language historian Sheldon Pollock observes, "[A] new language for communicating literarily to a [local] community of readers and listeners can consolidate if not create that very community, as both a sociotextual and a political formation."[13] Secondarily, as detailed in chapter 3, the implied context of the British-American contrast meant that vernacular expression signalled a particular kind of protagonist: an outwardly simple, uneducated, often uncouth figure who reveals deep moral truths—sometimes directly through plot actions, often also through ironies that exploit naïveté. Not surprisingly, just as European vernaculars helped produce and maintain individual nation-states, as Benedict Anderson showed in *Imagined Communities*, so Anglophone vernaculars acquired nationalist significance in former British colonies. Dohra Ahmad introduces her anthology of Anglophone vernacular writing, *Rotten English*, by arguing that such appropriations go to the core of the postcolonial politics of vernacular writing: "Puns, neologisms, musicality, orality, all function as weapons against cultural domination; all provide ways of making an imposed language one's own."[14] In the nineteenth-century U.S., regional, racial, and ethnic vernaculars became all the more politically significant to humorists and their audiences because differences between British and American literary language were so subtle.

Samuel Clemens grew up immersed in the idioms of vernacular humor, especially the lower Mississippi frontier tradition known as Old Southwestern humor, then joined his Nevada and California colleagues of the 1860s in writing western variations on the tall tale and hoax. Classic studies of Mark Twain's use of these comic traditions make clear that the vernacular style tickled humorists because it joined literary and political license. Most notably, as Henry Nash Smith emphasized, the "vernacular language" of Old Southwestern humorists expressed "vernacular values . . . at odds with the values cherished by accredited spokesmen for American society," and from their writings Twain took "themes, situations, a style, and above all a point of view hostile to the values ostensibly dominant in American culture."[15] Like today's theorists of the vernacular, Smith argued that Mark Twain's humor articulates "two ways of viewing the world," an idealized view ridiculed by a realistic one, because both implied and explicit comic contrasts between genteel and vernacular language reproduced broader cultural schisms: between received wisdom and local experience, as Emerson held in "The Young American" (1844), and between the genteel tradition and its antithesis, as George Santayana outlined in "The Genteel Tradition in American Philosophy" (1911).[16] The transgressions of vernacular writing generate humor as they critique social norms.

By embedding the high stakes of Huck's escape from Pap and Jim's escape from slavery within Huck's vulgar language and the pair's limited education and experience, Mark Twain mocks conventional beliefs about race and religion, blacks and whites, virtue and sin, ignorance and insight, language and meaning. The satire begins with the book's first sentence, which disdains formal grammar, narrative scene-setting, and other literary niceties by putting a marginally literate kid in the author's place. Sut Lovingood and other vernacular narrators who preceded Huck had told their stories through educated scribes,[17] but Huck presents himself without an intermediary: "You don't know about me, without you have read a book by the name of 'The Adventures of Tom Sawyer,' but that ain't no matter" (*HF*, 1). By the end of the opening paragraph, Huck has dispensed with the immorality of lying as well as the difference between fiction and truth, and in the next paragraph he complains that the Widow Douglas did him no favor by taking him in: "It was rough living in the house all the time, considering how dismal regular and decent the widow was in all her ways" (1). From this beginning, Twain's brand of vernacular humor in *Huckleberry Finn* emphasizes three main comic incongruities that satirize social norms.

First, each time Huck errs in judgement, the gap between his interpretations and an adult reader's yields humor at the youth's expense. Huck takes pride in his clever solution to the problem arising when some boys in Tom Sawyer's Gang reason that "it wouldn't be fair and square for the others" to let Huck join the gang since he doesn't have nearby kin to pledge when the boys decide to kill the family of anyone who betrays the gang's secrets: "I offered them Miss Watson—they could kill her" (*HF*, 10). This early evidence of his skill at escaping a tight spot coexists with his more obvious traits of half-knowledge and much superstition. For instance, though he understands that Jim's question "what use is half a chile?" (95) misses the point of the tale of Solomon and the contested baby, Huck's belief that handling the snakeskin brought them bad luck demonstrates that in a minstrel routine a white boy can be just as comically dense as a black man. So does Huck's inability to recognize a riddle when Buck Grangerford asks him where Moses stood when the candle blew out. Indeed, when Huck gives grudging admiration to Emmeline Grangerford's artwork, despite her obsession with death, by saying, "These was all nice pictures, I reckon, but I didn't somehow seem to take to them, because if ever I was down a little, they always give me the fan-tods," his remark sets up a comically literal critique of her work as a punch line: "a body could see by what she had done what they had lost" (138)—i.e., not much, or just more of the same bathos. Huck lacks a sense of humor himself, but his unwitting reports yield delicious irony.

Compounding these ironies, a second set of incongruities invests Huck's mistakes with kernels of meaning. His malapropism describing Harvey Wilks as "a dissentering minister" (*HF*, 207) instead of "a dissenting minister" becomes significant when Peter Wilks's coffin must be disinterred to recover the money that Huck hid next to the corpse in order to foil the con men posing as the deceased's brothers. The understatement that caps Huck's assessment of Emmeline Grangerford's poetry and drawings cuts through his polite pieties: "I reckoned, that with her disposition, she was having a better time in the graveyard" (138). Deadpan literalism not only adds to the lampoon of Huck's taste and Emmeline's pretensions, but also mocks readers who admire such art. The same literalism extends to Huck's admiration for Silas Phelps, Tom Sawyer's uncle, who built a church "at his own expense . . . and never charged nothing for his preaching, and it was worth it, too" (285)—a slap at down-home religion.

As this last example suggests, another set of incongruities satirizes society more broadly as Huck misuses, misunderstands, or misrepresents social conventions. His alliterative complaint about the Widow's "dismal regular and decent" life equates order and virtue with tedium, cloaking scorn for propriety in a child's restlessness. The novel's running ridicule of religion belongs to this pattern. By the end of chapter 1, Huck has sneered at recitations of grace ("you couldn't go right to eating, but you had to wait for the widow to tuck down her head and grumble a little over the victuals, though there warn't really anything the matter with them" [*HF*, 2]), Bible stories ("because I don't take no stock in dead people" [2]), and heaven ("I couldn't see no advantage in going where she [Miss Watson] was going" [4]). A religious reader can shake off these judgements as ignorance, or even proof of innate depravity, but Huck's portraits of believers don't advance the cause of traditional religion. He misses the hypocrisy in the Grangerfords' and Shepherdsons' praying in church with their guns between their legs, not to mention their ignoring the preacher's message about brotherly love while praising his "good sermon" for having "such a powerful lot to say about faith, and good works, and free grace, and preforeordestination, and I don't know what all" (147). Instead, when Huck returns to the church later to retrieve Sophia Grangerford's Bible (which shows her capacity to love her family's enemy even if she only uses it as a mailbox for communicating with her Grangerford beau), he observes only that the hogs enjoying the cool sanctuary in the summer were more loyal churchgoers than the humans: "most folks don't go to church only when they've got to; but a hog is different" (148).

Preachers don't come off well, either, in other details that Huck provides but doesn't interpret. The con men's success at running a fake revival meeting suggests marginal differences between the two professions, and honest preachers tend to be credulous or simple. The credulous category includes the preacher who falls for the duke and king's clumsy impersonation of the Wilks girls' British uncles. Among the simple is Tom Sawyer's sweet Uncle Silas—"the innocentest best old soul I ever see" (*HF*, 285), Huck calls him—who believes the boys' fantasy of an abolitionist raid to rescue Jim from the Phelps farm. When Huck famously decides, "All right, then, I'll *go* to hell" and tears up the letter telling Miss Watson where to find her slave, his choice adds to the satire of organized religion by finding irremediable sin in his rejection of slavery, convention, hatred, and heaven over freedom, friendship, love, and hell. Though Jonathan Arac has suggested that Huck's willingness to go to hell merely fulfills his wish from the opening chapter to avoid spending eternity with Miss Watson,[18] Huck's preference for the expedient solution in each case reinforces the parallels between comic and serious versions of his choice. Whether a reader sees circularity or growth in the parallels, their implications that Huck has not changed dramatically confirm Tom Quirk's reading that "good as Huck is, he is not so very good; he is only better than he ought to be."[19]

In Huck's decision that saving his friend is worth going to hell, as in other significant ironies in the novel, comic incongruity promotes a sense of truth as unstable, relative, and socially constructed. Humor based on the vernacular vision thus has a strong modern (and protomodernist) slant that explains its growing appeal over the past century. The novel's stature as a cultural icon (Arac has complained of its "hypercanonization") has whitewashed its transgressions: Huck's key insight about religion, society, and the state of nature when he decides, "All right, then, I'll *go* to hell" (*HF*, 271) resides in the satiric entanglement of right and wrong with their sentimental religious and political associations. Only an ignorant outcast child—someone like Huck—can tell a story that impugns civilization, from religion to democratic rule, as thoroughly yet indirectly as he does. Limits on his ability to change keep him a strong vehicle of naïve satire. Thus he clings to racist ideas and language even after declaring his allegiance to Jim above salvation; thus he resists Aunt Sally's attempts to "sivilize" him even after seeing Jim freed and learning that Pap has died. Incorrigible to the end, Huck understands that he remains outside society, concluding, "I reckon I got to light out for the Territory" (362). As James Cox points out, "If the 'incorrect' vernacular of Huckleberry Finn is to be more than décor, it must enact an equally 'incorrect' vision. Otherwise the style becomes merely a way of saying rather than a way of being."[20] That is, in the vernacular vision, verbal transgressions invite cultural insight.

In their very offensiveness, Huck's racial slurs belong to this pattern. As many readers have observed, use of the word *nigger* accelerates after Huck determines to do right by Jim. Modern readers object to Huck's continued use of a word that reasserts blacks' status as objects of white contempt—despite widespread use in North and South, by 1837 it was already identified as a term that "flows from the fountain of purpose to injure," according to Randall Kennedy, who wrote an authoritative study of its history[21]—as contrary to both the spirit of Huck's declaration and his efforts to free Jim. Jonathan Arac has found Huck's usage so disconcerting that he asked, "If Huck has such moral insight that he is willing to go to hell for Jim's sake, why does he not find new ways of saying his new sense of the world? Why not stop using a word that is part of the system he is, we suppose, rejecting?"[22] Twain might have resorted to *slave*, the substitute that Alan Gribben chose for the New South edition that caused such controversy in 2011 (although *slave* misrepresents Jim's real status at the end), or perhaps *colored*, Twain's respectful (if condescending) usage as the sentimental, misguided "Misto C" in "A True Story" (1874). But a better question takes the opposite tack: why *doesn't* Huck speak differently after accepting the consequences of deciding not to turn in Jim? To this question the last chapters of the novel suggest some answers: because Huck does not broadly repudiate racism, but sees mainly its injustice to his friend Jim; because Huck is "born again" (*HF*, 282) as Tom Sawyer, who cares about style and adventure, not justice; and because the epithet, by compounding both of these failings, sustains Huck's effrontery and, thereby, the book's satire. As David L. Smith points out, the epithet has significance for Jim as well as for Huck: a term that underlines white contempt "establishes a context against which Jim's specific virtues may emerge as explicit refutations of racist presuppositions" because his kindness, creativity, loyalty, and integrity assert his dignity in the face of cruelty and mistreatment from whites of all ages and classes.[23] The vernacular vision mocks social pieties from the inside, at the choice of individual words, and insensitivity by Huck and other characters can sting readers, moving them to new insights not modeled in the text.

In this context, Huck's use of the term *nigger* undercuts any claims to his nobility and complicates Twain's vernacular vision as stylistic transgressions with a politics in view. Each new appearance of the epithet forces another side or purpose of racism upon the reader as it violates rules for polite speech. Huck's first use, near the start of the novel, classes Miss Watson's slaves with dogs and other wayward animals with his offhand remark that they "fetched the niggers" (*HF*, 4) into her house for prayers each night; in addition to denying their humanity, Huck's word choice aligns him with his father, whose rant in chapter 6 against even free blacks' civil rights proves his own inhumanity. On their journey, Huck projects his own rhetorical failure onto Jim, claiming "you can't learn a nigger to argue" (98) when trumped by Jim's comically creative syllogisms to refute Huck's "Why ain't it natural and right for a *Frenchman* to talk different from us?"[24] Indeed, Huck's slurs mark the social gulf that remains as he grows closer to Jim. In the moral drama of the chapter following their burlesque argument about French, when Jim chides Huck for pretending to be dead, instructing him parentally that "trash is what people is dat puts dirt on de head er dey fren's en makes 'em ashamed" (105), Huck's response joins real contrition over hurting his friend with a lingering claim to racial superiority: "It was fifteen minutes before I could work myself up to go and humble myself to a nigger; but I done it, and I warn't ever sorry for it afterward, neither. I didn't do him no more mean tricks, and I wouldn't done that one if I'd a knowed it would make him feel that way" (105). Huck's other racist beliefs coincide with evidence to the contrary. He undercuts his left-handed compliment, "Jim had a wonderful level head, for a nigger," by adding "he could most always start a good plan when you wanted one" (107). The addition also reinforces criticism implied a few pages earlier, where Twain impugns "natural" as a category for generalizations about the races when Huck, mulling Jim's homesickness, concludes, "I do believe he cared just as much for his people as white folks does for theirn. It don't seem natural, but I reckon it's so" (201). By offering an ironic reading of Huck's standpoint, vernacular patterns subvert the received associations of the word *nigger* to oppose Huck's lingering racism.

But perhaps most important, Twain sustains Huck's status as an *eiron* by maintaining his transgressiveness and unrespectability to the very end. Unlike chapter 15, which ends with Huck's shame over playing with Jim's feelings, chapter 31 does not close on the dramatic high of Huck's rejection of racial and religious convention, despite many other parallels between the two scenes. Instead, Twain follows Huck's decision to sacrifice his soul by declaring it less a sacrifice than the easy way out, and the rhetorical move equates the boy's religious and linguistic transgressions: "It was awful thoughts, and awful words, but they was said. And I let them stay said; and never thought no more about reforming. I shoved the whole thing out of my head; and said I would take up wickedness again, which was in my line, being brung up to it, and the other warn't" (*HF*, 271). Twain promptly intensifies the comic incongruity of this vernacular version of Satan's "Evil, be thou my good" as Huck feigns a conventionally racist sense of ownership as rationale for recovering Jim. Seven times in a few lines Huck marks his commitment to sin with the racist slur, whining that the duke and the king "took my nigger which is the only nigger I've got in the world . . . my *nigger* . . . —the only nigger I had in the world, and the only property. . . . he was my nigger, and that was my money. Where is he?—I want my nigger . . . I got to turn out and find my nigger"(272–73). Considering his declaration of friendship, the repetitions not only stress the falseness of both Huck's performance and its racist premises (while limiting the extent of his moral growth), but also contrast Jim's public status as a body with a dark skin with his personal significance to Huck. The structure of the chapter, which ends as Huck leaves the duke to free Jim, cements his sincerity within this complex context.

Framed by this introduction, the final ten chapters set on the Phelps farm in Arkansas intensify ironies built on the epithet. Many readers have seen allegory of the Civil War or Reconstruction in this so-called "evasion sequence," in which the boys plot Jim's escape in a farce that burlesques white Americans' treatment of blacks along with Tom's fantasies of a life based on books.[25] Mark Twain further undercuts whatever nobility Huck acquired from his willingness to go to hell as he abandons his own identity (and his preference for a straightforward escape) to masquerade as Tom Sawyer and thereby double Tom's presence. But the subplot on Jim's freedom also travesties the history of American white-black relations. Jim's kidnapping by the duke and king, a reminder of slave traders' and European empires' plunder of Africa, leads first to his sale to the Arkansas farmer who turns out to be Tom's uncle. Soon the enslaved black man becomes a source of entertainment and self-aggrandizement to the white boys as well as their prisoner; Tom insists on a needlessly elaborate "evasion" based on Alexandre Dumas's *The Count of Monte Cristo* (1844–45), a performance made all the more grotesque when Tom admits in the final pages that Jim suffered needlessly because Miss Watson had already freed him in her will. Mock-torture turns into the real thing as the boys exploit the superstitions of the Phelpses' ignorant slave Nat and Tom delays the escape with new requirements for Jim to write in blood, entertain snakes, suffer spiders, and dig his way out. Jim's kindness and service to the wounded Tom, shot in the otherwise successful escape, earn him a return to slavery along with beatings, chains, and faint praise from the doctor: "a nigger like that is worth a thousand dollars—and kind treatment, too" (*HF*, 353). As framed by the evasion plot, Jim's freedom depends on white whim, whether young Tom's or old Miss Watson's, thieving con men's or expedient Huck's. In this ironic reading, repetition of the word *nigger* throughout these final chapters hammers home the injustice perpetrated on Jim and others.

Huck's vernacular rhetoric keeps the burlesque in high gear. By withholding details of Jim's manumission as the boys revel in the masquerade, the naïve narration dramatizes Huck's limited perspective and lets readers contrast his values with Tom's and their own, especially in that poignant moment when Jim counters Tom's enthusiasm for having Jim entertain spiders and rats with a plaintive "but what kine er time is *Jim* havin'?" (*HF*, 327). Taken together, Tom's guilt for keeping Jim enslaved and Huck's complicity in the evasion project (he has become Tom, after all, and withholds the information from us just as Tom kept it from him) clearly imply that all is not well just because it ends well.

Indeed, Twain frames the chapters at the Phelps farm with ironic jabs at the epithet. As soon as Huck arrives at the Phelps farm, he answers, "No'm. Killed a nigger" to Aunt Sally's question about whether anyone was hurt in the explosion on his steamboat, a remark that prompts her chilling reply denying personhood to those of African descent: "it's lucky; because sometimes people do get hurt" (*HF*, 279). As Kennedy points out, Twain "is seeking ruthlessly to unveil and ridicule" racism in this passage, "not branding blacks, but rather branding the whites" who so cavalierly dismiss black lives.[26] The satiric pattern continues as whites' contempt toward Jim and the Phelpses' slaves contrasts with the blacks' own innocence and generosity, ironically expressed when Huck reports Jim's response to Tom's evasion plans: "Jim he couldn't see no sense in most of it, but he allowed we was white folks and knowed better than him; so he was satisfied" (309). And it climaxes when Jim's refusal to save himself at Tom's expense spurs Huck to proclaim, "I knowed he was white inside" (341). If this last step in Huck's racial education makes his slurs all the more jarring, the effect demonstrates the power of satire to spur insight through indirect means. George Test's argument that satire blends "attack, judgment, play, and humor" supports such ironic use of the word *nigger*, though he does not mention it;[27] the epithet contributes both attack and judgment to the farce by which Tom plays with Jim's freedom. Whatever praise Huck intends by judging that Jim's goodness disproves claims of black inferiority, whatever growth Huck shows by rejecting his earlier belief that different skins imply different degrees of humanity, Mark Twain undercuts both with his collective portrait of white inhumanity and injustice and Huck's complicity with them.

I trace these threads as evidence of textual invitations to read the book ironically, but recognize that many readers, including some noted African American critics, find them insufficient. Ralph Ellison points out that "Jim's dignity and human capacity—and Twain's complexity—emerge" from ironic use of the same minstrel traditions that illustrate how "the white man's relish is apt to be the black man's gall."[28] John H. Wallace takes a less nuanced view: calling the book "the most grotesque example of racist trash ever written," he published a 1983 edition sans the words *nigger* and *hell* for use if the book absolutely had to remain in high school and college curricula.[29] But even some critics who appreciate Twain's satire find the end of the novel a dispiriting retreat. Bernard W. Bell, for instance, concludes that "Twain—nostalgically and metaphorically—sells Jim's soul down the river for laughs" through the farcical evasion sequence, while Rhett S. Jones finds that "in the final analysis, . . . Huck, for all his shrewd, sharpened insight, accepts the teachings of the society of which he is a part," and so does Mark Twain.[30] On the other hand, Richard K. Barksdale predicts that "American society—actually the same 'sivilization' castigated by Huck—will never fully comprehend Mark Twain's irony" unless readers see the paradox of having America's egalitarian ideal symbolized by the friendship of a black-white pair who have left a society that despises them.[31] The political tradition of vernacular humor relies heavily on incongruities between American ideals and local acts—in this case the conflicts between our nationalist ideology of freedom, equality, and virtue and our longstanding mistreatment of black Americans.

In addition to textual patterns, empirical research on the psychology of persuasion largely supports an ironic reading. Experiments showing that audiences accept a persuasive message most readily from an authority with whom they share a significant trait do not address the literary case of a somewhat unreliable narrator.[32] This similarity hypothesis does not, therefore, fully apply to *Huck*, but suggests that an adult reader who shares Mark Twain's ironic sensibility or literary background would incline toward an ironic reading of the novel, while a reader who shares Huck's claims to white privilege might receive a satiric lesson on white injustice if she were amenable to irony, but if not, might well feel licensed by Huck's example to use racist language, as some critics of the novel have charged. But other experiments do demonstrate that low-status communicators like Huck can exert influence when they make self-deprecating remarks, which evoke feelings of superiority in the audience, or when they project inexperience or vulnerability, which elicits rewarding feelings of reciprocity and social competence.[33] Readers who grant Huck's youth and ignorance may therefore absolve him of Jim's suffering in the last chapters considering his own repeated reports of "feeling pretty comfortable all down one side, and pretty uncomfortable all up the other" (*HF*, 282) when he masquerades as Tom and when Tom quashes his ideas to rescue Jim. In addition, experiments showing that humor makes a communicator more likeable[34] explain readers' positive attitudes toward Huck (and Tom and Twain) despite offenses against Jim. Keeping Huck's humor alive through the burlesque of literature, ridicule of Tom, and flummoxing of Aunt Sally enables readers to construct ironic humor from Tom's excesses and Jim's suffering, though readers who focus on Jim's mistreatment may find the humor deeply offensive or miss it altogether. Finally, researchers have found that irony increases the effect of humor on an audience, probably because the cognitive work required to decode irony promotes self-persuasion.[35] Readers attuned to irony surely appreciate Huck's dry scorn for Tom's insistence on the "principle" (307)—i.e., fiction—that he was digging beneath Jim's prison with a case knife, not a pick. Huck has similar deadpan sneers for the white farmers back at the Phelps farm after Jim's recapture. When they decide not to hang him in punishment as an example to the other slaves because his owner might expect compensation for lost property, Huck observes that "the people that's always the most anxious for to hang a nigger . . . is always the very ones that ain't the most anxious to pay for him when they've got their satisfaction out of him" (352). And when the men who have shackled Jim hand and foot with "rotten heavy" chains (354) finally yield to the doctor's argument that Jim proved "he ain't no bad nigger" by risking his freedom to take care of the wounded, Huck damns them with faint praise: "Then they all agreed that Jim had acted very well, and was deserving to have some notice took of it, and reward. So every one of them promised, right out and hearty, that they wouldn't cuss him no more" (354). In each of these cases, the word *nigger* invokes irony. Twain could not have known, of course, how empirical research would support vernacular ironies or a satiric reading of the evasion, but writers and speakers have exploited such rhetorical principles intuitively or deliberately since classical times, and here they uphold the power of Huck's naïve voice to move readers toward change.

Two other lines of argument also tilt *Huck*'s case toward satire. First is Twain's record of treating racial injustice ironically in earlier texts. "A True Story" (1874), Mark Twain's first literary experiment in dialect, characterized the author as the condescending "Misto C—" and the former slave Aunt Rachel as the vernacular hero who taught him a needed lesson about racist noblesse oblige. Five years before that tale, an unsigned editorial item in the liberal *Buffalo Express*, of which Clemens was managing editor and part owner, seethed over the lynching of the wrong African American man in "Only a Nigger" (1869): "Too bad, to be sure! A little blunder in the administration of justice by Southern mob-law; but nothing to speak of. Only 'a nigger' killed by mistake—that is all" (*MTBE* xix, 2–23). The piece refers to *negroes* [*sic*] in nonironic statements, but shifts to *nigger* enclosed in quotation marks to signify others' usage while mocking their racism. Some scholars attribute the essay to Mark Twain because its title echoes Huck's remark to Aunt Sally, and its caustic tone reappears in *King Leopold's Soliloquy* (1905) to protest mistreatment of Congolese men and women. Even if he did not write it, however, his revisions to the manuscript of *Huck* provide a second set of reasons for reading the epithet ironically.

As Victor Doyno has shown, late changes to the evasion sequence and elsewhere strengthened other structural, linguistic, and narrative parallels among Huck's three failed efforts to free Jim—through escape by river, under cover of the king and duke, and with Tom at the Phelpses' farm—that coalesce into an ironic anticlimax, "the ultimate impossibility of *winning* the slave's freedom gradually [becoming] more explicit as the novel progresses." Indeed, Doyno argues, the failures raise questions about freedom itself. In the context of Tom's climactic claim that Jim is "as free as any cretur that walks this earth!" (*HF*, 356), the failures suggest that freedom is not whites' to bequeath, nor a slave's to earn. Nor does nature act benevolently: challenges from currents, fog, snakes, and other natural forces also impede Jim's escape. The quasi-magical resolution to Jim and Huck's escape combines with the phrase "free as any cretur" to question the very origin and nature of freedom even as Tom assumes a role as liberator, distracting us and his sickbed audience from his role in keeping Jim enslaved for his own entertainment. Huck naïvely explains Tom's actions as appropriate to "his bringing up," which would permit him to liberate a free black man, but not an enslaved one, and Tom concedes having imagined that the evasion would make him a hero to "all the niggers around" (360).[36] The novel's last use of the epithet, attributed to Tom though it comes from Huck, confirms whites' own bondage to racial ideology and suggests—along with the unjust imprisonment of the legally free Jim—that freedom is elusive at best, a travesty at worst.

Many scholars have traced how Twain played with vernacular narrators across a series of experiments with naïve reportage and dialect until he wed vernacular voice and moral vision in the "fully felt complicity in the social and emotional condition of his created characters" in *Adventures of Huckleberry Finn*, as Tom Quirk put it. Quirk summed up *Huck's* vernacular vision as "a hopelessly old-fashioned liberal humanism,"[37] but critics who have considered the role of vernacular humor in Huck's narrative see more significant ethical implications in the comic friction between his commentary and his acts. As Cox points out, if not for his conviction that he does irredeemable wrong in helping Jim, Huck's tale would turn into the equivalent of a "sentimental . . . novel in our time about a boy in Hitler's Germany helping a Jew to the border"; in fact, Cox argues, "The more a book is committed to a vernacular hero, the more it necessarily must produce a vision which displaces the genteel values it plays upon."[38] This commitment provides perhaps the best reason for the grotesqueries of the literary burlesque in the evasion sequence, where the word *nigger* appears so prominently: the epithet encapsulates Twain's vernacular vision of American racism, religion, and romance.

The epithet's vulgarity also links the vernacular style of American humor to the international populist tradition of carnivalesque humor, which similarly upends social norms. As Mikhail Bakhtin described it in *Rabelais and His World*, the medieval carnival suspended taboos and sanctioned lampoons of secular and church authorities; carnival rituals gave voice to the lowest orders of society as elites briefly relaxed their control. More important for understanding of vernacular humor is how Bakhtin links the crude, often bawdy and grotesque popular humor of the carnivalesque mode to the development of the great literary, scientific, and philosophical works of early modern France as well as to the rise of vernacular languages and their sociopolitical challenges: vernaculars are vulgate languages, after all, both politically and socially demotic. He argues that early written humor grew from lives of the lower classes who lived in an oral culture "of the loud word spoken in the open, in the street and the marketplace." As the marketplace rose in political significance, so the demotic French language empowered people excluded from institutions and social relations bound by Latin.[39] Postcolonial American politics imbued vernacular humor with a similar ideology, as I've explained in chapter 3, "Humor and Empire." Bakhtin's analysis of the social functions of humor supports critics who see Mark Twain's vernacular writing, especially *Huckleberry Finn*, as a watershed in

American literary history because the mock-oral and dialect traditions of American vernacular humor honor vulgar speech and invert social hierarchies much as Bakhtin details.

Twain set his most famous work of vernacular humor in this oral world. Huck reports scene after scene of dialogue between characters within a narrative that presents itself visually as a text but retains the feel of talk, somewhat like a dictated letter (hence the sign-off, "THE END, YOURS TRULY HUCK FINN."). Misspellings like "sivilize" and "wuz" (*HF*, 1, 361) call attention to the textual form of Huck's tale and the dialect he records, yet the vocabulary, syntax, imagery, and content of his narrative all evoke the world of sensory experience and oral communication. Huck addresses us directly from his self-introduction, "You don't know about me," and the description of how his nose "itched till the tears come into my eyes" (7) to his concluding admission, "if I'd a knowed what a trouble it was to make a book I wouldn't a tackled it and ain't agoing to no more" (362). Attention to sensory experiences and details of what Walter Ong called the "life-world" is a hallmark of oral culture, which has no use for the classifications, abstractions, and other analytical structures of cultures grounded in writing.[40] In order to imitate oral communication between a narrative "speaker" and the implied, equally present audience, mock-oral writing incorporates details of sensory physical experience—especially feelings, sights, and sounds; the writer not only mimics speech through idiom, direct address, and topic, but also represents how words and noises sound through nonstandard spellings and punctuation. In this way, the craft of vernacular humor hinges on a representational paradox. Narrative displays of narrative incompetence and vulgarity depend on a writer's attention to minute orthographic and rhetorical details, and the joke is always on the reader who fails to recognize that the appearance of authenticity depends entirely on artifice.

Twain explained the technique as it applied to oral narration in "How to Tell a Story" (1895). Recalling a James Whitcomb Riley performance so hilarious that the audience laughed themselves to exhaustion and tears, Twain revealed the professional secret: "Simplicity and innocence and sincerity and unconsciousness . . . are perfectly simulated." And he inisisted, "This is art—and fine and beautiful, and only a master can compass it" (*CTS* 2:203). That is, by distracting an audience from the craftsmanship at its core, the simulated authenticity of vernacular humor conveys the artist's vision of truth.

The ambivalent view of self and society on which *Huckleberry Finn* ends its vernacular critique, stressing potential for good yet failure to achieve it, also sustains Twain's brand in contemporary graphic humor, which extends the demotic rhetoric of artlessness from the verbal to visual vernacular. Cartoons typically trade the first-person account of Twain's breakthrough novel for third-person representations, yet the speech balloons of print comics and synchronized voices of animated cartoons maintain the vernacular tradition of representing individual characters—and critiquing America—through mock-oral colloquial expression and vulgar acts. More important in terms of Twain's brand of humor, however, is how some cartoons exploit a visual aesthetic of amateurishness as a graphic counterpart for the simulated simplicity that Twain admired in Riley's performance and imitated in his own vernacular writings. Jokes about performance and realism in the verbal vernacular become jokes about representation and reality in the visual vernacular, and humor extends from ways of speaking and thinking into ways of seeing and knowing.

In referring to a visual vernacular style, I use the term *vernacular* more narrowly than is customary in art circles in order to stress how the fusion of technique and theme in this strand of graphic humor parallels its literary counterpart. Curators refer to the vernacular aesthetic practices of folk or outsider art in order to distinguish them from traditions based on formal education or apprenticeship and the high status bestowed by social and economic elites. In this sense, cartoons and comics qualify as vernacular art, as does most other graphic humor outside the fine arts traditions of realism and the grotesque, exemplified by William Hogarth (1697–1764) and Arnold Böcklin (1827–1901) or George Cruikshank (1792–1878), respectively. By contrast, graphic humor exploiting Twain's brand of the vernacular vision rejects high art tradition, providing visual parallels for the slang, vulgarity, dialect, and implied mispronunciations of vernacular writing—deliberate linguistic defects—through explicitly naïve or amateurish images. My usage builds on Özge Samanci's description of an "amateur aesthetic" that spurns the realistic anatomy, sophisticated coloration, and three-dimensional, linear perspective of mainstream narrative comics like *Superman* (which she characterizes as expressing a "professional aesthetic")—in favor of a crude, apparently untutored style of distorted anatomy, childish or otherwise unsophisticated colors, and two-dimensional compositions. Samanci's observations, analyses by Shelley Fisher Fishkin and M. Thomas Inge of Twain's influence on animators Chuck Jones and Tex Avery, and Kerry Soper's discussion of the Yellow Kid's carnivalesque impulse[41] together suggest to me why so many cartoonists have gravitated toward a vernacular style despite representational skill developed through formal art training. A vernacular aesthetic imbues graphic humor with an oppositional, carnivalesque frame for any theme or plot. Misshapen or ineptly rendered forms, cluttered or crude compositions, unconventional viewpoints, unnatural colors, parodic or deviant representational strategies—these and other devices constitute the visual vernacular style as a comically incongruous, counterhegemonic rhetoric. That is, just as the verbal vernacular rejects genteel values of conventional writing by valorizing regional vocabulary and pronunciation or semiliterate spelling or grammar, so the visual vernacular contests the refined values of mainstream art by debunking realism and other conventional ways of looking at the world. Together, the verbal and visual vernaculars of contemporary cartoons sustain humor when satire turns serious. Like the artless vernacular Huck, who does not catch the humor or significance of what Twain has him say, the amateurish vernacular artist appears unable to draw for deliberate effect—but does so nonetheless. Like the verbal vernacular, then, the visual vernacular turns style into content for comic and satiric effect, and it too is a political rhetoric, a style with a politics in view.

The historically low status of cartoons and comics, with their young or subliterate characters and audiences and their marginal place in the media environment, has let them trangress social rules with the boldness that marked Twain's greatest vernacular work in its own day, uniting the *eiron*'s naïve standpoint with the graphic artist's apparently naïve drawings in order to generate sophisticated satire. Doubtless the minimal literacy required for captioned graphic humor in print would have guaranteed an audience of children and less-educated readers—the demotic audience for the carnivalesque tradition of humor that Bakthin dates to the Middle Ages—even if American comics hadn't valorized children, immigrants, and other vernacular speakers. But they did, and American graphic humor quickly adopted the vernacular verbal and visual style when graphic reproduction became cheap enough for mass printing and distribution in the late nineteenth century.

Perhaps most notably, the Yellow Kid embodied vernacular values as the crudely shaped, vulgar, dialect-speaking urchin who first mocked upper-class urban manners in a panel by Richard Felton Outcault for the May 5, 1895, *New York World* entitled "At the Circus in Hogan's Alley," America's first modern newspaper comic, a decade after the publication of *Adventures of Huckleberry Finn*. Outcault saw the brand value of his iconic youth and sought copyright protection for his creation in September 1896, citing the character's design as "distinctly different from anything else" (see plate 2), but the figure's simple yet distorted shape shows how Oucault's graphic style, like the Kid's slang, drew on the familiar vernacular equation of an untutored manner with authenticity and insight. Indeed, Outcault's *Hogan's Alley* pages for the *New York World* consistently display vernacular antagonism to decorum and gentility, often in implied contrast with these middle-class values. Chaos reigns most obviously in the children's wild, often violent play, but it also appears in the semiliterate, clumsily hand-lettered signs posted on the Kid's oversized shirt and around the scene, with their mock-oral representations of slang. The Kid's simple shape reinforces other deviations from genteel norms of representation as it clashes comically with Outcault's detailed draftsmanship of other forms and neoclassical pyramid-composition of figures in the scene.[42] For instance, in "A Secret Society Initiation in Hogan's Alley" (Sept. 13, 1896, see plate 3), Outcault contrasts genteel social organizations such as the Elks and Masons with their wild, perverted imitations in Hogan's Alley, where kids fall from the fire escape, beat drums, throw bricks, and taunt animals and each other. Equally important, Outcault opens a nonthematic channel for social critique by directing the Yellow Kid's gaze at the viewer, bringing the imagined scene into the uptown viewer's world, even as the slum antics show that the residents of Hogan's Alley have turned their own gaze upon the behavior of their so-called betters uptown. As the Yellow Kid confronts the reader with his naïve eyes and urban dialect, the caption for the picture underlines its vernacular satiric impulse with its scorn for what Huck calls "sivilization."

Extending an antisentimental view of childhood into social satire has remained a mainstay of newpaper comics—think of the hijinks of the dialect-speaking *Katzenjammer Kids* (1897–), the preternaturally serious characters of *Peanuts* (1950–2000), and the hellion hero of *Calvin and Hobbes* (1985–95)—even as they left the slums that sanctioned (and contained) their carnivalesque vulgarity for more middle-class venues. But some of today's most innovative and important cartoons starring children have adopted a graphic style with a politics in view. Matt Groening's groundbreaking animated prime-time television cartoon *The Simpsons* (1987–), Lynda Barry's autobiographical graphic narrative *One! Hundred! Demons!* (2002), and Aaron McGruder's daily newspaper comic strip *The Boondocks* (1999–2006) deploy a vernacular style that scorns convention visually as well as thematically and converts amusement over children into satire of adults and American society at large.

Matt Groening confirmed his reliance on a vernacular aesthetic when he joked, "Cartooning is for people who can't quite draw and can't quite write. You combine the two half-talents and come up with a career."[43] *The Simpsons* began on *The Tracey Ullman Show* in 1987 as ninety-second animated short subjects in three acts, based on a simple slapstick formula: parents Homer and Marge could not control children Bart, Lisa, and Maggie. The series moved to the fledgling Fox network in 1989 as a half-hour animated sitcom, the first in prime time since *The Flintstones* (1960–66) went into reruns. Groening long ago turned over the task of drawing his characters to a cadre of animation professionals, but the show's visual style still depends on his apparent "half-talents" to create what he called "a hallucination of the sit-com" about a blue-collar family whom its creator conceived as "lovable—in a mutant sort of way."[44] As the Simpsons' antics reveal rottenness in schools, religion, government, and capitalism in the contemporary Middletown he called Springfield, U.S.A., the show's lower-middle-class characters and unsentimental attitudes toward work, family, and society also mock the aspirational and inspirational formulas of more conventional sitcoms. Targets include *The Cosby Show* (1984–92, broadcast opposite *The Simpsons* 1990–92) and *Father Knows Best* (radio, 1949–54; TV, 1954–60), that sentimental classic set in another Springfield, if not another America. In contrast to the typical kids in those families, ten-year-old Bart, whose name is an anagram for *brat*, is so antisocial that his eight-year-old sister Lisa calls him a "vile burlesque of irrepressible youth" ("War of the Simpsons," 7–20, 5/2/1991). Her complaint links Bart to the vulgar vernacular figures that influenced Twain's brand from Old Southwestern humor, most notably Sut Lovingood, the outrageous dialect-speaking prankster created by George Washington Harris; the critic Edmund Wilson found Sut so offensive that he called him "a peasant squatting in his own filth."[45] Just as verbal vernacular elements like slang and impolitic comments mark Bart and Homer's deviance from social norms, however, so by a related comic logic vernacular visual representation of characters' bodies and movements—and of *The Simpsons*'s places, objects, plots, and filmic style—gives us new ways of seeing the American family and society. The visual vernacular of *The Simpsons*'s satiric animation thus tweaks norms of social knowledge in much the same way that mock-oral vernacular writing mocks norms of literacy and class.

Like older vernacular American humor, *The Simpsons* targets book-learning, authority figures, and foreigners (especially Europeans) in favor of the lowbrow and low class, and viewers quickly recognized and split over the show's transgressions. Five months into the first season *Newsweek* called Bart "obnoxiousness incarnate" and marvelled that five "bug-eyed squiggles with hideous overbites" managed to "embody a genuine Sociological Force"; early focus groups confirmed that young people enjoyed Bart as "a misfit, but cool" hero in a world where parents don't know best, schools exist to torture kids, and happiness comes from retaliation and escape.[46] Not surprisingly, the vernacular vision of *The Simpsons* evoked the same humorless impulses toward condemnation and censorship that have shadowed *Huckleberry Finn*. In its first year, the show provoked the principal of a California elementary school to ban T-shirts of Bart proclaiming "UNDERACHIEVER AND PROUD OF IT," and William Bennett, director of the Office of National Drug Control Policy under President George H. W. Bush, warned teen addicts in rehab against the show because "[t]hat's not going to help you."[47] The satire soon proved too much for commercial broadcast television, which requires regular relicensing from the FCC: producers shifted the spotlight from Bart to Homer by the end of the third season in 1992, replacing the boy's anarchic impulses with the transgressions of an older vernacular character who nonetheless fulfills the basic expectations of a father and husband. (But the producers also lampooned censorship of cartoons in Season 2's "Itchy & Scratchy & Marge" [2–9, 12/20/1990].)[48] By 2010, when *The Simpsons* ranked as the longest-running prime-time American television series, English professors were praising it as "the greatest tv show ever,"[49] *Time* listed Bart among the one hundred most important figures of the twentieth century ("deplorable, adorable . . . a brat for the ages"), and nobody doubted the show's ability to hold a carnival mirror to American culture. In its representation of contemporary American life and its symbolic equation of vernacular hero and nation, *The Simpsons* brought Twain's brand of humor to the TV screen, especially in the early years focused on Bart, a Huck for our time.

Animating a sitcom signals rejection of realism along with other conventions of the form. Critical discussions of *The Simpsons* nonetheless emphasize its realism, as if it were not a cartoon but a live action show. Claims about realism, nicely surveyed by Jason Mittell, boil down to two: its antiromantic representation of American domestic life, especially as performed on television, and *The Simpsons*'s dramatically rich characterizations and plots.[50] While the antiromantic thrust of the series does link it to nineteenth-century literary realism, critics' focus on plot and character misses the core fact of animation: it replaces photography of live action and editorial manipulations after the fact with purely invented images and imagined camera angles. "We control every part of every frame, so we might as well put in the jokes," Groening told a reporter in 1991. "It takes six months to do a single show, so . . . we just cram it full of jokes."[51] An animated cartoon seldom adopts a first-person narrator's point of view in order to generate irony, but cartoons easily create satire from comic incongruities between other elements. Visual techniques for characterizing individuals and incidents include dynamic considerations of pacing and sequence or editing as well as static elements of shape, color, and composition (including allusions to other images), and these elements join music and other sound effects to cement *The Simpsons*'s satiric plots and vernacular dialogue. Particularly in the innovative early years, 1987–1992, when the show freely celebrated Bart's deviance, its animation featured the sort of carnivalesque violations of human dignity and resistance to social hierarchy that Bakhtin described in *Rabelais and His World* as the essence of satire. That is, the satire of *The Simpsons*—its very capacity for what John Alberti praised as "oppositional culture"[52]—originates in its animation, especially the cartoon's play with realistic representation. A crude graphic style matches colloquial speech and aberrant acts with the amateurish anatomy, perspective, and proportion of a colloquial graphic style.

Indeed, *The Simpsons*'s vernacular aesthetic sets humor in motion even before narrative, plot devices, characterization, and language define an episode's particular objects of critique. The main characters' distinctive profiles threaten their dignity from the outset: comically deformed shapes create opportunities for characterization and jokes (see plate 4). Marge's tall, bright-blue beehive hair, originally intended to conceal bunny ears, clashes with her conventional ethos of motherhood. Bart's picket-fence (or paper bag) head marks his extreme personality with the sharp edges of a shrieking speech balloon. Lisa's Statue-of-Liberty corona reduces the monumental to grade-school size. Homer's bowling-pin physique reverses 1980s yuppy athleticism and class consciousness. These and other hallmarks of *The Simpsons*'s graphic style remained intact from the characters' *Tracey Ullman* years. In conceding his "simple and crude" style, Groening credits the influences of James Thurber ("the only cartoonist that draws worse than I ever did") and *Rocky and Bullwinkle* (1959–61; 1961–64), for making "animation . . . crummy enough so that I could imagine doing something like that."[53] (Evidently he also absorbed the countercultural comic sensibility of *Rocky*'s "Fractured Fairy Tales" and satires of Cold War spycraft, which outlived *Rocky* in the pages of *MAD* magazine. *MAD*, a favorite of producer George Meyer,[54] likewise anticipated *The Simpsons*'s penchant for satire and parody.) Although Groening's characters lost their crazed looks and gained softer shapes when adapted for Fox, Gabor Csupo of the show's original animation studio Klasky/Csupo kept a style he described as "very two-dimensional, purposely primitive animation . . . [with] shocking colors" to signify "[t]hese are the craziest characters."[55] That is, even the more commercialized, professional design for the characters deliberately retained the antiprofessional vernacular style of Groening's original drawings: bug-eyed faces, distorted anatomy, three-fingered hands, and bright yellow skin. Their endurance despite commercial pressures against treating style as what Alberti called "a visible signifier of an identifiable artist"[56] shows how style contributes meaning to art.

From the standpoint of a style with a politics in view, *The Simpsons*'s vernacular aesthetic mocks traditions of realistic animation instead of caricaturing familiar figures in the manner of Hanna-Barbera (who based Fred Flintstone on Jackie Gleason) or imitating live action in the Disney mode. Even animal characters in Disney cartoons move in imitation of human and animal models, and they manifest recognizable human emotions and motivations as they confront explicitly moral dilemmas in recognizable scenarios.[57] *The Simpsons* upholds Disney's commitment to *narrative* realism by grounding each episode in the script, not in visual gags or graphic exploration, and critics' focus on the show's formal, situational, and verbal humor at the expense of its graphic elements demonstrates the success of this strategy as a thematic force. But Disney extended narrative realism into its graphic representation, and there *The Simpsons* did not follow. Whereas Disney developed the multiplane camera to create the impression of three-dimensional figures, motion, and environment, *The Simpsons* settles for crudely drawn linear perspective and characters that lack shading for depth of form (see plate 5). Moreover, in contrast to Disney's attractive protagonists set in a richly detailed environment, the Simpson family members have ill-proportioned, impossible bodies, bug-eyed faces, and bizarre hair, and the few objects in their spare surroundings offer visual jokes of their own. Finally, whereas Disney reinforced the realism of his plots by requiring characters to obey basic (if sometimes exaggerated) rules of physics, anatomy, and live motion, so that bunnies like Thumper can bounce and Bambi can talk but humans cannot fly, *The Simpsons* yields to the temptations of visual fantasy, and other impossibilities follow. In the world of *The Simpsons* actions and effects vary with their comic potential, so that the three-eyed fish in the plant's waste pond is funny rather than horrible, Homer can walk out of the nuclear power plant with radioactive materials with no ill effects, and Marge can crash the same car into the garage week after week. Animation more easily violates than obeys the laws of physics, anatomy, and biology, so antisocial acts and pain become funny. Indeed, visual assertions of fantasy in *The Simpsons*, such as the tidy slice off the top of Marge's blue beehive by a helicopter depositing Homer on his lawn ("Last Exit to Springfield,"

4–17, 3/11/1993 [see plate 5]), restore to animation what Disney realism removed: "the *ideological* freedoms of . . . both graphic and narrational anarchy," as Paul Wells put it.[58] *The Simpsons* rejects graphic realism, but nonetheless squashes and stretches its narrative realism in order to satirize social norms.

Vernacular comic play with narrative and graphic realism begins with the running gags of the opening sequence: brightly colored images set to sprightly music cheerfully present each family member's deviance and equate it with freedom. The clouds of heaven in the title shot give way to reveal the eccentric Springfield skyline, its cheerful welcome sign in the foreground incongruously introducing the grey cones of the nuclear plant that disrupt the otherwise bucolic scene. When the narrative zooms in on Springfield Elementary School and finally on Bart, the potentially sentimental scene of chalkboard punishment reveals Bart's latest vulgar, banal, or creative transgression, e.g., "I WILL NOT BELCH THE NATIONAL ANTHEM" ("Principal Charming," 2–14, 2/14/1991). The abstract shape of Bart's figure to the right of the text mitigates a realistic sense of punishment: bold colors on his body stop the eye, while spikes on his head point toward the text, with its comic incongruity between the typical schoolyard violation and Bart's latest crime. Indeed, the narrative lingers for five seconds to allow viewers to read and savor the details of the gag, whose apparently infinite variations on the theme week after week define *incorrigible*, characterize school as a humorless and petty penal institution, and frame Bart by contrast—that is, in opposition—as a funny, important, and fun embodiment of freedom. Reinforcing this implication is his flight out the door and into the air on his skateboard as soon as the bell ends his detention, and the sequence stays amusing through contrasts between his disruptive powers and narrative significance, on the one hand, and his social powerlessness and small size, on the other. The assertion of freedom in the opening comes partly from his transcending gravity to soar into the clouds above the school and its petty rules, but it also acquires subversiveness by showing him move right to left, against the norm of film movement from left to right. Parallels between school bell and factory whistle extend a similar sense of liberation to Homer's escape from work and, by establishing similarities between father and son, also juvenilize Homer and trivialize his mishandling of radioactive material at work and in the car. Links between liberty and transgression soon unite all the members of the family as they abandon their individual tasks to converge helter-skelter on the couch to watch TV. Wordlessly, the animation of the opening sequence, with its God's-eye view of the American scene, debunks the characters of the Simpsons individually and collectively.

FIGURE 6 The chaotic assemblage of the Simpson family on their couch at the start of each episode twits the orderly tableau of the typical TV sitcom family and specifically parodies the Williams family portrait, complete with telephone and lamp, from *The Danny Thomas Show*. ("Bart the Murderer," season 3, episode 4, 10/10/1991.)

Given the family unit as society in microcosm, deviations from TV realism represented by the couch gag announce by the end of the overture that America is in trouble. The tableau assembles the five bright-yellow, oddball forms into an image of collective aberration. Each week's details vary the room decor, asymmetrical pose of the group, the pratfall en route to the sofa, but they consistently start the show by portraying the household as a site of domestic chaos (figure 6). The tableau also operates, however, as a visual joke in the larger social sphere by parodying a visual convention of live-action sitcoms, the formal family portraits of *Ozzie and Harriet* (1952–66), *Father Knows Best* (1954–60), and especially *Make Room for Daddy* (*Danny Thomas Show*, 1957–64), which has *The Simpsons*'s signature phone and lamp. Like the picture on their wall, the Simpson clan—and the show about them—is a bubble off plumb.

As the spikes on Bart's head signify the rough edges of his personality, so other visual elements enhance his characterization as comic mischief personified. Bart's exploits are so vast that the school has a whole drawer, not just a file folder, documenting them (e.g., "Bart the Genius," 1–2, 1/14/1990). The punishment sentences that he writes in the chalkboard gag not only fail to fit his crimes but ridicule them, to boot. A hundred repetitions of "I WILL NOT WASTE CHALK" of course wastes chalk (1–2); "THE PLEDGE OF ALLEGIANCE DOES NOT END WITH HAIL SATAN" tweaks patriotic ritual ("Burns' Heir," 5–18, 4/14/1994); "MY PIGGIE BANK IS NOT ENTITLED TO TARP FUNDS" challenges federal policy along with his fib ("Wedding for Disaster," 20–15, 3/29/2009). The joke is visual, despite its basis in words, because it comes from writing instead of speech and because the animation implies (contrary to fact) that a camera has zoomed in on a preexisting scene. Chalkboard gags celebrate Bart's newest sin with vernacular humor's traditional scorn for book-learning, contempt for authority, and delight in trumping them, and the animation is similarly oppositional.

Compelling visual images drive early plots and their satiric targets. For example, the first season's "Crepes of Wrath" unfolds from a visually rich prank: Bart puts a cherry bomb down a toilet, producing delightful fountains of water for *Simpsons* viewers to enjoy along with him and his friends just as the principal's elderly mother sits down on the toilet in the girls' restroom next door (1–11, 4/15/1990). The episode follows Bart to France for a three-month suspension from school in the guise of an exchange program that Principal Skinner admits is "deportation," a political term whose nationalist context hints at the episode's satire of French culture. The gushing water of his bathroom prank portrays him in fairly conventional terms as a comic antagonist to the forces of civilization represented by adults, school, and the rules of society,[59] but the sitcom form requires a comic resolution in twenty-three minutes, so the plot and its visualizations restore the social order needed for comedy by reframing his relations to society. After being shown as an antisocial force, Bart becomes a victim of adults ranging from the inept Homer and Marge and mean-spirited Skinner to careless airport travelers and criminal French bootleggers until he finally emerges as a vernacular instrument of justice. Images emphasize juvenile behavior by Skinner and Homer, who jump in unison off the floor to celebrate Bart's banishment. Scenes at Bart's eye level in the airport show him battered by the knees of adults so tall that their torsos exceed the frame. Essentially kidnapped by his so-called hosts, he suffers neglect and abuse sleeping on hay in a barn, wearily stomping grapes for wine, and enduring other hardships of weather and work until he finally escapes. Then, with his stubbornness recast as spunk, this apparently uneducable American kid discovers that months of listening to his captors have enabled him to report their crimes *in competent French* to a gendarme underwhelmed by Bart's misery but galvanized by his report that the men have doctored wine with antifreeze. The plot engineers Bart's transformation from outlaw to hero, but images carry it out. Wordlessly they show him as victimized by adults: tossed on the plane like cargo, dwarfed by every adult he meets, mistreated by his captors, suffering in the barn and rain. Thus the animation mocks adult claims to deserve their power over kids—an ongoing theme of *The Simpsons*—as the plot ridicules French culture's wine worship.

Here and elsewhere visual jokes based on peculiar points of view highlight the incongruity between Bart's size and his ability to wreak havoc. One comic trope exaggerates other characters' animus toward him by playing with animation's capacity for representation (see plate 6). A scene imitating the view inside Mr. Burns's car, for example, creates a visual metaphor equating hood ornament and rifle sight to reinforce Burns's homicidal impulse as he tells his assistant Smithers to run over Bart ("Bart Gets Hit by a Car," 2–10, 1/10/1991). Another change in viewpoint exaggerates the size of forces against the boy. For instance, "Some Enchanted Evening," the Season 1 finale, shows an evil baby-sitter burglar looming hyperbolically large over Bart from the perspective of his subdued position on the floor. The scene comically reverses the show's formula of Bart terrorizing the person in charge; the unusual camera angle implied by the image extends the reversal by suggesting that Bart is getting a taste of his own medicine as a kind of poetic justice, yet information that the kids get about the sitter from TV's *America's Most Armed and Dangerous* makes her threat to Bart poignant, too (1–13, 5/13/1990). Still other scenes offer comically unlikely, if not impossible, viewpoints: a letter's-eye view of the mailbox slot from the inside and a view of Dr. Hibbert from the perspective of Bart's tonsils ("Bart's Dog Gets an F," 2–16, 3/7/1991). All these and similar variations on filmic point of view, distorted imitations of shots made by an oddly placed camera, debunk the idea of realism in animation.

Even as they stress how animation invents its subjects and scenes rather than captures bodies or movements in space, however, such images invite viewers to identify themselves with Bart, despite all his wrongdoing, as well as critique conventional mores by showing events through his eyes in a visual parallel to first-person vernacular narration.

Imitations of photographic realism likewise exploit the vernacular aesthetic's deliberate crudeness in order to lampoon realistic animation, a running visual gag since Season 1. Pseudorealism drives a purportedly backlit shot of Bart, emphasizing his distinctive shadow, in "Homer's Odyssey" (1–3, 1/21/1990), a scene so dark that only his eyes show clearly when he returns the statue of town founder in "The Telltale Head" (1–8, 8/25/1990), the refraction of his face as if photographed through a drinking glass in "Dead Putting Society" (2–6, 11/15/1990), and the imitation baby picture of him on the wall behind Marge in "Like Father, Like Clown" (3–6, 10/24/1991). Each case undermines realism by calling attention to differences between drawing and photography. In the process, parallels and incongruities between *The Simpsons*'s world and its viewers' tilt the representations toward a humor of critique.

Visual allusions take another route to this same end: putting a character in an incongruous graphic context calls attention to the artificiality of animation and injects humor or satire into the mood. The reference to Edward Hopper's famous painting *Nighthawks* (1942) in "Old Money" from Season 2 (see plate 7) comes as a classic two-stage joke: a close-up on Grampa, Homer's father, constitutes the setup; the punch line comes in a distance shot that puts Grampa in the diner by imitating an outward zoom shot and by merging high and low culture in one image (2–17, 3/28/1991). Within the plot, however, putting Grampa at the counter of Hopper's diner both underscores *and* undercuts how lonely he feels after the death of his girlfriend, Bea, from Springfield Retirement Castle. By countering his despair with an incongruous allusion, the visual joke restores humor to a sad tale of personal disappointment from lost love and family conflict. In addition, the joke provides a turning point that allows a sentimental end to the plot: Grampa uses his inheritance from Bea to upgrade the home, restore his own pride, and tell the other residents, "The dignity's on me." Across the early years, the crude *Simpsons* style cast allusions to well-known paintings and films as comically degraded imitations of already-imitated reality. For instance, the two-dimensional Van Gogh and Gaugin paintings that Bart and his French hosts race through on their motorcycles in "The Crepes of Wrath" mock the episode's premise that Bart has gone to France even as they invoke animation's origins in drawing and painting. At the same time, the basic vernacular contrast between genteel art and ordinary life sets up the episode's basic comic incongruity between the reputed sophistication of French culture and the lowlifes who put Bart to work. Nonetheless, whatever realism comes from parallels between *The Simpsons*'s world and ours fizzles amid comic contrasts between the foreground's animated vernacular images of a speeding motorcycle and the background's static reproductions of famous paintings, and the same incongruity drives film and celebrity caricatures that play with differences between animation and film.

By mocking everything, however, *The Simpsons*'s visual vernacular risks the bite of real critique. Fans hail Season 4's "Last Exit to Springfield" as the best episode ever made for its "stinging" and "savage" satire,[60] yet the graphic humor muddies as well as feeds its comic attacks. The episode opens by equating business with organized crime when a formal dinner to celebrate a powerfully addictive new drug becomes the scene of slaughter: following a toast to "human misery" by the mafioso host of the event, the Arnold Schwarzenegger lookalike McBain opens fire on the guests until the drug lord gleefully shoots him, too. After the scene shifts to Mr. Burns at the nuclear plant, parallel images of him smiling and the mafioso cackling link capitalism with crime again. The images also mock Homer for assuring Bart, as the scene identifies McBain as a fictional character, that "[t]here's nobody that evil in real life." The episode mocks management further in a madcap dancing sequence of Mr. Burns and his sidekick Smithers running the nuclear plant while their workers strike to keep their dental plan. Nonverbal ridicule continues after recently purchased robot scabs labeled as "100% loyal workers" carry the pair out of the plant, leading to a crisis symbolized by a close-up on the red button through which Burns plans to avenge the strike by causing a meltdown at the plant. However, (mock-) tension shifts to the comic anticlimax of ironic images: a blackout announced in neon lights, the reopening of an assembly line labeled "FAKE VOMIT INC.," where unnaturally happy workers, in a final slam at business, make a socially useless product, though it is comically valuable both for Springfield and for us.

The animation also takes pot shots at labor, especially the link between unions and organized crime dramatized in Homer's *Godfather* fantasy of himself as union president Don Homer, but targets its strongest attacks on the American health-care system. Lisa's need for braces satirizes the ideology that treats insurance as an employment benefit, subject to employers' whims or union standoffs, and the episode's graphic humor carries the theme through images of laughter that unite the business and family subplots. Midway through the episode Lisa delivers a parallel to the maniacal laughter of Burns and the drug king when she emerges from anesthesia with her new "affordable" braces, the only option in the absence of a dental plan. The appliance is so bulky that her profile looks monstrous and so archaic (not to say inadequate) that it will rust if it gets wet. The gothic image of her shadow, which alludes to the Joker's transformation in *Batman* (1989), mocks America's intertwined capitalist health care and insurance systems, a timely critique following Bill Clinton's election as president on a campaign of health care reform. Yet the animation counters all the episode's monstrous American smiles with a dentist's strategy for scaring patients into better oral hygiene, *The Big Book of British Smiles*, whose caricatures of Prince Charles and others with exaggerated overbites and other misalignments strike at the most obvious alternative to the American approach, a public system like Britain's National Health. Equally significant, both the labor dispute over health insurance and the episode itself end in comic ambiguity. Mr. Burns yields to union demands after mistaking Homer's incompetence for savvy strategy, yet the final representations of laughter do not signal viable solutions for U.S. health care. To be sure, workers at Fake Vomit Inc. have reason to cheer their restored jobs after a blackout caused by the union dispute, and the dentist joins Lisa's family in celebrating her new, nearly invisible braces, but the high spirits in the dental office owe at least as much to nitrous oxide inadvertently left on as to Homer's success in getting the dental plan restored. The implication that American workers, patients, employers, and health professionals are foolish at best, deluded at worst, and probably distracted by their need for paychecks puts the visual vernacular art of *The Simpsons* very much in the satiric tradition of Twain's brand of humor.

The parallel smiles behind the satire in "Last Exit" exploit a design principle based on the similarity gestalt, the psychological process by which parallels of shape, size, or position are perceived as likeness (see plate 8). Similar images lead easily to comic incongruity. Paired figures in the animated sitcom mimic the conventional "two-shot" of live-action TV, but *The Simpsons* gets great comic mileage from strategically drawn pairs that undercut social status or authority in the tradition of vernacular humor. When Principal Skinner and Homer jump in unison for joy after deciding to deport Bart to France in "Crepes," their childish high-fives portray the men as overgrown children and thereby knock down the principal's claims to the superior status implied by differences in their clothing: the contrasting shapes, colors, and social significance of his blue suit and Homer's red bathrobe mark their distinct levels of education and class. The critique implied by the pairing extends to American society more broadly by ridiculing two key authority figures as they exercise their power before a dubious Marge, who serves male prerogative to reframe Bart's exile as opportunity by suppressing maternal skepticism.

The series' most important pairings link Homer and Bart, who appear often in symmetrical poses that comically contrast big and little and double the thematic significance of their acts. In "Mr. Lisa Goes to Washington," the pair enjoy side-by-side massages from two attendants—one white, one black; one bald, one not—under portraits of two presidents in the Washington, DC, hotel where Lisa will deliver her patriotism essay (3–2, 9/26/1991). As shown in plate 8, near-doubles organize every component of the scene, from the clouds in the sky to the different drinks beside the beds. In addition to playing out adages about father-son likeness, the similarities reinforce their standing as vulgar males who, unlike Lisa, prefer physical indulgence at someone else's expense to improving their minds at the capitol's sights. Other pairings share the basic sentimentality of this scene while extending one individual's transgression to the other, as in "The Call of the Simpsons," where the animation lampoons Homer's bravado in traveling off-road in a recreational vehicle with a sequence of Bart and Homer running scared through the woods, falling off a cliff, and dog-paddling frantically through rapids (1–7, 2/18/1990). Father-son pairings often stress Homer's immaturity; in this case his cocky foray into the woods becomes a gauntlet of natural challenges that he fails at every turn until the excursion ends with a nearly unrecognizable Homer—his humanity invisible under a coat of mud, his tongue immobilized from bee stings, and (in the ultimate indignity) his consciousness stolen by a sedative dart intended for Big Foot. Most important, yoking Homer and Bart projects common character onto their common posture or purpose. A scene of the two sitting dejected outside the post office in "Blood Feud" symbolically caps a sequence in which Bart serves as Homer's surrogate, helping Homer write an angry complaint letter, taking his father's dictation, supplying a key insult ("you smell like an elephant's butt"), and finally dropping the letter in the mailbox (2–22, 7/11/1991). Early use of the gestalt and its durability across twenty years of plotlines show the significance of such pairings to conceptions of *The Simpsons*'s visual humor: the resolution of *The Simpsons Movie* (2007) also hinges on a scene of Homer and Bart riding together on a motorcycle to demolish the dome over Springfield and thereby save the town.

The device's significance shows also in the ease with which the series switched from son to father as the protagonist by 1992 as Bart's vernacular transgressions tested adult viewers' patience. Framing Homer and Bart as a pair not only extends the values of vernacular humor to a visual medium, but also doubles the opportunity for comic attack. Domesticating Bart's assaults on authority and social rules would destroy the show's antisentimental premise, whereas shifting the emphasis to Homer does not. A lowbrow hero in the vernacular tradition—hardly the epitome of the model husband, parent, wage earner, or citizen—Homer nonetheless bumbles into resolutions of the myriad problems that come his way, transforming comic ineptitude into unlikely success at the end of each episode in a parody that reinscribes sitcom morés and form.

By evading the censorship that still threatens *Huckleberry Finn*, *The Simpsons* gave up some satiric sting in plot and theme, yet its animation salvaged the satiric vision of its vernacular art. Like the narration of *Huckleberry Finn*, the visual vernacular of *The Simpsons*' clothes critique in humor. If viewers understand Bart as "an American icon, an updated version of Tom Sawyer and Huck Finn rolled into one," as Paul A. Cantor contends,[61] they do so because the show's visual rhetoric of apparent artlessness conveys its carnivalesque, demotic impulse. But art—that is, artifice—it is, a narrative style that is more than décor in the vernacular tradition of Twain's brand.

Art Spiegelman had comics' demotic origins in mind when he referred to "the cheerfully vernacular medium of comics" as the means by which underground cartoonists of the 1970s "unleashed their checkered demons" and so made way for his groundbreaking graphic Holocaust narrative *Maus* (1986),[62] but his remark also suggests the affinity of Twain's brand of vernacular humor for Lynda Barry's comics, especially her autobiographical narrative *One! Hundred! Demons!* (2002). Barry's nonliterary language and amateurish drawings have captured naïve patterns of expression and thought for ironic effect and social critique across many moods since she began publishing in the 1970s.[63] Yet even critics who recognize her kinship with Twain—*Comics Journal* editor Michael Dean credits her with "the uncanniest knack since *Huckleberry Finn* for unsentimentally capturing the perspectives and voices of kids"[64]—have missed her links to Twain's brand of vernacular humor as a style with a politics in view, revealing social ills by rejecting narrative norms.

Like *Huckleberry Finn*, Barry's tales of young people's inner lives and social experiences indict society at large and American adults in particular for their hypocrisies and betrayals. At the gothic extreme of Barry's vernacular work stands her illustrated novel *Cruddy* (1999), a confession of murder, castration, and survival by a young woman named Roberta, who calls her knife "Little Debbie" in a grimly comic allusion to a brand of lunchbox desserts. Janice P. Nimura's review of *Cruddy* hints at Mark Twain's influence on Barry's capacity to imply moral significance through a child's first-person narration: Nimura describes Roberta as "an ugly little masterpiece of a character, an anti-Huck Finn who no longer believes there's anything in the territories worth lighting out for."[65] At the opposite, exuberantly comic pole from *Cruddy*'s dark and scary ink-washed drawings, which leave little room for humor, stand Barry's upbeat and offbeat anecdotes of preteen Marlys Mullen, one of several youngsters who speak directly to readers from *Ernie Pook's Comeek* (1977?–), Barry's long-running four-panel comic strip published under varied titles in alternative weeklies such as *The Chicago Reader* and later collected in *The Freddie Stories* (1999) and *The Greatest of Marlys* (2000).[66] Roger Gilbert, who understands Barry's deliberately amateurish graphics as part of her transformation of the four-panel comic strip into "a kind of densely realized Proustian narrative . . . [of great] dramatic compression and emotional subtlety," nonetheless treats her relation to Mark Twain in primarily verbal terms, citing her ability to balance "the gawky idioms of childhood and adolescence and a more consciously literary level of speech that often approaches poetry in its compressed eloquence."[67] The *Ernie Pook* narratives certainly invite readers to laugh both with and at their narrators, as well as with and at the narrators' friends and antagonists, while evoking comic critique through dramatic irony, but the four-panel form limits satire by keeping the focus narrow even as the "four-panel epiphanies" (Gilbert's term) of individual strips coalesce into a larger context of characters, plots, and themes across the series and within volumes based on it. By contrast, Barry develops the vernacular vision more fully as she balances humor and moral insight in her most sustained and best-regarded narrative, *One Hundred Demons*, where social critique emerges from autobiographical tales of challenge and trauma fragmented across thematically organized chapters. Barry reordered and framed these graphic narratives, originally published serially online at *salon.com* in 2000, between "Intro" and "Outro" chapters when she published them in print. In this form, *One Hundred Demons* offers a hybrid verbal and visual rhetoric to match the hybrid form of stories she calls "autobifictionalography" (*OHD*, 5) whose ironic social commentary constitutes a vernacular vision in the tradition of Twain's brand of humor.

Barry has contested Dean's claim that "a lot of careful adult thinking" goes into her "naïve and spontaneous kid's perspective," as if no gradations existed between the poles of self-conscious and intuitive creativity,[68] yet she hints at the subversive and satirical potential of her vernacular aesthetic in the last chapter of *One Hundred Demons*: "Nobody feels the need to provide deep critical insight to something written by hand" (*OHD*, 216). Indeed, Barry's book as a whole has the feel of a homemade, handmade object. In addition to giving feminist pride of place to women's tradition of textile crafts, Barry's elaborate collages on the cover, title, and chapter-title pages—some made from glitter and glue—invoke children's art (see plate 9). So do the doodles on the endpapers and the borders of "Intro" and "Outro" on yellow legal paper. Barry likewise rejects conventional comics lettering, which imitates the regularity of letterpress (as in the Microsoft font *Comics Sans MS*), in favor of childish cursive or handprinting. The seemingly poor planning and execution of her figures and composition necessitates explanatory labels and arrows, as Özge Samanci has observed, noting that Barry's use of a brush rather than a pen produces uneven contours that further amateurish effects.[69] By casting her artwork as the authentic expression of an ordinary individual rather than the professionally trained artist that she is, Barry's style provides a graphic parallel to vernacular humor's basic incongruities. Humor in *One Hundred Demons* emerges from the contrast between her understated, often-pensive narration and her brightly colored vernacular images, with their mock-oral dialogue and dramatic, often chaotic scenes, perhaps epitomized when her narrative remarks about "someone's drunk uncle" in "Lost Worlds" introduce a bald, bug-eyed man whose belly jiggles out of his sloppy T-shirt as he waves his arms and yells, "Ahm open! Throw it to tha' swinger, kids! Looget me!" (see plate 10; *OHD*, 31). As her girlish style invokes the feminist mantra that the personal is political, her colorful, amateurish cartoons unite technique and theme in a vernacular vision of personal suffering and social discovery.

Verbal vernacular techniques augment these graphic elements. Speech balloons in Barry's panels reveal a virtuoso ear for colloquial voices, from the African American teenager who marvels at Lynda, "Girl, you got some strange hair" (*OHD*, 30) to the more direct challenge "How come you wave at planes, ya stupe?" (35). The misspellings known as eye-dialect occasionally intensify representations of her mother's vulgarity, her grandmother's spicy Tagalog, and children's slang. Confessions of childhood misdeeds, such as "Jennie and I would sneak out of her bedroom at 2 AM" (162), imitate the intimate dialogue of a letter, diary, or conversation. Colloquialisms in Barry's narration likewise imply a mock-oral sense of voice, but sometimes she explicitly speaks to her readers. In the chapter "Magic," for example, her ruminations about the strains of adolescence on a childhood friendship end with a photo of the two girls as Barry plaintively turns from her readers in general to the old friend in particular: "This is Ev and me in a photo booth in a Woolworth's a thousand years ago. Ev, if you're reading this, hello, it's me" (108). More commonly, however, Barry maintains the immediacy of her voice through questions that turn narrative monologue into dialogue. And these questions mimic oral voice to give her adult narrator the same comic inferiority as her childhood representations in the images. When the narrator asks, "Were we too toxic for head lice?" at the start of the first chapter, the naïveté and comic literalism behind her question show that the adult Lynda still gropes for knowledge. The comics medium enhances this characterization by depicting embodied actions that unfold before the reader: narration drags the past into the present, but the comics image gives mock-oral and mock-physical *presence* to childhood events. Thus the comics panel also carries past vulnerabilities into the present. As Barry asks questions both trivial and profound—"Was it all the TV dinners we ate?" (16), "Who knows which moments make us who we are?" (36)—she disclaims authority even over her own life. Word and image combine to put her adult and childhood selves in the comically inferior position of traditional vernacular innocents like Huck.

Unflattering portraits of Lynda emphasize her vulnerability as an outcast, though cheerful colors and comic details keep self-deprecation from becoming self-pity. A few images reveal poignant, not comic angst, but mostly Barry depicts her young self as physically foolish and often downright ugly, with unmanageable short red hair, ungainly legs and arms, buck teeth, a forlorn facial expression, and so many freckles that she looks pockmarked. Not even her mother loves how she looks, and the adult Barry takes revenge in portraying the mother as a comic grotesque while showing herself as yearning, struggling, and failing to win acceptance and friendship. Classmates ostracize her with taunts of "Cootie germs, no returns!" because of her status as someone "*so weird* that no one wanted to touch *anything* you touched" in a panel that dramatizes her alienation by placing her half out of picture, divided from her two classmates on the right by speech balloons (see plate 11, *OHD*, 17). Indeed, talk often separates Lynda from people with whom she seeks connection, as when her third-grade teacher refused to let her draw during recess (178). As a result of such widespread rejection, young Lynda's face typically shows fear, disappointment, frustration, loneliness, or sadness. She stands with shoulders hunched—her very person a sign of social exclusion.

From this vantage point, however, Barry reveals Americans' deep intolerance of difference. While plot details in the opening chapter trace her classmates' prejudice to cultural bias—they respond skeptically, "Oh *sure*" when she reports, "What I did on my summer vacation was went to the Philippines where I was slightly popular" (*OHD*, 20)—incidents spread across many chapters and from periods throughout Lynda's life show pervasive class prejudice. She reports in "The Visitor" in the middle of the book how one of her teenage boyfriends, son of "a slightly high-up person in the military," marveled at how "You're like me. You like to explore insane places. I never met a girl that was so much like me" as they wandered through slums, but then dropped her as soon as she confessed to "living in the 'insane places' he was only visiting" (113, 116, 120). Furthermore, as Melinda Luisa De Jesus has noted, Barry portrays femininity as a performance of class status and commodity display in the chapter titled "Girlness" toward the end of the book, where she contrasts her own empty Band-Aid box and "tomboy" clothes with a more well-off girl's pretty hair, dress, and doll (see plate 12).[70] Barry adds to this already-explicit visual contrast, stressing the importance of class to social acceptance, when she asks with a vernacular speaker's innocence, "If I had these things,*would I have been* a girlish girl *too*?" (185). The power of cartoon art to convey Barry's childhood wish with the poignance of lingering hurt also illustrates how humor emerges from incongruities between the traumas she faces and the trivial triggers to insight.

Barry's vernacular vision satirizes class bias most vividly in the opening chapter, "Head Lice and My Worst Boyfriend." Lynda's childhood immunity to lice, her unpopularity at school (especially in contrast to her friendships in the Philippines), her cruelly critical mother, and her quest to discover whether white people attract white *kuto* (head lice), as brown people have brown *kuto*—all these strands of Lynda's story come together in her twenties when she contracts lice and gives them to her self-absorbed suburban boyfriend, the butt of much of the chapter's humor. She tells us that "he had a pretty name" but does not share it, allowing her pictures and their labels to mock him as the effeminate ("he had a freaky ponytail") reader of the "LONELY GENIUS GAZETTE" (*OHD*, 21). After reporting how he called her "*little* Ghetto girl," she drips irony to add, "I'm sure he *meant* it in the *nicest* way" (21). Their conversation shows how his snobbery rests on assertions of difference; he so insistently resists comparison with anyone else that he takes offense when Lynda says that he reminds her of someone she can't pinpoint. The visual joke is on him, however, as parallels between panels of her with her mother and with him link him to her mother even before the turn of the page shows him shouting like the mother while he and Lynda stand as a matching pair lathered in lice-killing shampoo. And this revelation—that nemeses *and* social classes may be more alike than different—leads to a punning final panel, where her childhood friends from the Philippines, now grown up, demonstrate their enduring affection for Lynda as they provide a comic counterpart to her insight that "head lice are much easier to get rid of than bad love" (24). In the chapter's last bit of dialogue, her friend reads aloud Lynda's letter reporting, "I have found the white kuto!" By indirectly calling the boyfriend a louse, the conclusion attacks his claims to class privilege while she converts suffering to knowledge and wit. But fusing the various threads of the story at the end also implies that childhood sufferings last into adulthood because adults hold the same biases as children against "cootie girls."

Perhaps for this reason, like Mark Twain in the evasion sequence of *Huck*, Barry rejects the romantic vernacular theme that contrasts adult knowledge with childhood innocence in order to portray adult society as corrupt and youth society as virtuous. Across the length of *One Hundred Demons*, children enact their parents' racial and class prejudices. One of Lynda's acquaintances isn't allowed to come to her house (*OHD*, 55), while another reports that her mother doesn't want Lynda to touch her dolls (189). For her part, the young Lynda ponders how neither the adults nor the children on her block can tolerate the social differences manifested in the unique smells of each house. The chapter title "Common Scents" hints at the rarity of rationality about the differences portrayed in its pages. A speech balloon separating Lynda and a young neighbor reinforces the distance between the two girls who face off from opposite sides of the panel's borders, their heads framed by spiked bushes that give a sharp edge to the neighbor girl's report, "My mom says your people fry weird food and save the grease and also that you boil pig's blood which is the reason for the smell" (54). So little space remains in the panel after these comments and the narrator's introduction that Lynda seems barely to squeeze out her reply, "What smell?" Lynda classifies the neighborhood families by each house's smell, no more appalled by the dirty "cat pee smell" next door (52) than by the bleach fumes wafting down the block, leaving the kids "waiting for that house to explode" (53), but her classifications lack the racism of her friend's mother, "the most disinfecting, air freshener spraying person that ever lived," portrayed with arms and head madly swirling to spray all 360 degrees around her (55). Racist comments about the smells of different nationalities and ethnic groups spew from her mouth as readily as air-freshener sprays from her can, as she differentiates among the nationalities, with special venom for Lynda's family ("and don't get me started on your Filipinos," [56]). Adults in Lynda's family have their own prejudices, but the grandmother's charge that "white ladies smell bad too . . . she never wash her pookie!" comes from her faith in universal humanity: "God has made every people! . . . and every ta-ee smells bad!" (57).

Nonetheless, the chapter "Hate" excoriates adults of many colors as hypocrites. Barry points out that children's open verbal or physical antagonism is at least "honest" and "normal" (*OHD*, 76), but adults conceal theirs behind false claims to sociability. "Even my mother, who was obsessively enraged with at least one person at all times, would not admit to hatred," Barry recalls (77), and the predictable adult "hate lecture" ironically proves more disruptive to children's friendship than harsh words or actions. When Lynda and her friend fight over a toy rabbit, each declaring "I hate you," they at least remain engaged with each other, comically joined by the toy as by a rope in tug of war. By contrast, the friend's mother's warning, "The word *hate* will not be tolerated in this house," leads promptly to Lynda's being sent home after Lynda questions the mother's claim that *hate* is "the worst word you can say" by asking "worse than '#@!✗☉'?" (77). Children also accept the taboo. Outraged that "the drunk father of Huck Finn . . . beat him and starved him," Lynda confides to a friend, "Huck Finn must have hated him too," only to receive the girl's version of "a main rule of life": "You can never hate your own parents. No matter what. . . . If it was his step-father he could. But not his real dad" (79). The rule offers Lynda slim comfort because endless verbal and physical abuse from her own mother proved a constant problem: "I was terrified of her," she recalls in narration, "and it broke my heart that she didn't seem to like me much, but she meant more to me than anyone" (*OHD*, 93). As shown in plate 13, her mother's rage looms so large that it pushes Lynda's head half out of the picture. But even Lynda's research on *hate* in the dictionary gets her nothing but trouble, though in retrospect it provides anti-intellectual comic relief in the vernacular tradition. When she substitutes *execrate* for *hate* in a statement about the boy who bullies her, the teacher who publicly scolds her reveals her own ignorance by mistaking *execrate* for *excrement*. Young Lynda knows that "'I excrement Ronnie's guts' doesn't even make sense!" but the conspiracy leaves her with only one option: to pray for forgiveness each night for the day's hatreds. Indeed, so tightly does society repress hatred that a substitute teacher loses her job for a lesson trying to distinguish prejudice from other types of hate. Barry piles on ironies showing that everyone in Lynda's world—adults and children, school and religion, librarians and teachers—denies hatred as a legitimate emotion, while she feels and suffers hatred across her life.

Explicitly political satire appears only in a late chapter, "The Election," which pairs an account of the contested 2000 presidential election with another winter tale, *It's a Wonderful Life* (1946), while a mature Lynda ponders questions of justice. Images show her degenerating panel by panel, the increasingly frazzled portraits augmented by details like "STILL IN PAJAMAS AT 6 PM" and "LOOKING MORE AND MORE LIKE A CRACK-HEAD" (*OHD*, 202) as the controversy over the Florida vote count stretches to thirty-one days. Speech balloons with spiked borders convey urgent news reports that exacerbate her own rising tensions until she reaches "a full blown fugue state," so dazed that she confuses the election drama on her television with a rerun of *It's a Wonderful Life*. "MUST. KEEP. WATCHING. . . . MUST. HELP. AL. . . . MUST. FIGHT. MR. POTTER" (203). The movie celebrates the triumph of vernacular, democratic values of community, fairness, and the little guy over the evil opportunism of the local capitalist after an angel named Clarence persuades Jimmy Stewart's character to abandon suicide in order to rally the community and together prevent Mr. Potter from impoverishing and thus enslaving everyone. Visual self-ridicule gives Barry vernacular license for strong verbal ironies, as she contrasts the Republicans' and Democrats' lawyers in a classic comic standoff between cocky elites and homespun public: "[T]heir lawyer looks like an insane rooster while ours looks like Abe Lincoln. He says we should look at the ballots. The rooster says we can't. Is it a wonderful life or isn't it?" (203). But unlike early nineteenth-century humorists, Barry concludes that the answer to that question depends utterly on who asks. "For Mr. Potter, that movie is a tragedy. Lucky for him it's only a movie," she notes, but adds, "In real life, he rules." After all, she explains, "In real life there are no angels named Clarence"; there are "just judges who sit up on high" (204). This allusion to another Clarence, Clarence Thomas of the Supreme Court, who joined the majority opinion in *Bush v. Gore* opposing the communal good of counting every vote, implies disbelief in both poetic and human justice. This implication in turn casts a dark shadow on the final image, where a weary Lynda still exudes anxiety as she clings to her husband and urges, "Let's go see a movie, quick!" (see plate 14). In this context, although the color orange binds the couple, their embrace expresses not only the power of love and art to counter despair, but also the limits of love or art to affect public life. Furthermore, in a book that throughout has taken a feminist stance in stressing the personal as political, retreat from citizenship into private life and escape to the movies both signal failure of the democratic ideals behind American vernacular art. Retreat and escape also echo Huck's plan to light out for the territory. Barry offers a cheery verbal conclusion, exclaiming, "Merry Christmas everybody!" and asserting how hope endures like the Christmas spirit, of its own accord and for no rational reason (204). But the escapism of the last panel ends her most political tale on an ironic and ambivalent note.

Irony is a dominant form of humor in *One Hundred Demons*: even those chapters that end on a note of success undercut claims of triumph through contradictory narration, dialogue, or images. Vulnerability and narrative inferiority are essential to satire in the vernacular tradition, as Hank Morgan's demotion from Boss to slave illustrates in *Connecticut Yankee*, and Barry's structural choices follow a similar path. *One Hundred Demons* keeps trauma ever present by spreading incidents of shame and abuse, suffering and relief, across thematically organized chapters instead of sequestering them in the beginning of a bildungsroman that moves toward triumph. Psychic and other injuries pile up across the book, including a childhood rape by one of the few adults to speak nicely to her. As part of Barry's vernacular aesthetic, cheerfully colored pictures and two-dimensional scenes maintain a tone of naïveté even when they represent sad or troubling events. The panel revealing her rape provides a case in point (see plate 15). She reveals this horror by implication through silence and absence in a panel that hints at unspeakable memories that block the upper half of the man who asks her, as she plays happily outside, "Do you and your dolly want to go for a ride?" (*OHD*, 72). Deep and unsettling ironies emerge from a superficially bucolic scene: the innocent child in the flowers, her sweet smile as she looks up, the kindly offer that calls her "sweetheart" and includes her doll. But everything is wrong with the picture: the man is faceless, only his lower half is visible, words come from his waist and fill the space in front of his penis, and he looms over her, so large that he overflows the small space that Barry allows this memory, though the narration says, "I don't remember." The scene ends the chapter called "Resilience" with the event that began a dreadful chain of misery—leaving Lynda depressed, praying, "I wish I was dead" (70), and compelled to dangerous drinking, drugs, and sex (71). Earlier in the chapter, the narrator declares resilience a fantasy that lets "adults believe that children forget trauma" when it is actually just "the ability to exist in pieces" (70). By presenting these details and interpretations out of a conventional sequence of cause and effect, past and present, Barry rejects the idea of happy endings in a world in which adults speak of "resilience" yet fail to protect children from the abuse of strangers, family, or friends.

Like other vernacular *eirons*, Barry sustains her claims to moral and narrative innocence from the beginning to the end of her life story in *One*

Hundred Demons. The opening and closing frames wrap trauma in questions of art and disclosure in representations of reticence: her eyes in the opening frame's drawings are blank, while the photos at the end show just her hand and half her face. The last two chapters of her interior personal narrative both end on poignant notes despite visual and verbal evidence that the ungainly, depressed young Lynda grew into an attractive adult who found satisfaction in work as an artist and happiness with a loving husband and their dogs. The image of her adult despair over *Bush v. Gore* in "The Election" sustains her image of vulnerability, as does the final panel of "Lost and Found," which closes the inner tale. Barry remarks in this last panel that her younger self "would think that this [story] had a very happy ending" (*OHD*, 216), but she ends the chapter ambivalently by closing not with her successful adult self at the drawing board—the scene in the preceding panel—but with her child self lying on the floor pondering the anonymous misfortunes implied by classified ads for wedding dresses and lost dogs. And in this last panel, where young Lynda's face takes the same pose as her adult self in the adjacent image, the similarity gestalt suggests that the girl on the floor is the adult Lynda resuming childhood pleasures in a poignant take on storytelling that reveals what children sacrifice in growing up. "Lost. Somewhere around puberty. Ability to make up stories," she declares in the narrative's final speech balloon, and then adds a plaintive bit of advice for readers and herself: "happiness depends on it. Please write" (216). Here as elsewhere, Barry rejects chronology to create an anticlimactic form that, combined with lowly topics such as head lice and classified ads, keep her character in the vernacular mold of youthful comic inferiority.

There's nothing funny in the rape panel from "Resilience" except its violation of artistic and comics conventions, yet it sums up the power of vernacular humor generally and the visual vernacular in particular: to challenge norms, to express the ineffable, to convey through irony and implication what society or individuals repress. Barry testifies to the power of her vernacular vision and her skill in vernacular art as humor and horror, innocence and insight, satire and poignance emerge through ostensibly simple prose and colloquial dialogue combined with ostensibly clumsy drawings in cheerful colors on difficult topics. Her success in this complex endeavor puts her very much in the tradition of Mark Twain's brand of vernacular humor. *One Hundred Demons* fulfills not only Art Spiegelman's goal for "comix" as a hybrid medium *mix*ing "High Art and Low. Words and Pictures. Form and Content," but also Leo Marx's conception of the American vernacular tradition as uniting matter, manner, and meaning: "a style with a politics in view . . . of an egalitarian faith so radical that . . . [it] sweeps aside received notions of class and status—and of literature."[71]

The politics of the amateur aesthetic in visual vernacular satire shows perhaps most vividly, however, in Aaron McGruder's short-lived but highly influential comic strip *The Boondocks* (1999–2006). Hailed as a major contribution to contemporary American political discourse and African American popular culture, *The Boondocks* became a daily syndicated feature after several years in the student newspaper at the University of Maryland. It launched in April 1999 with a record-setting 150-plus newspapers nationwide and circulated in some 350, including campus papers, by late 2005. Despite winning a string of awards, the strip remained notorious for strident left-wing politics that constantly threatened its place on the funnies page, and some editors treated it as an editorial cartoon or dropped it altogether.[72] The strip became best known for its scathing critique of President George W. Bush's administration in the period following the 9/11 attacks of 2001, but McGruder also engaged topics of popular culture and racial identity through comic conflicts between the rhetorical and behavioral excesses of his pint-sized protagonists and the status quo of adult society: the strip pits left-wing black activist Huey Freeman and his hip-hop wannabe younger brother Riley against assorted representatives of older black generations and thoroughly clueless whites. For all the strip's originality, its humor belongs to Twain's brand of the vernacular tradition. Huey's idiom of black power and left-wing politics replaces an obviously inferior dialect such as Huck's with the language of the comic braggart, conventional target of comic attack and deflation, but *The Boondocks*' young hero speaks a language that flouts white literary rhetoric, and its art exploits an amateurish graphic aesthetic that rejects conventional visual representation and thereby fuses political critique into a vernacular vision.

Humor at Huey's expense satirizes the romantic ideal of black political leadership, but McGruder also targets Republican conservatism and white liberals through language, graphics, and a moral vision comically at odds with the norm. Conceptualizing the vernacular as an oppositional rhetoric, not merely as dialect, explains why Howard Rambsy II claims a place for Huey as a vernacular hero, classing him with Muhammad Ali and the other African American opinion makers whom Grant Farred calls "black vernacular intellectuals" for their "discursive turning away from the accepted, dominant intellectual modality and vocabulary and the adoption of a new positioning and idiomatic language."[73] In the absence of the naïve ironies and eye dialect of Huck's barely literate writing, however, the crude visual vernacular style of *The Boondocks* becomes all the more important to McGruder's vernacular vision, a challenge to ways of seeing and knowing in narratives that comically shrink political resistance and aspiration to child-size.

Like Bart, Huck, Lynda, and other young vernacular heroes, ten-year-old black radical Huey Freeman (who shares initials with Huck) provides plenty of humor at his own and society's expense. Society in this case means schools, neighbors, social rules, television and other media (especially Black Entertainment Television [BET]), and the federal government. Huey's paranoia gains credibility from an omnipresent FBI, which has tapped the family phone for so long that when the boy asks, "Hello? Is this the FBI's anonymous terrorism tip line?" he hears, "That's correct, Mr. Freeman. What have you got for us?" (*RBH*, 164). Huey knows so much about history and politics that McGruder often ridicules him for his *knowledge*, however, a variation of vernacular humor's scorn for book-learning. For instance, early in the strip, as a newcomer to suburbia, Huey takes the absence of a local Klanwatch group as evidence not of safety but of need and asks his grandfather to buy him a Humvee and other military equipment, including flamethrowers and night-vision goggles, on the ground that "a strong show of force is the best deterrent" and "a well-equipped neighborhood Klanwatch is an effective one" (*B*, 28). The joke tweaks hysterical activists who see racism everywhere, although McGruder indicates that racism remains alive and well through his portrait of the inept adults at J. Edgar Hoover Elementary School (its name a swipe at the FBI and right-wingers fearful of federal intrusions). After all, the punch line of one strip shows the principal responding to news that Jazmine DuBois has a white mother by telling the girl's teacher, "She's black," despite agreeing moments earlier to the mother's insistence, "It's up to Jazmine to construct her own identity. We don't want anyone doing it for her. Is that clear? . . . If she must be called anything, use the term 'multiracial.' Never 'white.' Never 'black.' OK?" (*B*, 71).[74] McGruder's jokes about identity politics gain a boost from his characters' names. *Thomas DuBois*, Jazmine's dad, recalls both the black intellectual advocate W. E. B. DuBois and the sell-out folk figure Uncle Tom; *Huey Freeman* alludes to Black Panther cofounder Huey Newton (1942–1989). But Huey Freeman differs from other vernacular heroes in that the traditional scorn for book knowledge undercuts, not elevates, the hero. He can lecture his grandfather about child labor laws and whine about "incredibly long hours . . . dangerous working conditions,

... little hope of bettering one's lot in life ... for virtually no compensation" (*B*, 47), but he still has to mow the lawn, and the triumph of the status quo proves his foolishness.

Rambsy overlooks such mockery in arguing that *The Boondocks* signifies a major mass-media "representation of a militant, brainy black boy" who challenges conventional American wisdom, although he recognizes a certain ambivalence in McGruder's presentation of "an African American hero whose struggles often place him at odds with official symbols of power and authority[,] ... a long-established tradition in black expressive culture."[75] But the homage to the FBI's wanted poster of Angela Davis in the portrait of Huey on the cover of *Public Enemy #2* (2005), a collection of daily *Boondocks* strips, is a double-edged joke that comically declares (and thus mocks) his threat to the U.S. while also suggesting official threats to *him* (see plate 16). Huey's earnestness exposes his ignorance of how the world works, for all his political knowledge. In this way, by generating satire from the ironic gap between ridicule and endorsement, Huey joins Twain's brand of vernacular *eirons*.

In this way also McGruder subverts Huey's bravado for vernacular humor's ironic ends. The strip's most pointed satire of government frames his earnestness as mock-naïveté, not the sincere puzzlement or misunderstanding of traditional *eirons* like Jack Downing, Huck, Bart Simpson, or Lynda Barry, yet Huey exposes corruption much as they do from the gap between viewpoints. Each of the three strips from October 4–6, 2001, shortly after al-Qaeda's attacks on the World Trade Center and Pentagon, opens with Huey calling the FBI with apparently new information on "Americans who have helped train and finance Osama bin Laden," and each ends with his naming a president as the culprit. In the first strip he pretends that they won't recognize the name, so he spells, "That's R-E-A-G-A-N"; in the last he pretends they need an address to locate the perpetrator, saying, "He lives at 1600 Pennsylvania Avenue" (*RBH*, 165). Here and elsewhere the satire of *The Boondocks* not only upholds vernacular trust that children may be wiser than adults, but also tweaks readers for their ignorance, frames Huey as the victim of his own obsessions, and scorns corruption at every level of society. Despite its inversions of traditional ideas about know-how and intellect, the strip's humor undercuts Huey in familiar ways for his romantic idealism and irrelevant book-learning, conventional targets of vernacular humor.

Likewise, McGruder favors a contemporary African American idiom that, notwithstanding Huey's engagement with sophisticated words and thought, also represents a style with a democratic politics in view. To be sure, he downplays traditional naïve vernacular ironies in the vein mined by Paul Laurence Dunbar, Zora Neale Hurston, and Langston Hughes, whose ironic Jesse B. Semple narratives for the Chicago *Defender* exemplify the African American variations on the nineteenth-century tradition.[76] Yet the vocabulary, syntax, and thought coming from Huey's ten-year-old mouth represent comic incongruities in their own right. They signal his intellectual superiority to the adults in the strip and join the varied speech patterns of other characters to generate linguistic contrasts—the basic joke of vernacular humor—in nearly every panel.

McGruder tweaks the full range of vernaculars: Huey's virtuoso range from legalese to slang, Riley's efforts to sound like a thug, Granddad's old-fashioned colloquialisms "friend" and "brotha," Caesar's propensity to signify, the DuBois family's political correctness and racial ambiguities, along with the languages of government, television news, and popular entertainment. From the start of the strip, McGruder used characters' different languages to reflect their different political positions, including gaps between white and black experience. For instance, the young white girl Cindy does not realize that she has already met one of the new residents of the neighborhood when she reports, right after inviting Jazmine to be her best friend, that she doesn't understand what it means when her father "keeps saying he's afraid of declining property values, juvenile delinquents and set-aside programs," to which Jazmine replies, "Lucky you" (*B*, 14). Jokes at Huey's expense, on the other hand, often target his black pride through the comic African American rhetoric known as the dozens. For example, in the July 4–5, 2003, strips, Caesar sets the trap by telling Huey, "July is 'Black English' month. When we take time to celebrate the richness and creativity of African-American language" (*PE*, 43). When Huey falls for it and asks, "Are you serious?," Caesar attacks with mocking nonsense, "F'shizzle, God. E'ything from mobbphonics to infamousbonics," before he finally concedes, "It's just an excuse to use excessive slang from different eras. You know . . . conversate like Negroes conversate." The two-day series ends in a draw with the boys' mock-oral dialect exchange: Huey's "A'ight. I'm down," and Caesar's "Cool. Holla at'cha, boy!" (*PE*, 43). Tia C. M. Tyree and Adrian Krishnasamy note that *The Boondocks* relies on a number of specifically Afrocentric discourses, yet the strip's variations on vernacular humor's conventional linguistic oppositions deserve special notice. *The Boondocks*' verbal contrasts not only align the strip with *Huckleberry Finn*, where Mark Twain claimed to have used seven dialects (*HF*, "Explanatory"), but also comically resist treating African American English—or its speakers—as a monolith.

FIGURE 7 Aaron McGruder's minimalist panels, many consisting only of head shots and speech balloons, do reflect his lost interest in detailed art, but they also contribute to his vernacular aesthetic through contrasts with the strip's comically extravagant approach to language. (Aaron McGruder, *A Right to Be Hostile*, 89.)

The crude visual style of the three-panel strip also signals the importance of Twain's brand of vernacular humor to McGruder's formal and verbal incongruities. Long an admirer of *Peanuts*, McGruder populated his strip with children as a deliberate strategy in the tradition of vernacular satire. A reporter for the (London) *Observer* compared the effect to "Charles Schultz by way of Nation of Islam" after McGruder confessed that he sought to "seduce the audience . . . You're taking someone [whom viewers] would maybe otherwise find unpleasant and making it pleasant to look at. And instantly, psychologically, the impact it has is tremendous."[77] McGruder's character designs borrow the kids' wide-eyed faces and oversized heads from manga, highlighting their youth and vulnerability, as well as reflect the influence of Bill Waterson's *Calvin and Hobbes*. Visual elements invoke a comic tone by resisting realistic anatomy and representation, especially in contrast to the comic exaggeration of the characters' language; Huey's huge Afro fills a panel or matches Jazmine's frizzy pony tail in a tableau that shows how small the two kids are (see plate 17). More to the point, the simplistic lines and forms of McGruder's amateur aesthetic counter Huey's harsh, elevated diction to leaven the tone and lighten the mood. But while McGruder draws well enough to caricature George W. Bush, John Kerry, and other figures, composition is not his strength, and the art serves his humor mainly by getting out of the way. That's why Robert C. Harvey called *The Boondocks* "a highly verbal enterprise" and declared that "very little of our comprehension of it depends upon understanding the pictures, which do little more than identify the speakers."[78] Panels often consist of a talking head or two and characters' speech balloons (figure 7). Facial expressions and a prop or two replace gesture, posture, or setting in weekday panels; slight changes in characters' poses have few if any direct or ironic links to the dialogue, thus adding little to it.

Always straightforward, the graphic style became still more minimalist as the strip aged and the rich watercolors of the Sunday panels became less important than the battle of wits between Huey and his various antagonists. McGruder told Harvey in January of 2003 that he loved to draw, but found after a year of doing the syndicated strip that he "just hated trying to make that little space look good in that small amount of time" and gave up trying. "People don't read newspaper comics to marvel at beautiful art," he insisted. "They read comics to laugh."[79] He began farming out the art in the fall of 2003, a decision he did not regret two years later when he turned his attention to developing *The Boondocks* into a weekly animated situation comedy for the Adult Swim division of cable television's Cartoon Network, where it ran 2005–2006, 2007–2008, and 2010.[80] Even before McGruder hired an outside artist, however, *Doonesbury*'s creator Garry Trudeau found the art disappointing. "'The Boondocks' is brand-new, relatively speaking," Trudeau griped to the *New Yorker*'s Ben McGrath in 2003, "and he's already stripped away the backgrounds . . . And he was using cut-and-paste images *before* he handed off the art. And he also stopped telling stories, for the most part, which I thought was a pity."[81] McGrath for his part lamented how artwork that "once stood out for its density" had now grown "spare: a lot of white space; little, if any, visual progression from panel to panel" and had "become an almost incidental vehicle for one-liners," a complaint shared by the London *Observer*, which noted "near-static panels of Huey slackly commenting on television."[82] A quick comparison of the style in *A Right to Be Hostile* (2003) and *Public Enemy #2* (2005) confirms the tendency toward minimalism, though a May 24, 2001, strip of Huey at his computer (*RBH*, 133) does not differ much from the panels of him on the phone from June 28, 2003 (*PE*, 43). More to the point, however, a number of newspaper funnies prefer to emulate McGruder's minimalism over *Doonesbury*'s richer representations—for instance, Jerry Scott and Rick Kirkland's *Baby Blues*, a child-based strip begun in 1990, a few years before *The Boondocks*. And as late as 2005 and 2006 McGruder's fans did not object to its graphic style of "anime-meets-hip-hop" any more than its tone of "Chris Rock-meets-Howard Zinn," as exemplified by the Florida reader who called *The Boondocks* "one of the most literate, well-drawn comics anywhere," although feminists resent its treatment of women.[83] Minimalism and static visual narration do contrast with the strip's extravagant approach to language, but that contrast, like the deviant style that it represents, fits the incongruities of visual vernacular humor.

Indeed, abundant white space around the talking heads dramatizes the figures in the foreground along with the relationships and political positions at stake. Absent rich backgrounds, the composition emphasizes the combat between Huey and his conversational adversary of the moment; panels portray the characters as overwhelmed, separated, and defined by words. Like Lynda Barry, McGruder fills up many panels with text as words spew from the Freeman TV and from Huey's computer, telephone, or mouth. McGruder does not follow Barry's example in extending his amateur aesthetic to his lettering style, but the visual emphasis on text highlights the role of language as the vehicle for the ideologies that *The Boondocks* lampoons. In this way, the visual and verbal vernacular techniques of *The Boondocks* coalesce into a satirical vernacular vision. No matter how spare it gets, McGruder's artwork undercuts his sophisticated critique of American politics, media, and identity by dramatizing the comic contrasts between Huey's small body and outsized voice, and between the strip's fantasies and daily realities. That Huey's fantasies are cynical and extravagant while others' are gullible or banal fuels satire of many kinds, which McGruder's amateur aesthetic ties to a vernacular vision.

Dissonance between McGruder's crude graphics and complex verbal humor parallels other clashes, most notably between Huey's progressive ideals and the conservative realities of the 2000s and between his highbrow politics and other characters' lowbrow or compromised values. Huey's chief antagonists are his trash-talking buddy Caesar, low-achieving younger brother Riley, unsentimental grandfather, and sell-out neighbor Thomas DuBois, along with Tom's white liberal wife and identity-challenged daughter Jazmine. Together the crew challenges Huey's romantic advocacy with an unsentimental pragmatism that inverts the conventional politics of vernacular humor, but Huey shares the vernacular hero's vulnerability to those in power (notably Granddad, who keeps the boy in line with various threats) and inability to change the status quo. And like the traditional *eiron*, Huey has a child's naïveté about the way the world works, for all his knowledge about American political life in general and racial politics in practice.

In the end, the oppositional rhetoric of *The Boondocks* depends on two comic incongruities that constitute a contemporary vernacular vision: the political and social impotence of the strip's most intellectual and politically knowledgeable character; the simple graphic style amid complex relationships, ideas, and speech. In the process the visual vernacular of *The Boondocks* conveys McGruder's deep pessimism about democracy in contemporary America, which he has described as a failure of left, right, center, and media: "Bush lost the election," he told an audience at the University of Illinois in 2003. "Over half the voters voted for Gore, but he lost. They stole the election, and nobody rioted! If we lived up to our responsibilities as Americans—lived up to the ideals we profess as Americans—we'd overthrow the government." In this environment, the humor of *The Boondocks* fills a void made by journalism that he sees as "so conglomerated that there really are very few avenues left for people to dissent."[84] McGruder's graphic aesthetic maintains the naïve faith in democratic potential at the heart of vernacular humor even as his plots and characters challenge its viability in our contemporary world. In this way, his visual vernacular fulfills the challenge for all vernacular humor that James Cox identified in *Huckleberry Finn*: a vision that substitutes radical democratic values for genteel ones. The deviant visual vernaculars of *Hogan's Alley*, *The Simpsons*, *One Hundred Demons*, and *The Boondocks* express such vernacular visions in "a style with a politics in view" as the amateurish representations of Twain's brand—naïve ways of seeing and knowing—mock approved ways of understanding the world.

The legacy of Twain's vernacular vision thus extends beyond the well-known first-person narrators of twentieth-century literature to social satire in contemporary American television and comics. Not that the vernacular strategy has escaped the notice of satirists in other media. Consider, for instance, Fanny Brice's radio character Baby Snooks, conceived as a solution to NBC radio's censorship of her adult dialect character Mrs. Cohen: "We'd be ready to rehearse, and they'd say: 'You can't do this, you can't do that. This will offend, and that will not sound nice.' And I knew this couldn't happen with a baby. Because what can you write about a child that has to be censored?"[85] Borrowing Brice's cynical pun, Yiddish for "dupes" (presumably the censors), Michelle Hilmes called this approach "the 'Schnooks' Strategy," and her account of Brice's rhetoric has the same outlines as Twain's brand of vernacular humor: "critique of adult hypocrisies, exploration of the pitfalls of the English language, and an inverted world seen through the eyes of a precociously resistant and troublesome child, whose deflation of some of the most respected traditions, concepts, and institutions of American culture provoked sympathetic laughter while remaining safely contained and corrected by her age and innocence."[86] "[T]hrough the eyes of a . . . troublesome child": here in an example of oral humor the double vision of vernacular humor stands out. Twain's brand of vernacular humor compounds sound with sight and meaning through irony. In the process, it not only provides humor and "suggests some indefinite *dis*-ease" about a world that the naïf does not quite understand, as Tom Quirk has observed.[87] Twain's brand of the vernacular vision satirizes conceptions of reality along with representations of it.

For this reason, emphasis on the language politics of vernacular humor, especially its association with literary realism, misses its epistemological charge to see and understand things anew. Adding irony to conventional meaning destabilizes representation and, thereby, challenges notions of reality itself. Mock-oral and other varieties of vernacular literature emphasize writing as a visual medium of representation. Conventional spelling renders writing a transparent medium that disappears from experienced readers' notice. By contrast, deviant spellings, whether attempts to mimic sound or mere eye-dialect (such as Huck's "sivilize"), expose how writing imperfectly approximates speech. In this way, vernacular writing follows the pattern that media theorists Jay David Bolter and Richard Grusin have called *hypermediacy*, in which a medium simulates nonmediated, direct experience (which they term *immediacy*) through representational practices that highlight their own artifice. Bolter and Grusin note that "hypermediated" representations operate paradoxically, that hypermediacy intensifies artifice in order "to rival or refashion them in the name of the real."[88] Twain's brand of vernacular artifice readily adapts to graphic art because American print comics from the start merged colloquial American language, vulgar American behavior, and demotic American ideology—the basis for America's tradition of vernacular humor. And animated cartoons followed suit as the two media shaped amateur aesthetics into oppositional narrative visions that reframe meaning. The standpoint of a troublesome child—Huck, Bart, young Lynda, Huey, or Baby Snooks—licenses an amateur aesthetic to lampoon the rhetorical, behavioral, and moral norms that have long stood at the heart of vernacular humor's critique. Innocence conveyed through the amateur aesthetic of any medium similarly asserts moral distance from the corruption its deadpan proffers. Indeed, as mock-oral vernacular writing ridicules norms of literacy and status, so the visual vernacular of contemporary satiric animation scorns norms of social knowledge and ideas about the world. Comic contrasts between fantasy and realism, piety and blasphemy, sentimentality and satire: these staples of Twain's brand of humor, visual and verbal, emerge from hypermediated representations—vernacular visions—that simulate realism to critique the real. Twain's brand of vernacular humor endures, despite its limits in conceiving American innocence as exempt from the corruptions of empire, because naïveté has power to expose our ills.

CHAPTER FIVE

Comic Brands

More than Funny Business

John Limon had it nearly right: America has experienced profound "comedification," but the process began a century before the stand-up comedy breakthroughs of the 1960s. Celebrity had already branded Mark Twain as the embodiment of "American Humour" when Samuel Clemens first visited England in 1872, allowing him to extend his comic brand internationally into commercial endeavors beyond writing. In January of 1879, for instance, the British *Westminster Review* greeted one of his serious money-making endeavors, duly registered as U.S. Pat. #140245 on June 24, 1873, as "Mark Twain's latest joke"; then, after describing Mark Twain's Patent Scrap-Book as "his own invention, gummed, ready for use," the *Review* declared, "A very good joke it is" (*CR*, 172). Some fifteen years later, Clemens capitalized on his international fame in a 1895–1896 global tour of live performances not only to pay off the debts of his bankrupt publishing house, Webster & Co., but also to convert his travel experiences into a new book, *Following the Equator* (1897). The book, in turn, could be sold back to those same Australian, Indian, and South African audiences as well as bring their worlds to American readers. In this way, he exported a U.S. comic sensibility throughout the British empire. His practice of trading on his Americanness for profit at home and abroad led Amy Kaplan to complain, "His famous 'homespun' qualitites were ... woven from the tangled threads of imperial travel,"[2] yet as shown in chapters 3 and 4, Twain's brand of humor both fed and fed off of America's postcolonial heritage. Indeed, Samuel Clemens

> The comedification of America ... is the most astounding fact about the American sensibility from 1960 to 2000.
> —**John Limon,**
> *Stand-up Comedy in Theory*[1]

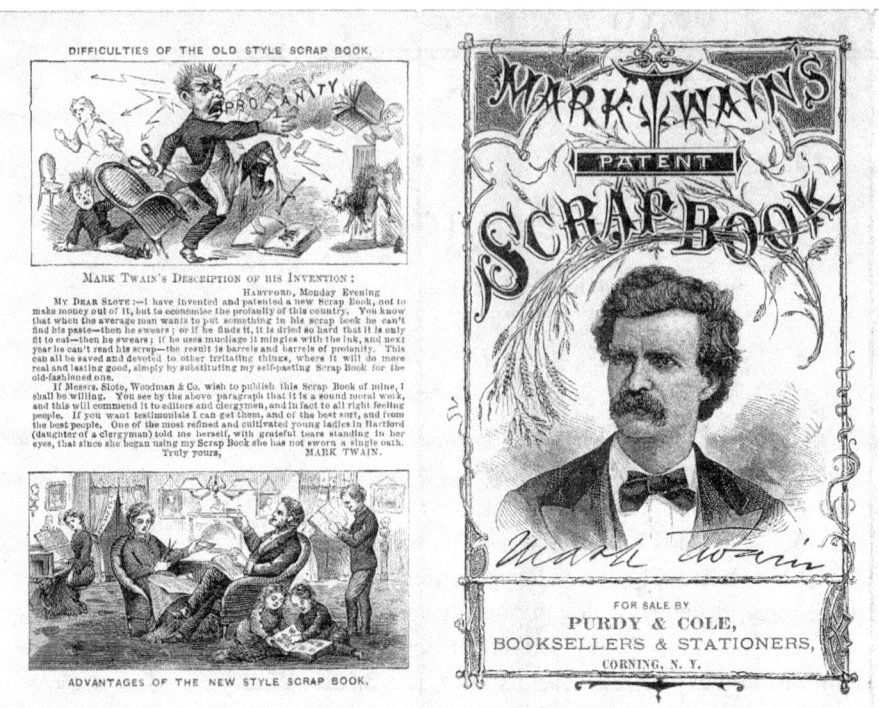

FIGURE 8 Sales of Mark Twain's Patent Scrap Book began in 1877, sold by stationers using eight-panel personalized brochures such as this one from an outlet near the Clemenses' summer home in Elmira, New York. Repetition of the name *Mark Twain* along with comic images and text brand the scrapbook with Twain's hallmark humor and fame. (Courtesy of Kevin Mac Donnell.)

reversed the imperial relations that gave American humor its distinctive postcolonial inflections by exporting American language and his comic sensibility through commerce.

Marketing for the scrapbook made humor central to the Mark Twain brand. A four-page sales brochure from 1877 branded the item by repeating the name *Mark Twain* four times (once as a signature) on two panels, graphically framing an image of his face on one and rhetorically framing jokes on the other, including a pair of cartoons and an equally humorous letter from the author-inventor (figure 8). The cartoon at the top depicts a domestic scene made frenzied by conventional scrapbooks, then restored to repose and harmony by "the new style scrap book," while the text between them presents the inventor's surprising pitch, in a letter to manufacturer Daniel Slote, for the product's moral value: "[B]arrels

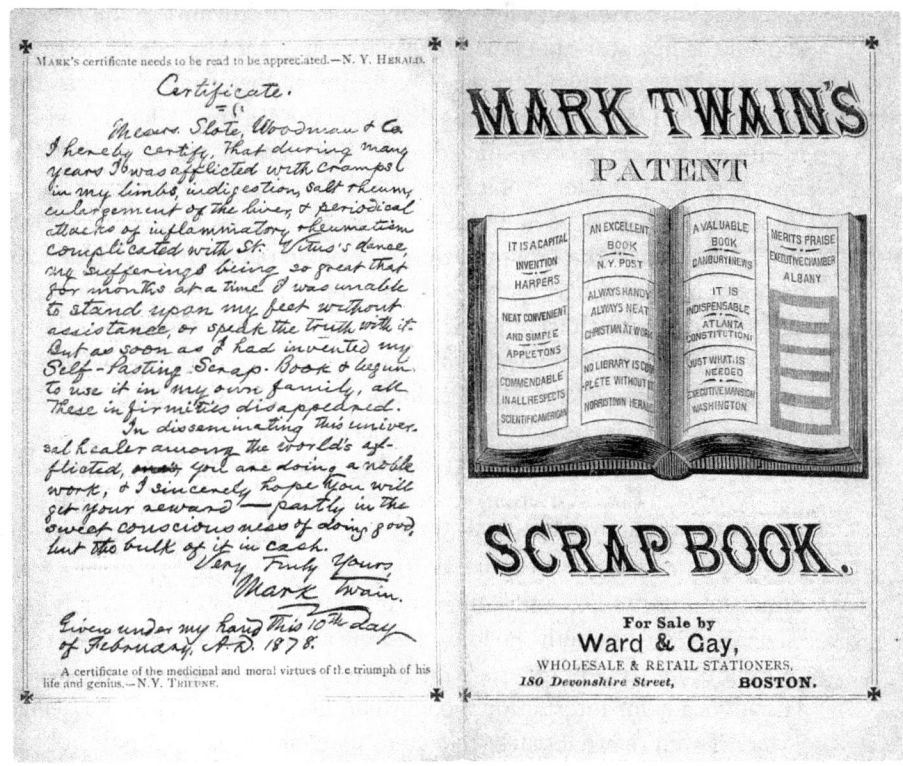

FIGURE 9 Marketing for the scrapbook also took advantage of reviews that appeared in newspapers across the U.S., as well as in England, as a result of Twain's celebrity. Reviews noted not only the product's practical merits, but also its comic sales strategy, featured here in the excerpts that frame Mark Twain's "Certificate." At bottom, the New York *Tribune*'s note: "A certificate of the medicinal and moral virtues of the triumph of his life and genius." (Courtesy of Kevin Mac Donnell.)

and barrels of profanity . . . can be saved and devoted to other irritating things, where it will do more real and lasting good, simply by substituting my self-pasting Scrap Book for the old-fashioned one." The claim mocks the nascent advertising genre of the commercial testimonial while adding a second extravagant assurance for good measure; the inventor reports that "one of the most refined and cultivated young ladies in Hartford (daughter of a clergyman) told me herself, with grateful tears standing in her eyes, that since she began using my Scrap Book she has not sworn a single oath" before he signs off with the humorist's symbolic wink, the name "Mark Twain."[3] Other publicity for the scrapbook likewise exploited Mark Twain's reputation for humor. Newspapers published the letter to Slote, and a sales flyer touting newspaper reviews of the product evoked the inventor's personal presence even in the absence of his image by reproducing his handwritten "Certificate" of the product's merits (figure 9). There he solemnly affirms that using the scrapbook had cured him of afflictions so extensive—including "indigestion, . . . enlargement of the liver, & periodical attacks of inflammatory rheumatism complicated by St. Vitus's dance"—that he had lost the ability (now presumably restored) to "speak the truth." The brochure thus revived an old Mark Twain joke, the confession of stretchers dating to his 1866–1867 lecture "Our Fellow Savages of the Sandwich Islands," where he reported that "the biggest liars in the world have got to visit the islands some time before they die" (*MTS*, 13), and made the joke a selling point of the item. Marketing branded the scrapbook with Twain's humor as well as his name.

Twain's brand thereby became a business strategy based on brand equity, or sign (i.e., symbolic) value, not simply a metaphor for a particular style of humor, and the examples of this chapter show how increasingly significant comic brands have become since Clemens pioneered this dimension of the U.S. and international information economy after the Civil War. Most notably, he identified the audience for humor as a community of customers for many products in markets around the world. His advocacy for international copyright, like his failed effort to declare "Mark Twain" a trademark, reflected his conception of the brand as a monetized symbol. And he exploited the brand by extending it to other products of his active mind—patented suspenders (1871, "Improvement in Adjustable and Detachable Straps for Garments," U.S. Pat. 121992) and a game for memorizing historical dates (1884, "Game Apparatus," U.S. Pat. 324535) as well as his "Improvement in Scrap-Books"—products whose only kinship to humor was the name *Mark Twain* on the label. But he also took care to distance some business activities from his brand. By naming his publishing house Charles L. Webster & Company after the nephew who managed daily operations, he enabled the firm to expand its list beyond humor and publish such serious works as U.S. Grant's *Personal Memoirs* (2 vols., 1885–1886) and the *Library of American Literature* (11 vols., 1888–1890), despite his public declaration to the Elmira, New York, *Herald*, "I am Webster & Co., myself, substantially."[4] Both strategies provided an early demonstration of today's dominant approach to marketing of all kinds, from widgets and films to universities and political candidates, and in this way Twain's brand anticipated one strand of contemporary American culture, though the branding phenomenon has spread worldwide.

Humor appears at the leading edge of both contemporary commercial opportunity and cultural innovation because playfulness flirts with seriousness *and* taboo. Copyright law specifically exempts parody from the list of infringements because parodists build new works from their sources, yet the equation of humor with triviality lets humorists experiment with new ideas, forms, and goals under the radar of critical notice. As Twain's brand exported American humor as a commodity in the nascent global information economy of the late nineteenth century, so contemporary American comic brands stake out new territories for colonization in the digital age. Branding leads today's marketing strategies because it assigns specific intrinsic value—distinction—to some symbols and messages in a time of communication and information overflow. Consultant Chuck Brymer put it this way: "If differentiation is the goal, branding is the process."[5] Brand-name humor identifies a quality that credits its consumers with class—all puns intended. In this way it depends utterly on capitalism, whatever its other ideologies.

Among comic brands born at midcentury, consider Second City. The Chicago nightclub opened December 16, 1959, featuring an impromptu theater company that specialized in creating skits based on suggestions from the audience. Its highly topical, often-intellectual humor always satirized American politics and social trends, reflecting its origins at the University of Chicago. Second City claims two generations of American comedy stars among its graduates: Barbara Harris, Alan Arkin, Elaine May, John Belushi, Bill Murray, Chris Farley, Tina Fey, Amy Sedaris, and Stephen Colbert all worked in the Chicago troupe. (Dan Aykroyd, Eugene Levy, and Gilda Radner started in the Toronto troupe, Nia Vardalos and Ian Gomez in the Northwest company.)[6] A series of breakthrough productions has enhanced the celebrity of these and other Second City performers, who burnished the brand's reputation with triumphs in more durable media. The most important, according to Sheldon Patinkin and Robert Klein's history of the club, were comedy recordings by Nichols and May, the television sitcoms *M*A*S*H* and *Cheers*, TV revues *Saturday Night Live* and *S[econd]C[ity]TV* (Canada), and the police procedural *Hill Street Blues*. From these successes came a series of Second City touring companies to compete with imitators across the nation and replication of the Second City formula in Toronto (1973–), Edmonton, Canada (1979–1982), Chicago's northwest suburbs (1988–1989, 2000), Las Vegas (2001–2008), Los Angeles (1983–), and Detroit (1993–, suburban Novi, 2005–), the last of these a sort of franchise operation with the owners of the Detroit Red Wings and Tigers.[7]

The Second City brand grew in the manner of more conventional branded commodities with the establishment of Second City, Inc., in 1985, a move that made the organization and its activities officially corporate. Twenty years later, in 2005, employees numbered three hundred, revenues ran about $8.6 million, and theatrical audiences exceeded 1 million.[8] In 2011 a corporate division, Second City Communications, was creating comic entertainment and training modules for live and video presentation at conventions, trade shows, and other corporate events, with marketing services as well as programs to promote employees' creativity and compliance with company policies. A separate educational division operates the Second City Training Center to teach acting, improvisation, and comedy writing in Chicago, Hollywood, and Toronto; the division serves thirteen thousand students annually, one thousand less than five years before, although units in Las Vegas, Detroit, and New York City have closed. Other educational activities include youth summer camps and a Comedy Studies program in conjunction with Columbia College Chicago. Second City Radio on Chicago's WCKG-FM (105.9) has given way to a variety format, but the Second City Network of 2011 offers original videos and podcasts online.[9] Like all good brand extensions, Second City Communications' corporate activities support the core product, the socially sophisticated satire of Second City's mainstage troupe, by colonizing new markets and creating new audiences for sketch comedy and improvisation. This task grows more important as live theater faces increasing claims on the recreational time of young adults, the audience who made the brand successful fifty years ago. Unlike lesser known comedy clubs, which tie their identities to a physical space, such as the Shadowbox Cabaret at Easton Mall in New Albany, Ohio, or Dad's Garage in Atlanta, brand-name humor such as Second City can break through the competition for leisure time by escaping *to* the work place. But dependence on corporate clients carries threats to a mainstage company celebrated for "risk-taking . . . and rebellion" and satire charged with "bite and importance."[10] Can humor remain funny when co-opted for corporate training? (After all, as Johan Huizinga put it, "Play to order is no longer play."[11]) More important, can mainstage satire bite the hand that feeds it?

Second City's success highlights a core principle of branding: evolving to remain relevant to the customer base.[12] Operations shrank during the Great Recession, and it's not clear how long the intellectually charged improv sketch can continue to draw crowds to live performances in the YouTube and TIVO era, yet the professional development model has managed to meet today's challenges with captive audiences of employees and other continuing education students. With activities for performers as well as corporate trainers and programs such as the University of Florida's 2006 Emerging Leader Certificate,[13] Second City surely has survived and thrived in part because it understands itself, as it boasts on its website, as "the leading brand in improv-based sketch comedy."

Despite its exceptional success in spawning comic careers, Second City has influenced modern American culture less dramatically and directly than two other comic brands, Disney and *MAD*. Indeed, Disney's exploitation of copyright and realization of fantasy make it an obvious heir to Twain's brand. The animated short subjects of 1927 led to feature films, then comic books and the *Mickey Mouse Club* television show, with its licensed mouse-eared beanies for kids and endless subsidiary rights for Annette Funicello, her comrades, and the producers. Then moving from media to physical communities, Disney developed the Disneyland theme park, followed by its East Coast cousins Disney World and Epcot and counterparts in Japan and France, and finally a suburban Orlando, Florida, neighborhood with utopian aims, evocatively named Celebration.

The Disney brand ranked seventh among worldwide brands in 2001 partly because it has mined and protected its intellectual property even more assiduously than Clemens did. Disney's brand equity stood at about $32.6 billion in 2001, barely half that of Coke or Microsoft, which topped the list at $68.9 and $65.1 billion, respectively,[14] but Disney's place points to the significance of comic entertainment—especially quality entertainment for children—in the information economy. Soft drinks and other goods get consumed, but intellectual property gets recycled. Consider the rerelease of the 1937 film *Snow White* in new media for successive generations, who become customers for DVDs, updated toys, and other licensed tie-ins long after the VHS cassette has turned obsolete. Investments in digital technologies brought Disney profits of $2.63 billion in the first half of fiscal 2007 as the firm partnered with Apple Computer's Pixar Animation and iTunes to program computer screens, iPods, and cell phones with content derived from its digitally enhanced live-action and animated films for theaters and DVD.[15] In fact, Disney's business model depends so heavily on intellectual property rights that the firm, faced with the prospect of having its first mouse film, *Steamboat Willie* (1928), enter the public domain, lobbied so intensively for the Sonny Bono Copyright Term Extension Act of 1998 that detractors called it the Mickey Mouse Protection Act. Nonetheless, the company has not taken action against the digital parodies made of the reedited cartoon snippets ("mash-ups") posted on YouTube.com, perhaps following the lead of Viacom, which sued YouTube for copyright infringement but apparently regards the popularity of a SpongeBob SquarePants mash-up, with more than seven million viewings in a few months, as free advertising.[16] Disney's notorious control over its brand image at its theme parks as well as in film content further secures its investment in brand identity.

Subsidiary rights alone can make humor a big business. Licensing and manufacturing income from products from Charles M. Schulz's *Peanuts* comic strip approximated $1 billion in 1999 alone, when the strip ran in more than twenty-six hundred newspapers worldwide, reaching more than 355 million readers in twenty-two languages each day, and *Peanuts* book sales topped 400 million copies since the first reprint appeared in 1952.[17] A comparison makes clear the dollar value of the Peanuts brand: $1 billion represents the total 2006 value of the rights owned by music publisher Sony/ATV, whose catalog then listed 251 songs by the Beatles, along with music by Hank Williams, Sr., Roy Orbison, Bob Dylan, and others.[18] By contrast, the name, image, and likeness of boxer Muhammad Ali, valued at $62.5 million in 2006, generate only $7 million in annual profits,[19] a mere 0.7 percent of *Peanuts*'s income. But these statistics highlight that prime comic commodities can have more lucrative resale than first-run value.

For instance, two decades have not exhausted licensing revenues from *The Simpsons*, which became a brand soon after its launch, with Bart's transgressiveness as its hallmark. Founder Matt Groening described the forty licenses sold within a week of the first regular episode as "the tail that wags the dog." Initial plans included a Bart Talking Doll that said "Kids in TV land, you're being duped" (but did not belch, apparently to avoid provoking parents) and blossomed by mid-1990 into Simpsons Mania, a marketing bonanza of licensed products. Bumper stickers showed Bart protesting, "Don't have a cow, man!" Campaign-style buttons labeled "UNDER-ACHIEVER" had Bart adding "and proud of it, man!" Baseball caps portrayed Bart as a devil with red wings and tail urging, "Go for it, Dude!!"[20] Even a towel with the Simpson family portrait depicted Bart aiming his slingshot at the viewer, and nice Jewish boys could sport a Bart Simpson skullcap with the devilish hero flaunting a halo.[21] Reruns began daily syndication on local U.S. television stations in the fall of 1994 at rates exceeding $1.5 million per episode.[22] As plots expanded to highlight Homer and other members of the family, licensing opportunities broadened as they also deflected criticism of the show's subversiveness. International sales of Simpson family consumer products exceeded $6 billion by 2008, when *Adweek* credited the show with the success of Hulu.com as a "groundbreaking online video model" that routinely "sells out its ad inventory" by delivering the total number of commercial screenings in its contracts.[23] In its 2010–2011 season, *The Simpsons* remained among broadcast television's top ten revenue producers, with an average rate of $253,170 for a thirty-second ad.[24] With gross revenues of more than $1 million per half-hour show, *The Simpsons* demonstrates the power of the comic brand in every corner of the humor business.

To be sure, subsidiary rights have become profitable for all genres, not just humor. The cable channel HBO cites DVD sales of *The Sopranos* as a reason that "new viewers discover the franchise every day . . . through season one."[25] Calling this breakthrough drama a *franchise* exposes the business model at work: a replicable concept defined as a brand. More to the point, however, the gross revenues of 1,660 comedy films topped $43 billion from 1995 to 2011, more than 24 percent of the industry total,[26] making comedy the top-ranked movie genre. Action films have the glamor, but comedies have the audience.

Recent licensing practices follow veins mined in the late 1920s by America's premier humor magazine, the *New Yorker*, within twenty years of Clemens's death. Founded in 1925 as a weekly of urbane wit whose verbal and visual commentary on the contemporary New York scene extended seasonally to the Hamptons, Florida, or Paris, the *New Yorker* discovered the brand value of subsidiary rights to humor in 1927, when editor Harold Ross began buying all rights to cartoons, instead of the first serial rights only, as typical, in order to reprint them in promotional materials. Almost simultaneously he began assembling the first cartoon reprint anthology, *The New Yorker Album* (1928), whose success proved that reprints augmented, rather than diluted, both publishers' *and* contributors' incomes. (The editors anticipated such substantial royalties that they asked the book's publisher to choose the cartoons so as to avoid appearing to favor one cartoonist over another.[27])

Subsidiary rights have been a mainstay of the *New Yorker*'s business model ever since. Cartoon collections soon led to literary anthologies, both light (*The New Yorker Book of Verse*, 1935) and heavy (*The New Yorker Book of War Pieces*, 1947). The magazine maintained good relations with its contributors by sharing royalties from its own resale projects and turning over all fees from licenses.[28] Today the magazine sells a wide range of products: consumable wares such as calendars in several formats, durable commodities such as thematic collections and gift books (*The New Yorker Book of Cat Cartoons*, 1990, and *The New Yorker Book of All-New Cat Cartoons*, 1997), and products in various electronic formats, including downloads from Cartoonbank.com and its firmware counterparts, *The Complete Cartoons of the New Yorker* (selected cartoons from the 68,647 on 2 CDs, 2004), *The Complete New Yorker* (more than 4,000 weekly issues on 8 DVDs, 2005), and its updates on an external hard drive (120 GB for $179 in mid-2011). Novelty products such as the $34.95 *New Yorker Cartoon Caption Game* (2007), a board game in which players invent new captions for drawings or identify their artists, demonstrate that the brand as much as the content is being sold. Emphasis on cartoons among the subsidiary rights products makes clear humor is central to the brand identity, and fiction collections such as the recent *Disquiet, Please!: More Humor Writing from the New Yorker* (2008) capitalize on it as well.

Even this brief survey explains why the magazine did not founder during either of its two postwar editorial crises and survived both the Great Depression and the more recent recession intact. Not that it lacked challenges: between 1967 and 1970, its appeal to "the wrong kind of reader," as Ben Bagdikian put it, led to a 50 percent plunge in ad pages and a two-thirds drop in annual profits, from $3 million to less than $1 million. Nonetheless, circulation remained constant at about 448,000,[29] an audience big enough to sustain its subsidiary products. Reprints also explain how the *New Yorker* weathered the financial difficulties of the 1980s, which bottomed out the year after the 1985 sale to Condé Nast, when annual ad pages dropped below 2,700 and circulation stood at 525,000.[30] Readership grew 25 percent in the next fifteen years, as William Shawn (1951–1987), Robert Gottlieb (1987–1992), Tina Brown (1992–1998), and David Remnick (1998–) cycled through the editor's office, but doubled to more than 1 million by the end of 2010, according to statistics from the Audit Bureau of Circulation; and the magazine remained profitable despite a 24 percent loss of 2009 ad revenues due to the recession. Such evidence of the *New Yorker*'s vitality affirms not only David Remnick's excellent editorial leadership, but also the magazine's brand management in today's media environment. Despite the challenges to print, the 2010 *New Yorker* boasted advertising revenues of $166 million, ranking thirty-seventh among American consumer magazines. But it has adapted to the ecosystem by mixing new and old media. The *New Yorker* brand reaches out to customers through an iPhone app as well as electronic editions for the iPad, Nook, and Kindle and through direct sales from its two websites, The New Yorker Store and Cartoonbank. At the same time, sales of books from thematic collections and an annual *New Yorker* festival of presentations by contributors and notable public figures personify the brand's commitment to literary humor and current affairs reporting while also—in the manner of Twain's brand of cross-media synergy—redirecting audiences back to the multiple platforms delivering its signature cartoons and other content.

Subsidiary rights dominate the *New Yorker*'s brand because its tangible comic commodity, the print magazine, has a shelf life of just one week, yet some contents—especially comic writing and cartoons—have the potential for much greater longevity in other media and forms. Other short-term comic commodities, such as the situation comedy and comic books, have sought similar solutions. Network sitcoms actually become most profitable when they cease production, which incurs expense, and enter syndication on cable and nonnetwork channels, which promote the brand at the wholesale level of advertising and at retail for sale and rent of recordings and downloads. Comic books' unique circulation challenges create greater difficulties and opportunities both. The youngsters who constitute the core audience for comics can't write subscription checks and depend on parents for the money and permission for purchases, especially in suburban communities where children no longer walk to the neighborhood newsstand with loose change for a cheap read. Moreover, the number of distribution outlets has declined, and many of those remaining limit casual reading by wrapping comics in plastic. Yet young fans grow up to control their own spending, giving comics more cultural capital than ever, to judge by the influence of comic books on blockbuster movies, which blend the nostalgia of superhero formulas with the realism of live action and the fantasy of computer graphics and gaming. Small wonder, then, that comic books represented just 16 percent of Marvel's $513 million net sales in 2004, while the remainder came from licensing: as one industry watcher put it, "comic books—the actual printed artifacts—have become little more than marketing materials." Thus Disney's CEO Robert A. Iger explained his 2009 purchase of Marvel for $4 billion as "a full price, but a fair price" for "Marvel's brand and its treasure trove of content" even without the comics company's film rights, already sold to Paramount Pictures and others. The success of *The Complete "New Yorker"* at $100 per set on DVD and $179 on external hard drive therefore bodes well for sales of a hypothetical *Complete "Batman"* even at three times the price.[31] To put it bluntly, the comics business model subsidizes young fans in order to cultivate lifelong interest in the brands, a strategy validated by the success of the comically inflected *Superman* films and, in 2011, the brand extension of Spiderman to Broadway.

Proof of concept came in 1999, when E. C. Comics partnered with Broderbund to bring out *Totally MAD*, every issue of the magazine from 1952 to 1998 on 7 CD-ROMs. Today Platinum Studios, a company dedicated to adapting comics for other media, works an extreme application of the approach, which its chairman calls "full-circle commercialization." Free original comics on its website DrunkDuck.com invite retail advertising direct to fans while also showcasing artists' productions for sale of subsidiary rights: video iPod and cellphone downloads; screen savers, wallpapers, and ring tones; durable goods from action figures to T-shirts; and production of print comics or films. Major comics publishers have followed suit. In July 2007, DC Comics launched the online imprint Zudacomics.com to augment its list of superhero titles, including *Superman* and *Batman*, by publishing (and copyrighting) the best electronic submissions from the public each month.[32] Inviting readers to vote for their favorites from each month's winners lets Zuda market-test the print and licensing prospects for each new comic.

As these examples illustrate, today's comic brands make the facts of the information economy central to their operation: they trade more in audiences, ideas, and experiences—the constituents of the symbolic or sign value that translates into brand equity—than in goods. Nowhere does this practice show more clearly than in television, which so blatantly sells audiences to advertisers. Situation comedy remains a staple of network broadcasting, yet cable has become its prime outlet and DVD sales a major profit center. Three of the four top-selling TV-DVDs in 2006 were humor: the animated sitcoms *Family Guy* and *South Park*, and the sketch-comedy *Chappelle's Show*.[33] In this context, it's not surprising that in the spring of 2006 the Cartoon Network ranked first among *all* ad-supported cable networks in several prized demographics (adults 18–34, adults 18–24, men 18–24, men 18–34). The network traced its success to its "Adult Swim" evening lineup of animated action and comedy shows, a strategy that soon drove MTV2 to replace music with the comic content suggested by its audience research: "short-form . . . weird and wacky, subversive humor."[34] But it's also not surprising in this context that television's leading comic brand is Comedy Central.

Created late in 1990, when MTV Networks and HBO merged their individual comedy channels, Comedy Central went live on July 1, 1991, to 500,000 potential subscribers and boasted 22 million within six months. In 2006 the channel reached more than 80 percent of all U.S. households.[35] This growth reflects the power of branding generally and Comedy Central's comic branding in particular. Cable channels need the differentiation that comes from branding far more than broadcast television does, because the broadcast spectrum limits each geographical market to a very few channels in order to avoid interference among their transmission

Comic Brands: More than Funny Business   171

signals. By contrast, dozens of cable channels compete in an ever-widening field, apparently limited only by producers' imaginations, subscribers' budgets, and available programming. And in this crowded mediascape, humor provides the distinctive differentiation needed to thrive.

Comically inflected public affairs—presented as a variant of socially conscious stand-up comedy—quickly became Comedy Central's signature. Cable TV's freedom from FCC supervision (because it doesn't use public airwaves) allowed edgier political discourse along with uncensored stand-up comedy, but the network also exploited two other developments. Rising partisanship in the politics of the mid-1990s generated passion and controversy, the seeds of satire. In addition, migration of young viewers from general-interest broadcasting to narrow-interest cable TV signaled the existence of an audience—that is, a market—for irreverence and novelty. They found it in Comedy Central. Stand-up comedian Al Franken hosted the network's live coverage of President George H. W. Bush's State of the Union address in January 1992, and anchored the *InDecision '92* election special that July. Political humor entered the regular schedule when Bill Maher debuted his *Politically Incorrect* talk show in July 1993. But the network's comic political programming found its contemporary form in 1996, when the Republican Congress increasingly clashed with President Bill Clinton (1993–2001). *InDecision* federal election specials hosted by Maher became a regular biannual feature, the network acquired Michael Moore's weekly investigative series *TV Nation* (1994, NBC–1995, Fox), and *The Daily Show* (1996–) debuted with host Craig Kilborn. By 2005, the network tied with ESPN as the year's top cable network among the free-spending demographic of males 18–24 years old. Four years later, the rebranding of the British kids' comedy channel Paramount Comedy as Comedy Central capped a deliberate, seven-year process of brand definition. The step illustrated a key principle of branding. As A. O. Scott put it when the 2007 *Simpsons* feature film came out, "Why mess with the formula when you can extend the brand?"[36]

Brand extensions began in 2002, when Comedy Central Records made a CD of recycled crank phone calls from its program *Crank Yankers* (2002–2007) and thereby revived the uncensored comedy recording business, which had died along with the 33⅓ vinyl audio LP. In that year the network also began sponsoring and managing performance tours for such comedians as Wanda Sykes, Dave Chappell, and Drew Carey.[37] The venture not only produced revenue and brand recognition, but also resulted in videotaped concerts for performance (and sale to advertisers) on Comedy Central and retail sale on video and DVD. Branding efforts intensified in 2004, with "branding guru" Doug Herzog's reappointment as president (1995–1999). Not that the brand lacked value before then: Viacom's 2003 purchase of AOL's stock in the channel established its equity at $2.5 billion.[38] But soon after Herzog's arrival, the licensing arm of sister channel Nickelodeon took over strategic development of Comedy Central's brand in order to increase retail sales, an arena increasingly marked by new media. The results, expected to add $150 million (more than 35 percent) to the network's $400 million in 2006 advertising revenues, included the Motherload broadband network of video clips from Comedy Central shows, original content, and downloads of *The Daily Show* and other programs from iTunes and cellphone carriers.[39] A strategy of cycling comic programming through multiple media formats fulfills the raison d'etre of branding by making Comedy Central a ubiquitous media presence as its transgressive humor inflects sitcoms such as *South Park* along with stand-up comedy. As Herzog told the *Wall Street Journal* in May 2006, "A guy can tell a joke Sunday night at the comedy club . . . and we can deliver it to our audience in six different ways the next day. We provide a brand and a platform."[40] Branding thus prevents the humor business from fragmenting into a series of unique experiences, too distinct and ephemoral for efficient marketing, by repackaging it as a commodity, the strategy pioneered by Mark Twain.

The prime product of Comedy Central's brand is, of course, *The Daily Show with Jon Stewart* (1999–). Indeed, branding consultant Seth Siegel considers Stewart "as important in shaping opinions today as Walter Cronkite was in the '70s and Huntley and Brinkley were in the '50s and '60s."[41] The show has become something of a brand itself since 2004, when it began spawning its own extensions. The most visible is *The Colbert Report* (2005–), produced by Stewart's Busboy Productions. The humor in this parodic political commentary program, starring Stephen Colbert as a gung-ho right-wing political pundit, begins with its self-inflated rhyming title, "Kol-béhr Re-póhr." As Stewart pointed out, speaking ironically in character, "We prefer not to think of it as a spinoff. We prefer to think of it as diverse marketing integration through spore reproduction."[42] But *Colbert* joins other brand products marketed as extensions of *The Daily Show*'s comic political critique, including Stewart's best-selling mock civics and anthropology texts, *America (The Book): A Citizen's Guide to Democracy Inaction* (2004) and *Earth (The Book): A Visitor's Guide to the Human Race* (2010), and DVDs such as the show's coverage of the 2004 Democratic and Republican conventions, *Indecision 2004* (2005).

Comic Brands: More than Funny Business

The Daily Show's basic televisual formula creates a comic frame for actual news from a video clip, photograph, or newspaper story. Three primary variations on this technique date back at least to 2006. The simplest version generates comic friction between Stewart's remarks and an image on screen. In the lead story from April 17, 2006, for example, Stewart shifts from reportage to ridicule after summarizing a *New York Times* article (duly displayed on screen) about the $400 million retirement package of Exxon CEO Lee Raymond, amounting to $144,573 for every day he worked: "Some might say, 'Hey, hey . . . *what?*'" And then Stewart moves into high comic gear by illustrating deadpan comments with absurd images.

> Let me show you this man. Let me show you Lee Raymond [traditional head shot]. Now some would say his face is the embodiment of—greed run amok, although it does have admirers: I suggest you check out jowlbangers.com [laughter]. But the truth is [hides a laugh]—they want to bang them some jowls!—but the truth is . . . those jowls are not an embodiment of anything. They are born of necessity [pause]. They're needed for storage. Can we get a cutaway view of his face [altered head shot, with junk in jowls]? Yes. A lot of the money that he has in there . . . it's where he keeps the doubloons, . . . and I believe Munch's *The Scream* is in there. [My transcription.]

A more sophisticated variation lets video clips speak comically to each other. In this same show, recent clips of three former military generals criticizing Secretary of Defense Donald Rumsfeld alternate with archival clips of Rumsfeld's earlier dismissals of critique: "Oh, goodness . . . ," "Well, my golly!," and "Oh, gosh!" And Stewart sets up the joke with the ironic declaration that the clips "[have] in no way . . . been manipulated to make Secretary Rumsfeld look at all foolish or out of touch" before capping the sequence with a sarcastic punch line based on Rumsfeld's own metaphor. If, as Rumsfeld claims, official resignations in response to public criticism would result in a "merry-go-round," then, Stewart suggests, the public is being "raped by carneys." Still more complex is a third variation, the sustained irony of a parodic feature story. In this episode, hyperbolically romantic narration about the bald eagle as an American symbol clashes with decidedly unromantic, realistic images of the problems caused by birds' infestation in Homer, Alaska—where most residents do not share reporter Ed Helms's view of eagle droppings as "a fresh glaze of freedom frosting." In all three variations, comic conflict between verbal and visual details also generates irony—and social satire—from the incongruity between conventional news and *The Daily Show*'s presentation.

The technique's success owes much to Stewart's commentary, which explains current events in an incongruously simplistic, literal, or metaphorical deadpan punctuated by pauses that symbolically wink at the audience. For example, the July 12, 2011, episode introduced the problem of the U.S. debt limit as the nation's inability to live within its means, reductively illustrated with a photo of four two-dollar bills and three piles of coins. Then Stewart identified the threats of default through a homely metaphor: "Unfortunately, while America figures it out, there is a . . . a . . . a repo man—let's call him 'China' [video cut to map of Asia] that on August 2nd could possibly . . . repossess us." And during the voice-over of President Obama calling for Congress to stop debating side issues, such as the standards for light bulbs passed in 2007, and raise the debt limit—"We may as well do it now. Pull off the Band-Aid. Eat our peas"—the video cut to a photo of bowl of peas, which remained on screen for nineteen seconds, exaggerating the literalism by dragging it out before cutting to a photo of a Band-Aid. Whereas in 2006 Stewart lamely ended the segment on Raymond by wishing him well in retirement ("here's hoping you get to spend some quality time—with your jowls"), by 2011 the *Daily Show* host sailed from one metaphorical zinger to another, lamenting congressional politics ("We are three weeks away from having to park our country down the street so China can't find it"), criticizing Obama ("the first president in history that begins every press conference with a heavy sigh"), and harpooning Speaker of the House John Boehner's approach to the negotiations ("It's not 'Awright, let's all chip in and we'll buy a keg for the party.' It's 'Buy me a keg and I won't burn your [bleep] house down'"). Such unvarnished attacks have won Stewart not only the loyalty of political progressives, but also coverage by the White House press secretary and traditional news organizations, as when he accused Jim Cramer, host of CNBC's *Mad Money*, who appeared on the March 12, 2009, *Daily Show*, saying, "You knew what the banks were doing, yet were touting it for months and months" and calling his explanations of the financial meltdown "disingenuous at best and criminal at worst." Here on a comedy show, viewers get news inflected with populist values but untainted by political correctness or objectivity.

The *Daily Show* formula may seem new because high-tech multiple video windows in some segments play out the show's signature comic reversal, putting authentic news in the audio background and "fake news" in the visual foreground. But the three techniques that Michael Cornfield cites as revolutionary—the use of video clips as the setup, parodies of conventional reportage, and "shambush" interview techniques[43]—all have predecessors in media new and old. After all, Will Rogers made a career as a Jack Downing for radio: he prefaced ironic political commentary with a faux naïve "All I know is what I read in the newspapers." A generation later, *MAD* magazine inspired the baby boomers by imagining politics as television parodies and comic strips. However, Stewart's ambush interviews also have recent antecedents in Michael Moore's variation on the vernacular naïf.

Television viewers of a certain age may trace *The Daily Show*'s satirical news format to the 1960s British import *That Was The Week That Was* and its *Saturday Night Live* descendent, "Weekend Update," but a nightly schedule separates *The Daily Show* from its weekly predecessors in several ways. First of all, commenting on very current events requires introducing unfamiliar topics as well as satirizing well-known individuals and incidents. The result is actual news coverage as well as parody, a context that explains why political authors and candidates appear on the show. The show's 11 p.m. time slot, soon after local news, ups the ante further and helps characterize *The Daily Show* as *alternative* news, not parodic or entertainment programming. Although Stewart has called the *Daily Show*'s formula "fake news," a more accurate label would be "comically interpreted news."

Such humor surely reflects "the objectivity and credibility crisis besetting mainstream media," as Michael Cornfield of the Pew Internet and American Life Project concluded in 2005.[44] But it is also more than that. The Pew project's 2004 survey found that 21 percent of adults 18–29 years old used late night comedy, including *The Daily Show*, as their chief source of news,[45] suggesting (especially in light of the success of conservative radio punditry) that Americans across the board want their news in some kind of evaluative context. Astute critics of American culture have long noticed that television program schedules have linked news and late night comedy since Steve Allen pioneered the genre as the first host of *The Tonight Show* in 1953.[46] Yet television's role in this process joins today's comic interpretations of news and politics with larger cultural shifts represented by electronic media's displacement of print culture. The rise of electronic media, begun with the telegraph in 1844 but accelerating with the spread of radio in the 1920s, explains why political humor has spread to shows like NPR's news quiz, *Wait Wait! . . . Don't Tell Me* (1998–), a successor to *Whad'ya Know?* (1985–). And it also explains why Tom and Ray Magliozzi have built careers, including a syndicated column and the "shameless commerce division" of their website, from a radio enterprise that began as a volunteer radio gig to promote their garage by giving humorous but helpful solutions to local listeners' car problems. Objectivity has lost ground as an American value.

Objective journalism has had a short career compared to the advocacy that dominated political rhetoric before and after the rise of periodicals in the eighteenth century. As an ideal, objectivity grew from the cultural penetration of literacy after print industrialized the power of writing and education spread. Walter Ong, Elizabeth Eisenstein, and others who have studied oral and literate cultures have shown how writing depersonalizes knowledge by detaching the knower from the known. Knowledge acquires an independent, autonomous character when writing replaces human memory as the storehouse of individual and collective experience. In western culture, autonomous information underlay the scientific empiricism that gave rise to positivist epistemology—and objectivity—along with divisions of government from the monarch's representation of the state into multiple organizations of government and bureaucracy.[47] Branding, which aims for sign value to displace exchange or use value as the basis of worth, represents an extreme case of the separation of symbol from referent. That's why the brand names Sharper Image and Halston live on after the companies themselves went out of business and why the naming rights business actually grew during the post-2008 recession: brand names and trademarks are assets with market value. In fact, liquidators have come to see themselves as "brand licensing experts," because, as one executive in the field observed, "It's not a capital-intensive business [like manufacturing or retail] . . . It's a royalty-driven business. It's like an annuity."[48] In its purest form, branding verges on fraud, as plaintiffs argued in filing suit against "the most coveted brand in real estate, synonymous with sky-piercing luxury and can't miss quality: Donald J. Trump." They charged that he "essentially rented his name" and public persona when the projects began, but withdrew them—and substantially lowered the properties' value—when the developers failed to complete the projects.[49] But the example also illustrates how branding can make even real property less real. The divorce of information from meaning represented by extreme forms of branding, in which a referent longer exists for the symbol, links it to postmodern culture as a phenomenon of what Fredric Jameson called the "cultural logic of late capitalism."[50]

Humor fits neatly with the decline of objectivity. Ong, Marshall McLuhan, and other media theorists, including most recently Jay David Bolter and Richard Grusin, have observed that the analytical powers spurred by literacy sowed the seeds of their own demise as science led to the development of electronic media.[51] Voices and pictures carried by radio, television, and the Internet have reattached information to the body, bridging the schism between knower and known while establishing the hybrid that Ong called "secondary orality," so called because electronic media mimic the sounds and sights of live experience through scientific knowledge and literate technologies. The blend of oral and literate values in secondary orality not only reflects the merger of image, sound, and text on the World Wide Web, whose most dramatic developments Ong did not live to see, but also explains the success of comically inflected news. The reunion of knower and known in secondary orality replaces objective reporting with interpretation, restoring the "agonistic tone" that Ong identified as a key feature of oral cultures. This phenomenon runs across genres from the persistent editorializing of MSNBC, CNN, and Fox cable news to the talk radio commentary of Rush Limbaugh and the parodic print and video news of *The Onion* (1988–). But the brand link between declining objectivity and rising political humor shows particularly well in the documentaries of Michael Moore.

Moore's documentary about the impact of globalization on American factory workers and communities, *Roger and Me* (1989), introduced his comic technique of using news clips and ambush interviews to ridicule contemporary political figures and policies. The technique became the foundation of his first television series, *TV Nation* (1994–1995), which took up matters ranging from the North American Free Trade Agreement (NAFTA) to racial profiling in fifteen episodes on NBC and Fox television before the networks' fears of alienating advertisers led to the show's demise on broadcast TV. The subscriber base of the Bravo! cable network offered a more congenial environment for Moore's alternative television magazine, renamed *The Awful Truth*, which ran for twelve episodes in each of two seasons in 1999–2000. His films *Bowling for Columbine* (2002), on gun control, and *Fahrenheit 9/11* (2004), on the Bush administration's war against terrorism, brought still broader attention to his comic technique as he turned archival footage against official sources of news. Since then, he has targeted his wry ironies at the larger tenets of neoliberalism, with its faith in the wisdom of free markets, especially in contrast to government. *Sicko* (2007) set up invidious comparisons between medical treatment in the U.S. and the supposedly inadequate, socialist single-payer health care systems of Cuba and France. *Capitalism: A Love Story* (2009) skewered Wall Street and Washington as an apparently bumbling Moore explored the people and forces shaping U.S. fiscal policy. The film drew little laughter from audiences stung by the Great Recession, but in turning comic technique into trademark, Moore branded the humor of his politically activist documentaries.

Critics such as Kevin Mattson scorn Moore's politics of entertainment as socially unproductive,[52] but his films' substitution of humor for action seems to me precisely the point. Moore's mock-naïve, proletarian persona, like his signature costume of baseball cap, blue jeans, and running shoes, belongs to the vernacular tradition of political humor outlined in chapters 3 and 4. Moore's cynicism has less in common with Mark Twain's best-known fiction, however, than with the philosophical quips from the apocryphal *Puddn'head Wilson's New Calendar* atop each chapter of *Following the Equator*. Likewise, Moore's approach to humor draws its energy from the belief that Twain late in his career attributed to the title character of "The Chronicle of Young Satan," one of unpublished *The Mysterious Stranger Manuscripts*. "This multitude [of humanity] see the comic side of a thousand low-grade and trivial things," he concedes, but overlook the "ten thousand high-grade comicalities" of a more cosmic type, especially the "engaging and delightful comicalities" of religion and government. "All forms of government—including republican and democratic—are rich in funny shams and absurdities, but their supporters do not see it," Young Satan goes on; "will a day come when the race will detect the funniness of [all] these juvenilities and laugh at them—and by laughing at them destroy them? For your race, in its poverty, has unquestionably one really effective weapon—laughter. . . . Against the assault of laughter nothing can stand"(*MSM*, 164–166). Moore produces laughter, not policy. His rhetoric has less in common with that of politicians and more in common with satirists like Rachel Maddow, who won a national radio audience as Al Franken's colleague on Air America radio and has hosted her own television commentary program for MSNBC since 2008.

But as an entertainer Moore also constructs a political community from the consumers who form the audience for his humor—at least for the duration of the movie, though Franken proved with his successful run for the U.S. Senate in 2008 that audiences can become political communities. Today, as politics and entertainment merge, especially in the ironic messages of the dispirited left, humor communicates the contemporary American paradox of technological progress and social conservatism. Just as electronic media merge literacy and orality, so contemporary American humor unites the literate values of constitutional democracy—grounded in documents and written law—with the anti-intellectual, oral values of vernacular tradition. Humor has a special affinity for orality, primary or secondary, because its most basic form is the oral anecdote. All of which leads me to conclude that one significance of comic brands lies in the invitation of America's capitalist postindustrial democracy to put our money where the laughs are.

When Fredric Jameson published his landmark *Postmodernism* in 1991, he expanded the economic component of an earlier argument about cultural shift and identified two "boundaries . . . washed over (in ways profoundly characteristic of the postmodern)": "identification of the commodity with its image (or brand name or logo)" and "symbiosis between the market and the media."[53] Mark Twain's brand of humor shows that the processes associated with postmodernism began a century earlier than most theorists have thought. By presenting a comically unmoored self, Twain's brand of stand-up comedy anticipated not only the modern identity theories of Willam James and Erving Goffman, but also an important strand of performances by contemporary comedians. By representing a youth's experience of American society in his own words, Twain's brand of vernacular vision wrought satire of deep cultural significance from the ironies of *Huckleberry Finn* and thus paved the way for some of today's most important graphic humor, cartoons and comics whose visual vernacular aesthetic likewise offers new ways to see and critique the world. By exposing vernacular humor's ideological complicity with imperialism, Twain's brand of humor and empire in *Connecticut Yankee* anticipated Philip Roth's satire of American exceptionialism as inherently corrupt. These achievements might have gone unnoticed, however, had Twain's brand of humor not also modeled the dominant commercial practices of modern popular culture and through them shown the centrality of humor to contemporary American life.

Notes

Chapter One

1. Henderson, *Mark Twain*, 43.
2. Annenberg Public Policy Center, *Daily Show Viewers*.
3. W., "Slick, Crockett, Downing, Etc," 137, 138–39.
4. Said, *Culture and Imperialism*, 18.
5. Nash Information Services, "Top-Grossing Genres 1995 to 2011."
6. Smuts, "Humor," offers an accessible introduction to humor theory. Aristotle introduces comedy in *The Poetics* (I–IX) and incongruity theory in *The Rhetoric* (III, 2). Other sources noted are in the bibliography.
7. Walker, *Very Serious Thing*, 82. An example of neuroscientific research into humor is Mobbs, et al., "Personality"; Caron, "From Ethology" surveys other scientific and anthropological approaches to humor.
8. The phrase "the damned human race," often attributed to Twain, was coined by Bernard DeVoto as a section head for posthumous works collected in Twain, *Letters from the Earth*.
9. Leach, *Land*, 150.
10. U.S. Census Bureau, "Census Bureau Reports Steady Growth"; Bureau of Economic Analysis, "Table 1.1.5."
11. "Mark Twain Left Daughter $611,136"; "Purchasing Power of Money in the United States."
12. Bureau of Statistics, "Progress of the United States," inside cover.
13. For recent books discussing Twain's newspaper writing and his professional and imaginative engagement with the printing industry, see Caron, *Mark Twain*, and Michelson, *Printer's Devil*.
14. Boorstin, *Americans*, 146.
15. Hartman Center for Sales, "Timeline"; Ohmann, *Selling Culture*, 101.
16. "Twain's Fancy Suit."
17. According to Bureau of the Census, *Historical Statistics*, 808, the number of book titles published in the U.S. rose from 2,076 in 1880 to 4,559 in 1890, and reached 13,470 in 1910.
18. For a general introduction to brands, see Arnold, *Handbook*, or Landa, *Designing Brand Experiences*. More detailed analyses of branding include Clifton, et al., *Brands and Branding*, and Holt, *How Brands Become Icons*.

19. For statistics on brand to total market values, see "Editorial," *Brand Management*. What accountants call the equity or "asset value" of a brand equals the difference between the market value of its stock and the net asset (or "book") value of the business—somewhere between $70 and $125 billion in the case of Coca-Cola, the world's most valuable brand; see Blackett, "What Is a Brand?," 5. A more detailed account is Lindemann, "Brand Valuation."

20. A self-reflexive example is the British book series Great Brand Stories, which includes Milligan, *Brand It Like Beckham*.

21. Hilton, "The Social Value of Brands," 64.

22. For documents in the case, see Schmidt, "Special Feature: *Samuel L. Clemens Vs. Belford, Clarke & Company*," http://www.twainquotes.com/ClemensVsBelford.html.

23. See, for example, Arac, *Huckleberry Finn*, 141.

24. "Mark Twain," *Once*; Frear, *MTH*, 176–77, 188–89, notes that the illustration, used to promote Twain's only lecture at the Brooklyn Academy of Music, has been erroneously dated 1877 (*Modern Eloquence*, 1900), 1866–67 (New York *Independent*, May 5, 1910), and 1869 (Paine, *MTB*). For details of Clemens's London visit, see *MTL* 5:151–230.

25. "Mark Twain," 519, 521.

26. Twain, *MTL* 5, 163–64.

27. "Matthew Arnold," 320–21.

28. Locker, "Two American Humorists," 310, 324.

29. Kirch, et al., "Producing."

30. Louis J. Budd, *Interviews*, ix. Budd identified 278 interviews in this 1977 volume but later estimated in "Interviews," 402, that Twain gave at least 50 more, although only 258 apppear in the comprehensive 2006 collection *CI*.

31. Boorstin, *Image*, 57.

32. "Dinner at Delmonico's."

33. Ohmann, *Selling Culture*, 82.

34. Budd, "Talent," 79.

35. Vaidhyanathan, *Copyrights*, 55–80.

36. Twain, *MTS*, 158, 160.

37. Glass, "Trademark Twain," 688.

38. Clemens, SLC to HMS, 1 Sept. 1872, ALS, AS. #2734, Henry M. Stanley Archives. Collection King Baudouin Foundation on Deposit at the RMCA Tervuren. Royal Museum for Central Africa, Tervuren, Belgium.

39. Gribben, "Autobiography"; Gribben, "MT, Business Man," 32.

40. Leach, *Land*, 3, 150.

41. Hemingway, *Green Hills*, 468.

42. Blair, *Native American Humor*, 147–62.

43. I take up the nationalist ideology of Blair's scholarship in "International Twain."

44. Rodgers, "*Great American Novel*."

45. U. S. Census Bureau, *Table 4. Population: 1790 to 1990*, www.census.gov/population/censusdata/table-4.pdf.

46. Applebee, "Stability," Table 1, Most Frequently Required Titles, 28.

47. A search of Lexis-Nexis for "Mark Twain" in major newspapers in the two years from February 7, 2004, to February 6, 2006, yielded 889 hits, a rate of 1.2 per day. New Zealand, Singapore, England, and Scotland were represented in the sample's 40 most

recent hits. Within a mere two weeks Twain was invoked to comment upon the trial of Enron Corporation officials ("The jury system puts a ban [up]on intelligence and honesty, and a premium upon ignorance, stupidity and perjury"), mine safety ("there are three types of lies, lies, damned lies, and statistics"), exotic travel ("heaven was copied from Maritius"), and a California restaurant ("Golf is a good walk spoiled"). Barbara Schmidt, compiler and editor of www.twainquotes.com, attributes the observation on lies to Benjamin Disraeli and notes that the golf quip is not among Twain's published writings. See Bennett, "The Doltish Dozen"; Boselovic, "Workplace Safety Not Always Easy to Measure"; Cole, "The Best of Mauritius"; Pierleoni, "A Bit Off Course." More recently, the *New York Times* referred to Twain on both sides of a single page. While one article reported a controversy over the annual frog-jumping contest inspired by his famous tale, the other cited his opinion of Cairo, Illinois (see McKinley, "Calaveras County"; "Where Two Rivers").

48. Twain's works continue to inspire films, comic books, children's adaptations, and other versions. Among the more notable are the musical *Big River: The Adventures of Huckleberry Finn*, which opened on Broadway during the novel's centennial year, 1985, and has since had regional, community, and international productions in addition to a 2003 Broadway revival; and playwright Charles Smith's recent dramatization of *Pudd'nhead Wilson*, which opened off Broadway and toured briefly in 2002.

49. Burns, dir., *Mark Twain*. Recent biographies include Kaplan, *Singular*; Powers, *MT Life*; Loving, *MT Adventures*; Morris, *Lighting Out*; Trombley, *MT Other*; Shelden, *MT White*.

50. Budd, *Our Mark Twain*, 25.

51. Hutton, "Scholarly Mark Twain Edition."

52. Dinkelspiel, "With Twain a Bestseller."

53. Kennedy Center, "Mark Twain Prize for American Humor."

54. Holt, *How Brands Become Icons*, 8, 14, quote 9–10.

55. Clark, *Brandscendence*, 6, 33–34; Holt, *How Brands Become Icons*, 22–27. Clark attributes the failure of New Coke, a 1980s innovation that turned the original Coke into a "classic," to "brandicide."

Chapter Two

1. Seinfeld, "Playboy Interview," 56.

2. Kurtzman, "Jon Stewart 'Crossfire' Transcript."

3. Carlson attacked Stewart on his treatment of John Kerry: "Well, I'm just saying, there's no reason for you—when you have this marvelous opportunity not to be the guy's butt boy, to go ahead and be his butt boy. Come on. It's embarrassing." And Stewart retorted to Carlson's charge, "I do think you're more fun on your show," with one of his own: "You know what's interesting, though? You're as big a dick on your show as you are on any show."

4. Mintz, "Stand-up Comedy," 576; Marc, *Comic Visions*, 16.

5. Marc, *Comic Visions*, 13.

6. Rothenbuhler, "Church," 96, 95.

7. See, for example, early articulations of the genre, such as Stahl, "The Personal Narrative as Folklore," and Stanley, "The Personal Narrative and the Personal Novel: Folklore

Notes

as Frame and Structure for Literature"; more recent studies include Gaudet, "Telling It Slant," and the special issue of *Western Literature* edited by Dolby-Stahl, "Personal Narrative in Literature"

8. See, for instance, Mintz, "Standup Comedy As," 74–75, which invokes the comedian as a "negative exemplar" and "our contemporary *anthropologist*"; and Bakhtin, *Rabelais and His World*.

9. Caron, *Mark Twain*, 20–21.

10. Huizinga, *Homo Ludens*, 22.

11. Bakhtin, *Rabelais and His World*, 196–277, esp. 266ff; Budd, "Been There," 13.

12. See, for example, Budd, "Been There," 13, and Wickberg, *Senses of Humor*, 126; Marc, *Comic Visions*, 15–16, doesn't mention Mark Twain, but includes the nineteenth-century public lecture among the sources of stand-up.

13. Wickberg, *Senses of Humor*, 153, 146.

14. In addition to Gilbert, critics who have explored stand-up as the performance of marginality include Schulman, "House That Black Built," and Price, "Humorous Hapas."

15. House, "Mark Twain as a Lecturer."

16. "MT's Lecture."

17. For a survey of the phenomenon, see Cawelti, *Apostles*.

18. Emerson, "Strange," 143.

19. No definitive texts of the lectures exist. I rely on Fatout's lecture composites in *MTS* unless otherwise cited, because his version of the "Sandwich Islands" lecture includes political comments about America's intentions toward Hawaii omitted by Lorch, *Trouble Begins at Eight*. Frear's *MTH*, Appendix M, includes more of Twain's political remarks, including a letter to the New York *Daily Tribune* published January 6, 1873.

20. De Quille, "Reporting with Mark Twain," 178; Seinfeld, "Playboy Interview," 51.

21. Knoper, *Acting Naturally*, 67, argues for the influence of the deadpan theatrical style, especially as popularized by the famous comic actor Joseph Jefferson III (1829–1905), whose portrayal of Rip Van Winkle relied on an unconscious humor parallel to that of Simon Wheeler and the Twain narrator in "Jim Smiley and His Jumping Frog" (1865). However, Jefferson enacted dramatic monologues in a conventional theatrical performance requiring willing suspension of disbelief, rather than the direct author-audience communication of the lecture or stand-up comedy.

22. Twain, "MT in Washington."

23. Knoper, *Acting Naturally*, 65; Carton, "Speech Acts," 162.

24. DeVoto, "The Lineage of Eustace Tilley," 20.

25. Branch, "Babes," 962.

26. Clemens first used *Mark Twain* in a comic letter from Carson City, Nevada, published in the *Territorial Enterprise* of February 3, 1863. His remarks as president of Carson City's burlesque "Third House" have not survived, but his December 13, 1863, account of the event ran in the *Enterprise* (see Twain, *Mark Twain of the* Enterprise, 102–110). The fullest account of Ward's visit to Virginia City is Pullen, *Comic Relief*, 78–99.

27. Budd, *Our Mark Twain*, 59.

28. Caron, "Satirist."

29. Johnson, *19th C*, esp. 125–26.

30. Twain, "My Ancient."

31. "Mark Twain on the Platform."
32. Longstreet, "Georgia Theatrics," 288.
33. One might argue from a rhetorical standpoint that the contrast between a narrator's and audience's perceptions underlies all humor of pain and embarrassment, including slapstick, and that the bewilderment of the narrator in "Jim Smiley and His Jumping Frog" (1865) falls into this category as well, but here I am talking about this contrast as a matter of theme, not rhetoric.
34. Berkove, "Nevada Influences," 163–64. Berkove, *Sagebrush*, provides a broad introduction to this group of humorous writers.
35. One hallmark of a mature science, according to Thomas Kuhn, *Structure* is the exclusion of amateurs.
Clemens followed a number of sciences, although his interest in psychology is less well known than his reading in those nineteenth-century favorites, geology (from his mining years) and biology. Sherwood Cummings details the importance of these two, but not psychology, in *Mark Twain and Science*. Clemens met James in 1892, the same year he purchased *Principles of Psychology* (1891), and mentioned James's ideas both in an 1894 letter to his wife, Olivia, urging her to seek hypnosis in Paris, and in the 1898 notebook entries for the psychological tale "My Platonic Sweetheart" (Gribben, *MTLib* 1:351; Gillman, *Dark Twins*, 153; "James, William," *MTEncy*). No evidence links Clemens's reading directly with Freud's texts (though Freud attended at least one of his performances), but the men traveled in the same circles, and Clemens may have consulted him regarding his daughter Jean's epilepsy when the family was in Vienna for twenty months in 1897–1899 ("Austria," *MTEncy*). Clemens's understanding of psychology, including what we would now call psychosomatic illness and the placebo effect, was one reason for his attack on Mary Baker Eddy in *Christian Science* (1907).
36. Gillman, *Dark Twins*, 139.
37. James, "Remarks," 17.
38. James, *Principles of Psychology*, 1:294, 337.
39. Goffman, *Presentation*, 252–53. Goffman traces his conception to Mead, whose *Mind, Self, and Society* was profoundly influential, but Mead's sources included James (whose legacy also includes the concept of the double-consciousness described by W. E. B. DuBois).
40. Budd, "Talent," 79.
41. Rothenbuhler, "Church."
42. Popular sources persist in claiming that the idea for *A Prairie Home Companion* came to Keillor at *The Grand Ole Opry* while on assignment to write for the *New Yorker*, but Twin Cities newspaper coverage from August 1973 shows that plans for a live Saturday night variety hour were already afoot before Keillor had left KSJN to begin that work ("Keillor to Quit"). His hiatus from radio after *A Prairie Home Companion* went off the air in 1987 lasted only through November 25, 1989, when his New York–based *American Radio Company of the Air* replaced it. He restored the title *A Prairie Home Companion* when the show returned to St. Paul in 1993 following a brief run as *Garrison Keillor's American Radio Company*.
43. Roback, "*PW* Interviews," 138.
44. Mitchell, "Homespun," 7.
45. Garrison Keillor, untitled typescripts, 1971. Prairie Home Companion Archives (St. Paul, MN: Minnesota Public Radio). For a history of the Lake Wobegon monologue,

see Lee, *Garrison Keillor*, 28–36, 67–87. In 1982, *A Prairie Home Companion* joined the national lineup of American Public Radio (APR, now American Public Media), a network invented to syndicate the show after National Public Radio (NPR)declined to carry it.

46. Fedo, *Man*, x.
47. Keillor, *Leaving*, xx.
48. Keillor titled the monologue "Aprille" in *Leaving Home*. Quotations from "Aprille" here come from my transcription of the monologue broadcast on April 26, 1986; this version differs in a number of respects from the published version, as detailed in Lee, "Five Ways."
49. Chaucer, *Works*, 17.
50. Gerber, "MT's Comic Pose"; Lee, *Garrison Keillor*, 49–76.
51. He began the program on KSJR in Collegeville, then moved with it to Minnesota Educational Radio's new flagship station KSJN in St. Paul in October 1971 after a nine-month hiatus resulting from his dispute with management.
52. Keillor, *Ten Years on the Prairie*, 1A.
53. Second, third, and fourth annual farewell performances followed ("it's a pretty good excuse to get together and toss a party," noted the program for the 1988 show at New York's Radio City), but the series ended after Keillor returned to live radio in his old Saturday night slot in November 1989.
54. Keillor, "Perils," 100, 104.
55. Roback, "*PW* Interviews," 139.
56. On Keillor and Twain in the traditions of midwestern culture, see Lee, "Introduction," and Bernt et al., "Literature."
57. Fox and Frederiksen, "Video Reviews (*Notorious C.H.O.*)."
58. ACLU of Southern California, "ACLU/SC Honors"; Keepnews, "There Was Thought in His Rages."
59. Rachel C. Lee, who does not cite Gilbert, presents a similar argument in her "'Where's My Parade?'"
60. Bakhtin, *Rabelais and His World*, 240–41.
61. Limon, *Stand-Up*, 6, 13.
62. Cho, *I'm the One* [Book], 37, 30.
63. Navarro, "Returning in Her Favorite Role," 19.
64. Stahl, *Literary Folkloristics*, 15, 17.
65. Raskin, *Semantic Mechanisms of Humor*.
66. Stahl, *Literary Folkloristics*, 24.
67. Ibid., 21, 23.
68. 1999 Performance of the Year, *New York* magazine; one of the Great Performances of 2000, *Entertainment Weekly*.
69. Mandese, "'Seinfeld' Rates Soar," 1.
70. Marc, *Comic Visions*, 12–13.
71. Bushman, "Stand-Up," 30.
72. Seinfeld and David, *Seinfeld: Seasons 1 & 2*, commentary, 1:55. The pilot aired in the undistinguished slot of 9:30 p.m. EDT on July 4, 1989.
73. Oppenheimer, *Seinfeld*, qtd. 279.
74. Myers, *Seinfeld: A XXX Parody*.
75. Bruce, *The Lenny Bruce Performance Film*.

Chapter Three

1. Celayo, Shook, and Díaz, "In Darkness," 17.
2. For the African heritage of African American humor, see Gates, *Signifying Monkey*; Watkins, *On the Real Side*.
3. Díaz, *Brief*, 1.
4. Marx, "Vernacular," 8, 3.
5. Pollock, "Cosmopolitan and Vernacular," 592.
6. Arac, *Huckleberry Finn*, 162.
7. Foner, *Mark Twain, Social Critic*, 310–12; Zwick, *Confronting Imperialism*, 79–87; Caron, "Blessings."
8. Kaplan, "Anarchy of Empire," 52. McBride, *Colonizer Abroad*, 61, expands Kaplan's argument when he interprets Twain's Sandwich Islands lectures as evidence of "the conflict between satire and imperialism that Clemens faced" in mocking business interests that paid his way.
9. Roth, *Facts*, 123.
10. On the relation between Twain's scatological narrative *[Date, 1601.]* (comp. 1876) and his vernacular breakthrough in *Huckleberry Finn*, see Jong, "Intro to *1601*," and Lee, "Mark Twain: [Date, 1601]."
11. Webster, *Dissertations*, 406.
12. Blair, *Native American Humor*, 17, traces the history of "Yankee Doodle," showing that the term *Yankee* began as British scorn for the New Englander's rustic speech, coarse clothing, penny-pinching, and general ignorance of the world.
13. W., "Slick, Crockett, Downing, Etc," 137.
14. According to the *OED*, the term *Americanism* acquired all these senses between its coinage in the 1781 *Pennsylvania Journal* by Scottish immigrant John Witherspoon as an adaptation of *Scotticism* and its 1833 (re)migration to the United Kingdom via the *Edinburgh Review*.
15. Twain, *Mark Twain to Mrs. Fairbanks*, 257–58.
16. Howells, "Editor's Study," 319, 320. Henry Nash Smith, *Mark Twain*, 170, saw *Connecticut Yankee* as evidence that Twain had lost "contact with the vernacular affirmations" responsible for "the climax of his achievement in *Huckleberry Finn*," a position he later expanded: "[T]he [vernacular] values embodied in the character of the Yankee are too largely taken for granted," he observed, "and the 'say against monarchy' replaces the imaginative mode of comedy with mere rhetoric" (Smith, *Mark Twain's Fable*, 76). Cox, *Mark Twain*, 219–20, went further, arguing that "Hank's supposed vernacular is not really vernacular at all" because his slang neither displaces genteel values with "a new reality of form and action," as in *Huck*, nor allows Hank enough distance on his predicament to produce a satire. By contrast, Allen Guttmann, "Mark Twain's *CY*," 237, concluded that Twain ultimately "could *not* affirm wholeheartedly the vernacular tradition as embodied in The Boss and his Colt's Arms factory." Critics' own positions on Manifest Destiny affect their evaluations of the novel, as Jennifer O'Neill, "Twain's *CY*," 3, suggests when she observes that Fred Lorch missed Twain's critique of imperialism in *Connecticut Yankee*, despite recognizing its origins in the writer's experience of Hawaii, because of "his own inflexible understanding of missionaries and colonizing forces as nothing but a blessing for feudal Hawaii."
17. Baetzhold, "Well, My Book,'" 69.

18. Driscoll, "'Man Factories.'"
19. Lee, "International Twain"; Howells, "Editor's Study," 321.
20. Custer, *My Life*, 5.
21. Ibid., 64, 65.
22. Sumida, "Reevaluating"; Caron, "Blessings"; Rowe, "How"; Oliver, "New Manifest Destiny"; and O'Neill, "Twain's *CY*," also advance an imperialism thesis.
23. Twain lectured at Mercantile Library Hall in St. Louis on March 25 and 26, 1867. About one thousand attended the first lecture; Stanley transcribed the second, from which the quote is taken (Stanley, "Mark Twain at Mercantile"). Bad weather apparently reduced this second audience to about eighty (*MTL* 2: 19n.2). Kaplan, "Anarchy of Empire," 61, identifies Clemens's meeting with Stanley as part of "an international circle of other travelers and writers, who were serving and selling the rapidly expanding empires to their audiences at home" but Stanley had barely begun his career as a journalist at this point and had not yet left St. Louis to cover the U.S. Army's Plains Indians mission, much less imagined his role in the colonization of Africa. See Wheeler, "H. M. Stanley's Letters."
24. Samuel L. Clemens to Henry Morton Stanley, September 1, 1872, ALS, AS. #2734, Henry M. Stanley Archives, Royal Museum for Central Africa (Tervuren, Belgium); *MTL 5*: 202, 201, includes Clemens's drawing of seating at the head table.
25. In a letter to Stanley as *Connecticut Yankee* came out, Clemens mentions his memories of both lectures, though he introduced Stanley only at the Boston performance (SLC to HMS, December 16, 1889, TLS (copy), #3378, Henry M. Stanley Archives, Royal Museum for Central Africa [Tervuren, Belgium]).
26. Between November 1886 and January 1889 Robert Smith is Hank Smith (Twain, *CY*, Intro, 8n.23).
27. "Remarkable," 4.
28. According to a *New York Times* account of his 1886 lecture, Stanley "surrendered . . . about 400 treaties to King Leopold of Belgium," suggesting that the explorer claimed credit for them ("Stanley's Exploits," 2), but Tim Jeal, *Stanley*, 280–88, 524n.13, argues that Leopold abrogated or destroyed Stanley's treaties and secured others more to his liking via other agents after Stanley wrote him to warn that his treaties left Congolese chiefs in control of the land and that "[t]hey are not subjects—but it is we who are simply tenants."
29. "Stanley in New York," 4
30. Jeal, *Stanley*, 313–31.
31. Rowe, "How," 180, 191n.17; Bierman, *Dark Safari*, 265.
32. Most correspondence between Clemens and Stanley has not been published, although three letters from 1885–86 in *MTBM*, 330, 369, 379, show the men's ongoing relationship. In the summer of 1885, Clemens asked Stanley to guide nephew Charles Webster in negotiating contracts for European translations of Grant's *Memoirs* (SLC to HMS, July 9, 1885, SA. 3243, Henry M. Stanley Archives, Collection King Baudouin Foundation on deposit at the Royal Museum for Central Africa, Tervuren, Belgium). I am grateful to Robert Hirst of the Mark Twain Papers and Project at the Bancroft Library, University of California, Berkeley for copies of unpublished letters to Stanley from Clemens (November 18, 1886, June 18, 1889, November 22, 1889) and Webster (August 15, 1885, December 7, 1886) seeking a book, which Stanley declined in a letter to Clemens dated January 24, 1887. See also Notebook 27, August 1887–July 1888

(*N&J* 3:304); Notebook 28, July 1888–May 1889 (*N&J* 3:438); Notebook 29, May 1889–August 1890 (*N&J* 3:494–95, 551); Notebook 30, August 1890–June 1891 (*N&J* 3:587, 588, 590, 616, 645).

33. Baetzhold, "Well, My Book,'" 53–54.

34. On Twain's response to Arnold's 1882 essay, see Baetzhold, *MTJB*, 110. The 1887 response had an ideal venue, a banquet by the Hartford Army and Navy Club commemorating Grant on his birthday (*MTS*, 225–30). For the notebook commentaries, see *N&J* 3:383–84, 391, 392, 394, 398, 403, 406, 411, 467, 468, 541. Arnold's death in February 1890, after *Connecticut Yankee* appeared, precluded a direct public response by Clemens as unseemly.

35. Arnold, "Civilisation," 488, 489.

36. Editions of Stanley's books listed in *MTLib*, 658–59, postdate *Connecticut Yankee*. I found the inscription to Jervis Langdon, Jr., dated "Jany 26, 1887," the boy's birthday, in the copy in the library at the Clemenses' summer home, Quarry Farm, whose archivist Mark Woodhouse confirmed that family members constantly exchanged books. I have not yet identified who purchased the book or inscribed it, but it joined other tales of exploration among the young man's books. I am grateful to Woodhouse for his generous assistance with this question.

37. "Through," 2; "Stanley's Exploits," 2.

38. See, for example, "Through."

39. "Free," 1.

40. "In the Congo," 14.

41. Newman, *Imperial Footprints*, qtd. 350; Jeal, *Stanley*, 294–95.

42. Jeal, *Stanley*, qtd. 173, 512n.16.

43. Baetzhold, *MTJB*, 108–9.

44. Buell, "American Literary Emergence," 435.

45. Caron, "Blessings."

46. Lee, "From the Sublime."

47. Roth, "Second Dialogue in Israel," 74.

48. Rodgers, "*Great American Novel*," 12.

49. Blair, "'Man's Voice,'" 190.

50. Rothberg, "Roth and the Holocaust," 67n.23.

51. Roth, *Reading Myself and Others*, 89–90. When Roth described this goal, he could not know that historical figures from the Nixon administration (1968–1974), most notably Dick Cheney and Donald Rumsfeld, would return to government thirty years later and apply their resentments against congressional interference with what they perceived as Nixon's proper exercise of presidential powers, especially in wartime, to shape U.S. domestic and international policies in response to the attacks of September 11, 2001. Historical links between the Nixon and Bush administrations provide another reason to see Roth's two novels as a pair.

52. For examples of critics' domestic focus on *The Great American Novel*, see, for example, Ahearn, "'Et in Arcadia'"; Royal, "Fouling"; Ardolino, "Americanization of the Gods"; Daniel, "Philip Roth, MVP"; on *The Plot Against America*, see, for example, Graham, "On the Possibility."

53. Roth, *Reading Myself and Others*, 91.

54. I am indebted to the late Professor Terence Malley of Long Island University–Brooklyn for sharing his knowledge of baseball lore with me.

55. Spurr, *Rhetoric of Empire*, 127–28.
56. Said, *Culture and Imperialism*, 42.
57. Ibid., 29–30.
58. Graham, "On the Possibility," 120.
59. Wirth-Nesher, "Roth's Autobiographical Writings," 171.
60. Roth, *The Dying Animal*, qtd. 60.
61. Roth, "On *GAN*," 91.
62. Posnock, *Philip Roth's Rude Truth*, 268n.6.
63. Royal, "Fouling," 159–60.
64. Roth, "Writing American Fiction," 224, 227.
65. Díaz, *Brief*, 335.

Chapter Four

1. Benjamin, "The Storyteller," 89.
2. Marx, "Vernacular," 8, 3.
3. The phrase comes from Cox, *Mark Twain*, 219; Quirk, *Coming to Grips*, 125.
4. Cox, *Mark Twain*, 176, 168.
5. My coinage does not derive from Buhle, "The Left," 348, who uses the phrase without comment or explanation in the subtitle of a review essay on political comics.
6. Marx, "Vernacular," 8.
7. Webster, who also had the dubious distinction of proposing what we now call an "English only" policy to bind people of different regions and national origins and generate "political harmony" through a nationally uniform language, vacillated between recognizing that language originates and operates as a local phenomenon and urging the adoption of national, uniform standards (Webster, *Dissertations*, 19–20, 26–27). Leonard Tennenhouse, *Importance*, esp. ch. 1–2, discusses the British side of these language debates.
8. The history of "Yankee Doodle" shows that the term *Yankee* began as British scorn for the New Englander's rustic speech, coarse clothing, penny-pinching, and general ignorance of the world. See Blair, *Native American Humor*, 17.
9. Smith, *My Thirty Years*, 10.
10. Marx, "Vernacular," 17, 16.
11. From his name to his dress, Robin personifies the pure, virtuous New England youth at his most sentimental and conventional and thus makes Hawthorne's ridicule clear:

> He was clad in a *coarse gray coat, well worn but in excellent repair*; his under garments were *durably constructed* of leather, and fitted tight to a pair of *serviceable and well-shaped limbs*; his stockings of blue yarn were the *incontrovertible work of a mother or a sister*; and on his head was *a three-cornered hat*, which *in its better days* had *perhaps sheltered* the *graver brow of the lad's father*. Under his arm was a heavy cudgel formed of an *oak sapling*, and retaining a part of the *hardened root*; and his equipment was completed by a wallet, not so abundantly stocked as to incommode the *vigorous shoulders* on which it hung. Brown, curly hair, *well shaped features*, and *bright cheerful eyes* were *nature's gifts*, and worth all that art could have done for his adornment [my italics]. (Hawthorne, "My Kinsman, Major Molineux," 1209–10)

12. Much controversy centers on usage in which *vernacular* refers to language variation among American-born whites while *dialect* refers to American language variation among immigrants and persons of color. (I rebut this argument in detail in "International Twain.") From a technical standpoint, all are dialects, and all colloquial forms are vernaculars.

13. Pollock, "Cosmopolitan and Vernacular," 592.

14. Ahmad, "Introduction: 'This is Ma Trooth,'" 29.

15. Smith, *Mark Twain*, vii, 4. Smith specifically credits Lynn's book on the politics of American humor, though he also cites other humor scholarship. A recent comprehensive bibliography of the frontier tradition is Inge and Piacentino, *The Humor of the Old South* (2001); Justus, *Fetching the Old Southwest* (2004), provides an encyclopedic analysis.

16. Smith, *Mark Twain*, 1–2; Santayana, "Genteel," 40.

17. See, for example, Harris, *Sut Lovingood's Yarns*.

18. Arac, *Huckleberry Finn*, 35.

19. Quirk, *Coming to Grips*, 144.

20. Cox, *Mark Twain*, 176.

21. Kennedy, *Nigger*, qtd. 5. Fishkin, "Mark Twain and Race," contextualizes Twain's usage and its controversies through 2001.

22. Arac, *Huckleberry Finn*, 34.

23. Smith, "Huck, Jim," 108.

24. Ibid., 111.

25. See, for example, Schmitz, "Twain"; and Doyno, *Writing*, 129.

26. Kennedy, *Nigger*, 109.

27. Test, *Satire*, 5.

28. Ellison, "Change," 104.

29. Wallace, "Case."

30. Bell, "Twain's," 138; Jones, "Nigger and Knowledge," 185.

31. Barksdale, "History," 55.

32. See Pornpitakpan, "Persuasiveness."

33. Pratkanis and Gliner, "And When Shall a Little Child Lead Them?," 285, 300; Walster, Aronson, and Abrahams, "On Increasing Persuasiveness," 341; Pornpitakpan, "Persuasiveness," 268.

34. See, for example, Hampes, "The Relationship Between Humor and Trust."

35. Lyttle, "Effectiveness of Humor," 213.

36. Doyno, *Writing*, 246–49.

37. Quirk, *Coming to Grips*, 117, 144.

38. Cox, *Mark Twain*, 170, 219.

39. Bakhtin, *Rabelais and His World*, 182.

40. Ong, *Orality and Literacy*, 42.

41. Samanci, "Lynda Barry's Humor," 185–90; Fishkin, *Lighting Out*, 147–50; Inge, "Mark Twain"; Soper, "From Rowdy," 158.

42. Couch, "The Yellow Kid and the Comic Page," 68.

43. Groening and Solomon, "Screen," 15.

44. Stanley, "Simpsons," 47.

45. Wilson, *Patriotic Gore*, 510.

46. Waters and Buckley, "Family Feuds."

47. "Eat My Shirts"; Kimsley, "Bart for President."

48. Episodes are cited by title, season and episode number, and first broadcast date.

49. Cantor, "The Greatest TV Show Ever."
50. Mittell, "Cartoon Realism," 23. See also, for example, Berkman, "Sitcom Reality," and Gray, "Imagining," 142. Among the most influential arguments about realism in *The Simpsons* are Berlant, "Theory," also rpt. in Berlant, *Queen*; Alberti, *Leaving Springfield*; Pinsky, *Gospel*; Irwin, Conrad, and Skoble, *Simpsons*.
51. Kettman, "Creator."
52. Alberti, "Introduction."
53. Shales, "Groening of America." Groening also credits the opening animated sequence of the short-lived sitcom *Dennis the Menace* (1959–1963), which he remembers as "this Tasmanian devil–like cyclone spinning out. I was so excited that there was an actual menace on television. If I had to go back to the first impetus for *The Simpsons* it would be that night in 1959 when that pilot episode was broadcast and this cyclone of a menace came out. It was a kid! I was so excited. It turned out to be this fairly namby-pamby pseudo–bad boy who had a slingshot but didn't ever seem to use it. Bart Simpson is basically what Dennis should have been." See Groening and Sheff, "Playboy Interview," 145.
54. Owen, "Taking," 70.
55. Turner, *Planet Simpson*, qtd. 26.
56. Alberti, "Introduction," xxi.
57. Wells, *Understanding Animation*, 23.
58. Ibid.
59. See Caron, "Call," on the convention of children's water pranks in American graphic humor.
60. Turner, *Planet Simpson*, 71; Carvell, "The Simpsons Top 25," 31.
61. Cantor, "*The Simpsons*," 738.
62. Spiegelman, *Breakdowns*, Afterword, n.p.
63. See "Barry, Lynda," *Current*, for a reliable summary of her career through the early 1990s.
64. Barry and Dean, "Interview," 34.
65. Nimura, "My."
66. The years 1977, 1979, and 1980 have all been proposed as the start of the strip, which acquired the title *True Comeek* in *Ernie Pook's Comeek* in 1984, long after Barry began the four-panel series as a college student and some four or five years after she began publishing it professionally in *The Chicago Reader*. See "Barry, Lynda," *Current*, 41; "Barry, Lynda," *Notable*.
67. Gilbert, "Four-Panel Epiphanies," 78, 90.
68. Barry and Dean, "Interview," 41.
69. Samanci, "Lynda Barry's Humor," 185–87.
70. De Jesus, "Of Monsters," 15–17.
71. Spiegelman, *Breakdowns*, Afterword, n.p; Marx, "Vernacular," 8.
72. Statistics from Sony Pictures, "About the Show," *The Boondocks* Official Site, accessed March 8, 2011; McGrath, "Radical."

The Boondocks strip won a 2002 N.A.A.C.P. Chairman's Award; the cartoon won a 2005 N.A.A.C.P. Image Award for Outstanding Comedy Series and a 2007 Peabody Award for "Return of the King," an episode imagining Martin Luther King's dismay over the debasement of contemporary American culture manifested in phenomena ranging from gangsta rap to the war on terror. The *Atlanta Constitution* moved *The Boondocks* to the editorial page before the comic was three months old; other papers, including the *New York Daily News* and *Washington Post*, refused to publish strips they found offensive. See Croal and Pan, "What's the Color of Funny?," 59; Blair, "Media"; Hoad, "Talk of the Toon"; Tucker, "Like."

73. Rambsy, "Shine"; Farred, *What's My Name?*, 11.
74. McGruder comes down hard on all adults.
75. Rambsy, "Vengeance," 651; Rambsy, "Shine," 147.
76. For details on African American and other iterations of vernacular literary humor, see my "From the Sublime." Hughes's Semple stories are collected in *Simple Speaks His Mind* (1950) and other volumes.
77. Hoad, "Talk of the Toon."
78. Harvey and McGruder, "Encountering," 165.
79. Ibid., 166.
80. McGrath, "Radical," 160; Tucker, "Like."
81. McGrath, "Radical," qtd. 160.
82. Ibid., 160; Hoad, "Talk of the Toon."
83. Pozner, "On My Bookshelf"; Flynn, "Boondocks' Candor is Needed"; Jordan, "Huey."
84. Harvey and McGruder, "Encountering," qtd. 157, 163.
85. Hilmes, "Fanny," qtd. 15.
86. Hilmes, "Fanny," 16.
87. Quirk, *Coming to Grips*, 116.
88. Bolter and Grusin, *Remediation*, 65.

Chapter 5

1. Limon, *Stand-Up*, 79.
2. Kaplan, "Anarchy of Empire," 51–52.
3. Editors at the Mark Twain Project date this style of advertising pamphlet, with a spot for the sales agent's name, to 1877. The comic text reproduces a September 1876 letter to Daniel Slote, whose firm manufactured the scrapbook and who probably released a copy of the letter to the New York *Herald*, which published it on December 11. See SLC to Daniel Slote, 11 Sept.? 1876, http://www.marktwainproject.org/xtf/view?docId=letters/UCCL11146.xml;style=letter;brand=mtp. I am deeply grateful to Kevin Mac Donnell for his generosity in sharing his remarkable collection of Twain-branded artifacts and sales materials with me, and for providing the images reproduced here.
4. Camfield, *Oxford Companion*, qtd. 642.
5. Brymer, "What Makes Brands Great," 68.
6. Patinkin, *Second City*, passim.
7. Ibid., xii–xv, 178–79.
8. Second City Communications, "Who We Are."
9. Second City Network, "About Us."
10. Patinkin, *Second City*, xi–xiii.
11. Huizinga, *Homo Ludens*, 7.
12. Brymer, "What Makes Brands Great," 70.
13. Rexrode, "UF Theater."

14. Twitchell, *Branded*, 13.
15. Steptoe, "Building."
16. "Disney," C4.
17. Caswell, "Charles M. Schulz and *Peanuts*," 9.
18. "Changes: Jacko Bankrupt?," 14.
19. "CKX Punches up $50 Million Deal for Ali Licensing."
20. Dale and Tritsch, *Simpson Mania*, 30.
21. Ibid., 31; "Lifestyle."
22. Shales, "Groening of America."
23. Stanley, "The Simpsons and BK"; Wilensky, "103 Leading Licensing Companies," 20; "Top."
24. Steinberg, "Simon."
25. Atkinson, "What?," C4.
26. Nash Information Services, "Top-Grossing Genres 1995 to 2011."
27. Lee, *Defining New Yorker Humor*, 13.
28. Fleishman, "New Yorker Cartoons Go on Line." Fleishman reports that the *New Yorker* originally lacked interest in Mankoff's Cartoon Bank because its policy of turning over all resale revenue to cartoonists deprived it of a pecuniary interest in these royalties.
29. Bagdikian, "Wrong," 52.
30. Mahon, *Last*, 327, 325.
31. Barnes and Cieply, "Disney," B1; McClusky, "Free Spidey!," 36.
32. Marriott, "For One," C8; Gustines, "Escape," C5.
33. Freierman, "Most Wanted."
34. "Expanding TV's Impact"; Dana, "Cut," 44.
35. Viacom, "2nd Quarter '06," 6.
36. Comedy Central, "Milestones"; "Expanding TV's Impact"; Johnson, "Paramount Shifts," 6; Scott, "We'll Always Have Springfield," B15.
37. Flint, "Comedy," B3.
38. Comedy Central, "AOL's 50 Per Cent"; Comedy Central, "Stop Us."
39. Shields, "Comedy Central"; Flint, "Comedy," B3; "Comedy Plans Series for Cellphones."
40. Flint, "Comedy," B3.
41. Flamm, "Jon Stewart."
42. Goetz, "The TV of Tomorrow," 105.
43. Cornfield, "'The Daily Show' Revolution."
44. Ibid.
45. Pew Internet and American Life Project, *Perceptions of Partisan Bias*.
46. Pinsker, "Tradition," 93.
47. Ong, *Orality and Literacy*; Eisenstein, *The Printing Press*; McLuhan, *Understanding Media*.
48. Zipkin, "Stores," B8.
49. Barbaro, "Buying."
50. Jameson, "Postmodernism," 87.
51. Ong, *Orality and Literacy*; McLuhan, *Understanding Media*; Bolter and Grusin, *Remediation*.
52. Mattson, "Perils."
53. Jameson, *Postmodernism*, 275.

Bibliography

ACLU of Southern California. "ACLU/SC Honors Civil Liberties Advocates at Annual Garden Party." Http://www.aclu-sc.org/releases/view/100755.

Ahearn, Kerry. "'Et in Arcadia Excrementum': Pastoral, Kitsch, and Philip Roth's *The Great American Novel.*" *Aethlon: The Journal of Sport Literature* 11, no. 1 (Fall 1993): 1–14.

Ahmad, Dohra. "Introduction: 'This is Ma Trooth.'" In *Rotten English: A Literary Anthology*, edited by Dohra Ahmad, 15–32. New York: W. W. Norton & Company, 2007.

Alberti, John. "Introduction." In *Leaving Springfield: The Simpsons and the Possibility of Oppositional Culture*, edited by John Alberti. Contemporary Approaches to Film and Television, xi–xxxii. Detroit: Wayne State University Press, 2004.

———, ed. *Leaving Springfield: The Simpsons and the Possibility of Oppositional Culture*. Contemporary Approaches to Film and Television. Detroit: Wayne State University Press, 2004.

Anderson, Benedict R. O'G. *Imagined Communities: Reflections on the Origin and Spread of Nationalism*. London; New York: Verso, 1991.

Annenberg Public Policy Center. *Daily Show Viewers Knowledgeable About Presidential Campaign, National Annenberg Election Survey Shows*. NAES 04: National Annenberg Election Survey, 2004. Http://www.annenbergpublicpolicycenter.org/naes/2004_03_late-night-knowledge-2_9-21_pr.pdf.

Applebee, Arthur N. "Stability and Change in the High-School Canon." *English Journal* 81, no. 5 (September 1992): 27–32.

Arac, Jonathan. *Huckleberry Finn as Idol and Target*. Madison: University of Wisconsin Press, 1997.

Ardolino, Frank R. "The Americanization of the Gods: Onomastics, Myth, and History in Philip Roth's *The Great American Novel.*" *Arete* 3, no. 1 (Fall 1985): 37–60.

Arnold, David. *The Handbook of Brand Management*. International Management Series. Reading, MA: Addison-Wesley, The Economist Books, 1992.

Arnold, Matthew. "Civilisation in the United States." *The Nineteenth Century*, no. 134 (April 1888): 481–96.

Atkinson, Claire. "What to Watch? How About a 'Simpsons' Episode from 1999?" *New York Times*, 24 September 2007, C4.

Baetzhold, Howard G. *Mark Twain and John Bull: The British Connection*. Bloomington: Indiana University Press, 1970.

———. "'Well, My Book Is Written—Let It Go . . .': The Making of *A Connecticut Yankee in King Arthur's Court.*" In *Biographies of Books: The Compositional Histories of*

Notable American Writings, edited by James Barbour and Tom Quirk, 41–77. Columbia: University of Missouri Press, 1996.

Bagdikian, Ben H. "The Wrong Kind of Readers: The Fall and Rise of *The New Yorker*." *Progressive* 47, no. 5 (May 1983): 52–54.

Bakhtin, Mikhail. *Rabelais and His World*. Translated by Helene Iswolsky. 1965. Bloomington: Indiana University Press, 1984.

Barbaro, Michael. "Buying a Trump Property, or So They Thought." *New York Times*, 13 May 2011, A1, A23.

Barksdale, Richard K. "History, Slavery, and Thematic Irony in *Huckleberry Finn*." In *Satire or Evasion? Black Perspectives on* Huckleberry Finn, edited by James S. Leonard, Thomas A. Tenney, and Thadious M. Davis, 49–55. Durham: Duke University Press, 1992.

Barnes, Brooks, and Michael Cieply. "Disney Swoops Into Action, Buying Marvel for $4 Billion." *New York Times*, 1 September 2009, B1, B7.

Barry, Lynda. *Cruddy: An Illustrated Novel*. New York: Simon & Schuster, 1999.

———. *One! Hundred! Demons*! Seattle [Berkeley, Calif.]: Sasquatch Books Distributed by Publishers Group West, 2002.

"Barry, Lynda." *Current Biography Yearbook* 55, no. 11 (November 1994): 40–44.

"Barry, Lynda." In *Notable Asian Americans*. Gale Biography in Context. New York: Gale, 1995.

Barry, Lynda, and Michael Dean. "An Interview with Lynda Barry." *Comics Journal*, no. 296 (February 2009): 34–46.

Bell, Bernard W. "Twain's 'Nigger' Jim: The Tragic Face Behind the Minstrel Mask." In *Satire or Evasion? Black Perspectives on* Huckleberry Finn, edited by James S. Leonard, Thomas A. Tenney, and Thadious M. Davis, 124–40. Durham: Duke University Press, 1992.

Benjamin, Walter. "The Storyteller: Reflections on the Works of Nikolai Leskov." In *Illuminations*, edited and introduction by Hannah Arendt, translated by Harry Zohn, 83–109. New York: Schocken Books, 1969.

Bennett, Drake. "The Doltish Dozen." *Boston Globe*, 5 February 2006, E1.

Berkman, Dave. "Sitcom Reality." *Television Quarterly* 26 no. 4 (1993): 63–69.

Berkove, Lawrence I. "Nevada Influences on Mark Twain." In *A Companion to Mark Twain*, edited by Peter Messent and Louis J. Budd, 157–71. Malden, MA: Blackwell, 2005.

———. *The Sagebrush Anthology: Literature from the Silver Age of the Old West*. Columbia: University of Missouri Press, 2006.

Berlant, Lauren. *The Queen of America Goes to Washington City*. Durham: Duke University Press, 1997.

———. "The Theory of Infantile Citizenship." *Public Culture: Bulletin of the Society for Transnational Cultural Studies* 5, no. 3 (Spring 1993): 395–410.

Bernt, Joseph P., Joseph Csicsila, Patrick S. Washburn, and Edward S. Watts. "Literature." In *The Midwest*, edited by Joseph W. Slade and Judith Yaross Lee, 349–95. Greenwood Encyclopedia of American Regional Cultures. Westport, CT: Greenwood Press, 2004.

Bierman, John. *Dark Safari: The Life Behind the Legend of Henry Morton Stanley*. New York: Knopf, 1990.

Blackett, Tom. "What Is a Brand?" In *Brands and Branding*, edited by Rita Clifton, John Simmons, and Sameena Ahmad, 13–25. The Economist Series. Princeton, NJ: Bloomberg Press, 2004. Rpt. http://www.interbrand.com.

Blair, Jayson. "Media: Some Comic Strips Take an Unpopular Look at U.S." *New York Times*, 22 October 2001, Bus. 9.
Blair, Walter. "'A Man's Voice, Speaking': A Continuum in American Humor." In *Veins of Humor*, edited by Harry Levin, 185–204, Harvard English Studies, vol. 3. Cambridge, MA: Harvard University Press, 1972.
———. *Native American Humor*. 2nd ed. Scranton, PA: Chandler Publishing Company, 1960.
Blount, Roy, Jr. "America's Original Superstar." *Time* 172, no. 2 (14 July 2008): 46–53.
Bolter, Jay David, and Richard Grusin. *Remediation: Understanding New Media*. Cambridge, MA: MIT Press, 1999.
Boorstin, Daniel J. *The Americans: The Democratic Experience*. New York: Random House, 1973.
———. *The Image: A Guide to Pseudo-Events in America*. 1962. New York; Evanston: Harper & Row, Harper Colophon, 1964.
Boselovic, Len. "Workplace Safety Not Always Easy to Measure." *Pittsburgh Post-Gazette*, 8 January 2006, A14.
Branch, Edgar M. "'The Babes in the Wood': Artemus Ward's 'Double Health' to Mark Twain." *PMLA* 93, no. 5 (October 1978): 955–72.
Bruce, Lenny. *The Lenny Bruce Performance Film*. 1965. Santa Monica, CA: Rhino Home Video, 1992. Videocassette.
Brymer, Chuck. "What Makes Brands Great." In *Brands and Branding*, edited by Rita Clifton and John Simmons, 65–76. The Economist Series, Princeton, NJ: Bloomberg Press, 2004.
Budd, Louis J. "Been There, Done That (Not): Stalking Mark Twain." In *Mark Twain Among the Scholars: Reconsidering Contemporary Twain Criticism*, edited by Richard Hill and Jim McWilliams. Albany, NY: Whitson Publishing, 2002.
———. "Interviews." In *The Mark Twain Encyclopedia*, edited by J. R. LeMaster and James D. Wilson, 401–3. New York: Garland, 1993.
———. *Our Mark Twain: The Making of His Public Personality*. Philadelphia: University of Pennsylvania Press, 1983.
———. "'A Talent for Posturing': The Achievement of Mark Twain's Public Personality." In *The Mythologizing of Mark Twain*, edited by Sara deSaussure Davis and Philip D. Beidler, 77–99, 167–68. University: University of Alabama Press, 1984.
Buell, Lawrence. "American Literary Emergence as a Postcolonial Phenomenon." *American Literary History* 4, no. 3 (Fall 1992): 411–42.
Buhle, Paul. "The Left in American Comics: Rethinking the Visual Vernacular." *Science & Society* 71, no. 3 (July 2007): 348–56.
Bureau of Economic Analysis. "Table 1.1.5, Gross Domestic Product." *National Income and Product Accounts Tables*. U. S. Department of Commerce, 2011. Http://www.bea.gov/iTable/iTable.cfm?ReqID=9&step=1.
Bureau of Statistics, U. S. Department of Commerce and Labor. "Progress of the United States in Its Area, Population and Material Industries, December, 1909." Table in *Monthly Summary of Commerce and Finance of the United States*. Washington, DC: U. S. Government Printing Office, 1910.
Bureau of the Census. *Historical Statistics of the United States, Colonial Times to 1970*. Bicentennial ed. Washington, DC: U. S. Department of Commerce, 1975.
Burke, Kenneth. "Poetic Categories." In *Attitudes Toward History*, 34–75. 1937. 3rd ed. with a new afterword. Berkeley: University of California Press, 1984.

Burns, Ken, director. *Mark Twain*. Alexandria, VA, and Hollywood: PBS and Paramount Home Entertainment, 2004. Videocassette.

Bushman, David. "The Stand-up Comedian on Television." In *Stand-up Comedians on Television*, 18–49. New York: Abrams [in association with] The Museum of Television & Radio, 1996.

Camfield, Gregg, ed. *The Oxford Companion to Mark Twain*. New York: Oxford University Press, 2003.

Cantor, Paul A. "The Greatest TV Show Ever." *American Enterprise* 8, no. 5 (September–October 1997): 34.

———. "*The Simpsons*: Atomistic Politics and the Nuclear Family." *Political Theory* 27, no. 6 (December 1999): 734–49.

Caron, James E. "The Blessings of Civilization: Mark Twain's Anti-Imperialism and the Annexation of the Hawai'ian Islands." *Mark Twain Annual*, no. 6 (2008): 51–64.

———. "A Call from the Wild: Tigers, Monsters, and Other Beastly Fantasies in *Calvin and Hobbes*." *Inks: Cartoon and Comic Art Studies* 4, no. 1 (February 1997): 2–19.

———. "From Ethology to Aesthetics: Evolution as a Theoretical Paradigm for Research on Laughter, Humor, and Other Comic Phenomena." *Humor: International Journal of Humor Research* 15, no. 3 (2002): 245–81.

———. *Mark Twain: Unsanctified Newspaper Reporter*. Mark Twain and His Circle Series. Columbia: University of Missouri Press, 2008.

———. "The Satirist Who Clowns: Mark Twain's Performance at the Whittier Birthday Celebration." *Texas Studies in Literature & Language* 52, no. 4 (Winter 2010): 433–66.

Carton, Evan. "Speech Acts and Social Action: Mark Twain and the Politics of Literary Performance." In *The Cambridge Companion to Mark Twain*, edited by Forrest G. Robinson, 153–74. New York: Cambridge University Press, 1995.

Carvell, Tim, et al. "The Simpsons Top 25." *Entertainment Weekly*, no. 694 (7 February 2003): 31–35.

Caswell, Lucy Shelton. "Charles M. Schulz and *Peanuts*." In *Peanuts*. Exhibit catalog, edited by Lucy Shelton Caswell, 9–33. Columbus: Ohio State University Cartoon Research Library, 2000.

Cawelti, John. *Apostles of the Self-Made Man*. Chicago: University of Chicago Press, 1964.

Celayo, Armando, David Shook, and Junot Díaz. "In Darkness We Meet: A Conversation with Junot Díaz." *World Literature Today* 82, no. 2 (March/April 2008): 14–19.

Chabon, Michael. *The Amazing Adventures of Kavalier and Clay: A Novel*. New York: Random House, 2000.

"Changes: Jacko Bankrupt?" *Rolling Stone*, 4 May 2006, 14.

Chaucer, Geoffrey. *Works*. 2d ed. Edited by F. N. Robinson. Boston: Houghton Mifflin, 1961.

"CKX Punches up $50 Million Deal for Ali Licensing." *Wall Street Journal*, 12 April 2006, A8.

Cho, Margaret. *Assassin*. Port Washington, NY: Koch Vision, 2005. DVD.

———. *I'm the One That I Want*. 2000. Fox Lorber, 2001. DVD.

———. *I'm the One That I Want*. New York: Ballantine, 2001. Book.

———. *Margaret Cho: Beautiful*. Directed by Lorene Machado. Image Entertainment, 2009. DVD.

———. *Notorious C.H.O.: Margaret Cho Filmed Live in Concert.* Wellspring Media, 2002. DVD.

———. *Revolution.* Filmed live at the Wiltern Theatre, Los Angeles, May 2–3, 2003. New York: Wellspring, 2004. DVD.

Clark, Kevin A. *Brandscendence: Three Essential Elements of Enduring Brands.* Chicago: Dearborn Trade Publishing, 2004.

Clemens, Samuel L. Letter to Henry Morton Stanley, 1 September 1872, ALS, AS. #2734, Henry M. Stanley Archives. Collection King Baudouin Foundation on Deposit at the Royal Museum for Central Africa, Tervuren, Belgium.

———. Letter to Henry Morton Stanley, 9 July 1885. SA. 3243. Henry M. Stanley Archives. Collection King Baudouin Foundation on Deposit at the RMCA Tervuren. Royal Museum for Central Africa, Tervuren, Belgium.

———. Letter to Henry Morton Stanley, 16 December 1889. SA. 3378. Henry M. Stanley Archives. Collection King Baudouin Foundation on Deposit at the Royal Museum for Central Africa,Tervuren, Belgium.

Clifton, Rita, and John Simmons, eds. With Sameena Ahmad and Tony Allen. *Brands and Branding.* The Economist Series. Princeton, NJ: Bloomberg Press, 2004.

Cole, Teresa Levonian. "The Best of Mauritius." *Daily Telegraph* (London), 22 January 2006, travel section, 6.

Comedy Central. "AOL's 50 Per Cent Interest in Comedy Central Sold for $1.225 Billion." *Comedy Central,* 20 October 2006. Http://www.comedycentral.com/press/bios /index.jhtml?pg=milestones.

———. "Milestones." *Comedy Central,* 20 October 2006. Http://www.comedycentral. com/press/bios/index.jhtml?pg=milestones.

———. "Stop Us If You've Heard This One Before . . . Comedy Central Names Doug Herzog as New President." *Comedy Central,* 16 March 2004. Http://www.comedycentral .com/press/press_releases/2004/031604_dougherzog_hiredpresident.jhtml.

"Comedy Plans Series for Cellphones." *Broadcasting & Cable* 136, no. 9 (27 February 2006): 28.

Cornfield, Michael. "'The Daily Show' Revolution." *Campaigns and Elections* 26, no. 8 (September 2005): 34.

Couch, N. C. Christopher. "The Yellow Kid and the Comic Page." In *The Language of Comics: Word and Image,* edited by Robin Varnum and Christian T. Gibbons, 60–74. Jackson: University Press of Mississippi, 2001.

Cox, James M. *Mark Twain: The Fate of Humor.* 1966. Columbia: University of Missouri Press, 2002.

Critchley, Simon. *On Humour.* London; New York: Routledge, 2002.

Croal, N'Gai, and Esther Pan. "What's the Color of Funny?" *Newsweek* 134, no. 1 (5 July 1999): 59.

Cummings, Sherwood. *Mark Twain and Science: Adventures of a Mind.* Baton Rouge: Louisiana State University Press, 1988.

Custer, (Gen.) George A. *My Life on the Plains.* New York: Sheldon and Co., 1874.

Dale, Steve, and Shane Tritsch. *Simpson Mania: The History of TV's First Family.* Lincolnwood, IL: Publications International, 1990.

Dana, Rebecca. "Cut the Music! MTV$_2$ Drops Vids for Frat-Boy-Targeted Humor." *Rolling Stone,* 10 August 2006, 44.

Daniel, Anne Margaret. "Philip Roth, MVP: *Our Gang, The Breast,* and *The Great American Novel*." In *Philip Roth: New Perspectives on an American Author,* edited by Derek Parker Royal, 59–74. Westport, CT: Praeger, 2005.

De Jesus, Melinda Luisa. "Of Monsters and Mothers: Filipina American Identity and Maternal Legacies in Lynda J. Barry's *One Hundred Demons*." *Meridians: Feminism, Race, Transnationalism* 5, no. 1 (2004): 1–26.

De Quille, Dan. "Reporting with Mark Twain." *California Illustrated Magazine* 4, no. 2 (July 1893): 170–78.

DeVoto, Bernard. "The Lineage of Eustace Tilley." Review of *Native American Humor,* edited and introduction by Walter Blair. *Saturday Review of Literature* 16 (25 September 1937): 3–4, 20.

Díaz, Junot. *The Brief Wondrous Life of Oscar Wao.* New York: Riverhead Books, 2007.

Dinkelspiel, Frances. "With Twain a Bestseller, UC Press' Withey Steps Down." *Berkeleyside: Berkeley, CA's Independent News Site,* 20 December 2010. Http://www.berkeleyside.com/2010/12/20/with-twain-a-bestseller-ucpress-withey-steps-down/.

"Disney Tolerates a Rap Parody of Its Critters. But Why?" *New York Times,* 24 September 2007, C4.

"The Dinner at Delmonico's in Honor of Mark Twain's Seventieth Birthday." *Harper's Weekly* 49 (23 December 1905): 1884–1912.

Dolby-Stahl, Sandra, ed. and intro. "The Personal Narrative in Literature." *Western Folklore* 51, no. 1 (January 1992): 1–107.

Doyno, Victor A. *Writing Huck Finn: Mark Twain's Creative Process.* 1991. Philadelphia: University of Pennsylvania Press, 1993.

Driscoll, Kerry. "'Man Factories' and the 'White Indians' of Camelot: Re-Reading the Native Subtext of *A Connecticut Yankee in King Arthur's Court*." *Mark Twain Annual* 2 (2004): 7–24.

"Eat My Shirts! Pesky Bart Simpson Tees Off a California Principle—and Gets Kicked Out of School." *People* 33, no. 20 (21 May 1990): 130.

"Editorial: Brands and Our Times." *Brand Management* 9, no. 3 (January 2002): 157–61.

Eisenstein, Elizabeth R. *The Printing Press as an Agent of Social Change: Communication and Cultural Transformation in Early Modern Europe.* 2 vols. New York: Cambridge University Press, 1979.

Ellison, Ralph. "Change the Joke and Slip the Yoke." 1964. In *The Collected Essays of Ralph Ellison,* edited by John F. Callahan, with a preface by Saul Bellow. 100–12. New York: Random House, 1995.

Emerson, Everett. "The Strange Disappearance of Mark Twain." *Studies in American Fiction* 13, no. 2 (Autumn 1985): 143–55.

"Expanding TV's Impact." *New York Times,* 8 May 2006, TVupfront 2.0, ZS4.

Farred, Grant. *What's My Name?: Black Vernacular Intellectuals.* Minneapolis: University of Minnesota Press, 2003.

Fatout, Paul. *Mark Twain on the Lecture Circuit.* Bloomington: Indiana University Press, 1960.

Fedo, Michael. *The Man from Lake Wobegon.* New York: St. Martin's, 1987.

Fishkin, Shelley Fisher. *Lighting Out for the Territory: Reflections on Mark Twain and American Culture.* New York: Oxford University Press, 1997.

———. "Mark Twain and Race." In *A Historical Guide to Mark Twain,* edited by Shelley Fisher Fishkin, 127–62. New York: Oxford University Press, 2002.

Flamm, Matthew. "Jon Stewart Builds an Empire on Comedy Central." *New York Business.Com*, 14 November 2005. Http://www.newyorkbusiness.com/news/cms?id=12265.
Fleishman, Glenn. "New Yorker Cartoons Go on Line." *New York Times*, 29 October 1998, G10.
Flint, Joe. "Comedy Central Corners the Laughs Business." *Wall Street Journal*, 8 May 2006, B1,3.
Flynn, Richard. "Boondocks' Candor Is Needed." Letter to the editor. *St. Petersburg Times* (Florida), 16 January 2005, 2P.
Foer, Jonathan Safran. *Everything Is Illuminated: A Novel*. Boston: Houghton Mifflin Co., 2002.
Foner, Philip S. *Mark Twain, Social Critic*. 2d ed. 1958. New York: International Publishers, 1966.
Fox, Bette-Lee, and Linda Frederiksen. "Video Reviews (*Notorious C.H.O.*)." *Library Journal* 128, no. 1 (1 January 2003): 177.
Frear, Walter Francis. *Mark Twain and Hawaii*. Chicago: Lakeside Press, 1947.
"Free State of Congo. Stanley's African State Does Not Seem to 'Go.'" *The News* (Frederick, MD), 11 December 1886, 1.
Freud, Sigmund. "'Humour.'" 1928. In *Character and Culture*, with an introduction by Philip Rieff, 263–69. New York: Collier, 1963.
——. *Jokes and Their Relation to the Unconscious*. Edited and translated by James Strachey. 1905. New York: W. W. Norton, 1963.
Freierman, Shelly. "Most Wanted: Popular Demand, Television on DVD." *New York Times*, 8 May 2006, C7.
Gates, Henry Louis, Jr. *The Signifying Monkey: A Theory of Afro-American Literary Criticism*. New York: Oxford University Press, 1988.
Gaudet, Marcia. "Telling It Slant: Personal Narrative, Tall Tales, and the Reality of Leprosy." *Western Folklore* 49, no. 2 (April 1990): 191–207.
Gerber, John C. "Mark Twain's Use of the Comic Pose." *PMLA* 77, no. 3 (June 1962): 297–304.
Gilbert, Joanne R. *Performing Marginality: Humor, Gender, and Cultural Critique*. Detroit: Wayne State University Press, 2004.
Gilbert, Roger. "Four-Panel Epiphanies: The Art of Lynda Barry." *Northwest Review* 34, no. 1 (1996): 78–108.
Gillman, Susan. *Dark Twins: Imposture and Identity in Mark Twain's America*. Chicago: University of Chicago Press, 1989.
Glass, Loren. "Trademark Twain." *American Literary History* 13, no. 4 (Winter 2001): 671–93.
Goetz, Thomas. "The TV of Tomorrow." *Wired*, September 2005, 102–5.
Goffman, Erving. *The Presentation of Self in Everyday Life*. New York: Anchor, 1959.
Goldberg, Whoopi. *Whoopi Goldberg: Direct from Broadway*. DVD. 1985. HBO video, 2005.
Graham, T. Austin. "On the Possibility of an American Holocaust: Philip Roth's *The Plot Against America*." *Arizona Quarterly: A Journal of American Literature, Culture, and Theory* 63, no. 3 (Autumn 2007): 119–49.
Gray, Jonathan. "Imagining America: *The Simpsons* Go Global." *Popular Communication* 5, no. 2 (2007): 129–48.
Gribben, Alan. "Autobiography as Property." In *The Mythologizing of Mark Twain*, edited by Sara deSaussure Davis and Philip D. Beidler, 39–55. University: University of Alabama Press, 1984.

———. "Mark Twain, Business Man: The Margins of Profit." *Studies in American Humor* n.s., 1, no. 1 (June 1982): 24–43.

———. *Mark Twain's Library: A Reconstruction.* 2 vols. Boston: G. K. Hall, 1980.

Groening, Matt, and David Sheff. "Playboy Interview: Matt Groening." *Playboy* 54, no. 6 (June 2007): 57–60, 145–46.

Groening, Matt, and Deborah Solomon. "Screen Dreams." *New York Times Magazine*, 22 July 2007, 15.

Gustines, George Gene. "An Escape from the Slush Pile: A Web Site Tries Out New Comics." *New York Times*, 9 July 2007, C5.

Guttmann, Allen. "Mark Twain's *Connecticut Yankee*: Affirmation of the Vernacular Tradition?" *New England Quarterly: A Historical Review of New England Life and Letters* 33, no. 2 (June 1960): 232–37.

Hampes, William P. "The Relationship Between Humor and Trust." *Humor: International Journal of Humor Research* 12, no. 3 (1999): 253–60.

Harris, George Washington. *Sut Lovingood's Yarns.* Edited by M. Thomas Inge. New Haven: College & University Press, 1966.

Hartman Center for Sales, Advertising, and Marketing History. "Timeline." *Emergence of Advertising in America, 1850–1920.* Http://scriptorium.lib.duke.edu/eaa/timeline.html.

Harvey, Robert C., and Aaron McGruder. "Encountering Aaron McGruder." In *All the Rage:* The Boondocks *Past and Present*, by Aaron McGruder. 2003, 157–72. New York: Three Rivers Press, 2007.

Hawthorne, Nathaniel. "My Kinsman, Major Molineux." 1832. In *The Complete Novels and Selected Tales of Nathaniel Hawthorne*, edited by Norman Holmes Pearson. 1209–23. New York: Modern Library, 1937.

Hemingway, Ernest. *The Green Hills of Africa.* 1935. In *The Hemingway Reader*, edited by Charles Poore. 453–75. New York: Charles Scribner's Sons, 1966.

Henderson, Archibald. *Mark Twain.* Photographs by Alvin Langdon Coburn. 1911. New York: Frederick A. Stokes Co., 1912. Http://www.gutenberg.org/files/6873/6873-h/6873-h.htm.

Hilmes, Michelle. "Fanny Brice and the 'Schnooks' Strategy: Negotiating a Feminine Comic Persona on the Air." *Spectator: The University of Southern California Journal of Film and Television* 25, no. 2 (Fall 2005): 11–25.

Hilton, Steve. "The Social Value of Brands." In *Brands and Branding*, edited by Rita Clifton and John Simmons, 47–64. The Economist Series. Princeton, NJ: Bloomberg Press, 2004.

Hoad, Phil. "Talk of the Toon." *The Observer (London) Magazine*, 31 October 2004, 32+.

Holt, Douglas B. *How Brands Become Icons: The Principles of Cultural Branding.* Boston: Harvard Business School Press, 2004.

House, Edward H. "Mark Twain as a Lecturer." *New York Tribune*, 11 May 1867. *Mark Twain in His Times*, edited by Stephen Railton. Http://etext.lib.virginia.edu/railton/onstage/houserev.html.

Howells, William Dean. "Editor's Study: Mark Twain's New Wonderful Book [rev. of *Connecticut Yankee*]." *Harper's* 80 (December 1889): 319–21.

Hughes, Langston. *Simple Speaks His Mind.* [New York]: Simon and Schuster, 1950.

Huizinga, Johan. *Homo Ludens.* 1944. Boston: Beacon Press, 1955.

Hutton, C. "The Scholarly Mark Twain Edition." Http://www.Amazon.Com/Autobiography-Mark-Twain-Vol-1/Dp/0520267192/Ref=Sr_1_1?Ie=UTF8&Qid=1304617763&Sr=8–1 (accessed 21 October 2010).
"In the Congo Free State. Henry M. Stanley's Idea of Its Future Trade." *New York Times*, 28 November 1886, 14.
Inge, M. Thomas. "Mark Twain, Chuck Jones, and the Art of Animation." *Studies in American Humor* n.s. 3, no. 17 (2008): 11–17.
Inge, M. Thomas, and Dennis Hall, eds. *Greenwood Guide to American Popular Culture*. Westport, CT: Greenwood Press, 2002.
Inge, M. Thomas, and Edward J. Piacentino, eds. *The Humor of the Old South*. Lexington: University Press of Kentucky, 2001.
Irwin, William, Mark Conrad, and Aeon J. Skoble. *The Simpsons and Philosophy: The d'Oh! of Homer*. Popular Culture and Philosophy. Chicago: Open Court, 2001.
James, William. *The Principles of Psychology*. 2 vols. London: Macmillan, 1891.
———. "Remarks on Spencer's Definition of Mind as Correspondence." *Journal of Speculative Philosophy* 12, no. 1 (January 1878): 1–18.
Jameson, Fredric. "Postmodernism, or the Cultural Logic of Late Capitalism." *New Left Review*, no. 146 (July–August 1984): 53–92.
———. *Postmodernism, or, the Cultural Logic of Late Capitalism*. Post-Contemporary Interventions. Durham: Duke University Press, 1991.
Jeal, Tim. *Stanley: The Impossible Life of Africa's Greatest Explorer*. New Haven: Yale University Press, 2007.
Johnson, Nan. *Nineteenth-Century Rhetoric in North America*. Carbondale: Southern Illinois University Press, 1991.
Johnson, Sarah. "Paramount Shifts to Central Brand." *Marketing*, 4 March 2009, 6.
Jones, Rhett S. "Nigger and Knowledge: White Double-Consciousness in *Adventures of Huckleberry Finn*." In *Satire or Evasion? Black Perspectives on* Huckleberry Finn, edited by James S. Leonard, Thomas A. Tenney, and Thadious M. Davis, 173–94. Durham: Duke University Press, 1992.
Jong, Erica. "Introduction: 'Deliberate Lewdness' and the Lure of Immortality." In *1601, and Is Shakespeare Dead?*, edited by Shelley Fisher Fishkin, xxxi–xlii. New York: Oxford University Press, 1996.
Jordan, Jennifer A. "Huey and Riley in *The Boondocks*: Sometimes I Feel Like a Womanless Child." In *African American Humor, Irony, and Satire: Ishmael Reed, Satirically Speaking*, edited by Dana A. Williams, 131–43. Newcastle, UK: Cambridge Scholars Pub., 2007.
Justus, James H. *Fetching the Old Southwest: Humorous Writing from Longstreet to Twain*. Columbia: University of Missouri Press, 2004.
Kaplan, Amy. "The Imperial Routes of Mark Twain." In *The Anarchy of Empire in the Making of U.S. Culture*, 52–91, 223–26. Cambridge, Mass: Harvard University Press, 2002.
Kaplan, Fred. *The Singular Mark Twain: A Biography*. New York: Doubleday, 2003.
Keepnews, Peter. "There Was Thought in His Rages [Lenny Bruce]." *New York Times*, 8 August 1999, Arts 27.
Keillor, Garrison. *Leaving Home: A Collection of Lake Wobegon Stories*. New York: Viking, 1987.

———. "The Perils of Success." In *Farewell to A Prairie Home Companion*, edited by Daniel Kelly, 100–104. St. Paul: Minnesota Public Radio, 1987.

———. *Pilgrims: A Wobegon Romance*. New York: Viking, 2009.

———. *Ten Years on the Prairie: The Anniversary of the Home Companion*. 2 sound cassettes, 105 min. St. Paul, MN: Minnesota Public Radio, 1984.

———. Untitled typescripts. 1971. Prairie Home Companion Archives. St. Paul, MN: Minnesota Public Radio.

"Keillor to Quit Daily Show, Others Leave KSJN." *Minneapolis Tribune*, 24 August 1973, 14B.

Kennedy Center. "Mark Twain Prize for American Humor." Http://www.kennedy-center.org/programs/specialevents/marktwain/.

Kennedy, Randall. *Nigger: The Strange Career of a Troublesome Word*. New York: Pantheon Books, 2002.

Kettman, Steve. "The Creator of Simpson Mania." *San Francisco Chronicle*, 27 October 1991, This World 3.

Kimsley, Michael. "Bart for President." *New Republic* 203, no. 4 (23 July 1990): 4.

Kirch, Claire, Judith Rosen, Marc Schultz, and Wendy Werris. "Producing a Holiday Miracle." *Publishers Weekly* 257, no. 48 (6 December 2010): 6–8.

Knoper, Randall. *Acting Naturally: Mark Twain in the Culture of Performance*. Berkeley: University of California Press, 1995. Http://ark.cdlib.org/ark:/13030/ft4n39n9g5/.

Kuhn, Thomas S. *Structure of Scientific Revolutions*. 2nd ed., enlarged. Chicago: University of Chicago Press, 1970.

Kurtzman, Daniel. "Jon Stewart 'Crossfire' Transcript: Stewart Slams Tucker Carlson and Paul Begala." *Daniel Kurtzman's Political Humor Blog*, 2004. Http://politicalhumor.about.com/library/bljonstewartcrossfire.htm.

Landa, Robin. *Designing Brand Experiences*. Clifton Park, NY: Thomson Delmar Learning, 2006.

Leach, William. *Land of Desire: Merchants, Power, and the Rise of a New American Culture*. New York: Pantheon, 1993.

Lee, Judith Yaross. *Defining New Yorker Humor*. Jackson: University Press of Mississippi, 2000.

———. "Five Ways of Looking at 'Aprille' (with Apologies to Wallace Stevens): Analysis of Storytelling in the Twenty-First Century." In *Eye on the Future: Popular Culture Scholarship Into the Twenty-First Century in Honor of Ray B. Browne*, edited by Marilyn F. Motz, John G. Nachbar, Michael T. Marsden, and Ronald J. Ambrosetti, 91–106. Bowling Green, OH: Bowling Green State University Popular Press, 1994.

———. "From the Sublime to the Ridiculous: Comic Traditions in the American Novel." In *The Blackwell Companion to the American Novel*, edited by Alfred Bendixen, 218–40. Oxford, England: Blackwell, 2012.

———. *Garrison Keillor: A Voice of America*. Studies in Popular Culture. Jackson, Mississippi: University Press of Mississippi, 1991.

———. "The International Twain and American Nationalist Humor: Vernacular Humor as a Post-Colonial Rhetoric." *Mark Twain Annual* 6 (2008): 33–49.

———. "Introduction." In *The Midwest*, edited by Joseph W. Slade and Judith Yaross Lee, xiii–xxx. Greenwood Encyclopedia of American Regional Cultures. Westport, CT: Greenwood Press, 2004.

———. "Mark Twain: [Date, 1601.] Conversation, as It Was by the Social Fireside in the Time of the Tudors." In *Encyclopedia of Erotic Literature*, 1320–22. 2 vols. London: Fitzroy Dearborn, 2006.

Lee, Rachel C. "'Where's My Parade?': Margaret Cho and the Asian American Body in Space." *Drama Review* 48, no. 2 (Summer 2004): 108–32.
Levine, Lawrence W. *Highbrow/Lowbrow: The Emergence of Cultural Hierarchy in America*. Cambridge, MA: Harvard University Press, 1988.
Lewis, R. W. B. *The American Adam: Innocence, Tragedy, and Tradition in the Nineteenth Century*. Chicago: University of Chicago Press, 1955.
"Lifestyle: The Yarmulke Is Now a Fashion Item." *New York Times*, 23 September 1990, 54.
Limon, John. *Stand-up Comedy in Theory, or, Abjection in America*. Durham: Duke University Press, 2000.
Lindemann, Jan. "Brand Valuation." In *Brands and Branding*, edited by Rita Clifton and John Simmons, 27–45. The Economist Series. Princeton, NJ: Bloomberg Press, 2004.
Locker, Arthur. "Two American Humorists—Hans Breitmann and Mark Twain." *Graphic* (London), 5 October 1872, 310, 324.
Longstreet, Augustus Baldwin. "Georgia Theatrics." 1937, In *Native American Humor*, edited by Walter Blair, 287–89. 2d ed. Scranton, PA: Chandler Publishing Company, 1960.
Lorch, Fred W. *The Trouble Begins at Eight: Mark Twain's Lecture Tours*. Ames: Iowa State University Press, 1968.
Loving, Jerome. *Mark Twain: The Adventures of Samuel L. Clemens*. Berkeley: University of California Press, 2010.
Lyttle, Jim. "The Effectiveness of Humor in Persuasion: The Case of Business Ethics Training." *Journal of General Psychology* 128, no. 2 (April 2001): 206–16.
Mahon, Gigi. *The Last Days of* The New Yorker. New York: New American Library, 1988.
Mandese, Joe. "'Seinfeld' Rates Soar." *Advertising Age* 65, no. 39 (19 September 1994): 1, 6.
Marc, David. *Comic Visions: Television Comedy and American Culture*. Boston: Unwin Hyman, 1989.
"Mark Twain as a Pedestrian." *Boston Evening Journal*, 14 November 1874, 2.
"Mark Twain." Illustrated by F[rederick] W[addy]. *Once a Week* n.s. 10 (14 December 1872): 519–21.
"Mark Twain Left Daughter $611,136." *New York Times*, 27 October 1910. *Mark Twain Quotations, Newspaper Collections, & Related Resources*, edited by Barbara Schmidt. Http://www.twainquotes.com/19101027.html.
"Mark Twain on the Platform." *The Sketch*, 27 November 1895. *Mark Twain Quotations, Newspaper Collections, & Related Resources*, edited by Barbara Schmidt. Http://www.twainquotes.com/OnThePlatform.html.
"Mark Twain's Lecture on the Sandwich Islands." *New York Times*, 6 February 1873, 5.
Marriott, Michel. "For One Publisher, the Life of Every Comic Book Starts on the Web." *New York Times*, 25 September 2006, C8.
Marx, Leo. "The Vernacular Tradition in American Literature." 1958. In *The Pilot and the Passenger: Essays on Literature, Technology, and Culture in the United States*, 3–17. New York: Oxford University Press, 1988.
Mathews, Mitford M., ed. *Americanisms: A Dictionary of Selected Americanisms on Historical Principles*. 1951. Chicago: University of Chicago Press, 1966.
"Matthew Arnold." Illustrated by F[rederick] W[addy]. *Once a Week* n.s. 10 (12 October 1872): 320–22.
Mattson, Kevin. "The Perils of Michael Moore: Political Criticism in an Age of Entertainment." *Dissent* 50, no. 2 (2003): 75–80.

McBride, Christopher Mark. *The Colonizer Abroad: American Writers on Foreign Soil, 1846–1912*. Literary Criticism and Cultural Theory. New York: Routledge, 2004.

McClusky, Mark. "Free Spidey! How Digital Distribution Can Save Comics from Infinite Crisis." *Wired*, May 2006, 34–36.

McGrath, Ben. "The Radical: Why Do Editors Keep Throwing *The Boondocks* Off the Funnies Page? [Profile of Aaron McGruder]." *New Yorker*, 19 and 26 April 2004, 152–61.

McGruder, Aaron. *All the Rage:* The Boondocks *Past and Present*. New York: Three Rivers Press, 2007.

———. The Boondocks*: Because I Know You Don't Read the Newspapers*. Kansas City: Andrews McMeel, 2000.

———. *Public Enemy #2: An All-New* Boondocks *Collection*. New York: Three Rivers Press, 2005.

———. *A Right to Be Hostile: The* Boondocks *Treasury*. New York: Three Rivers Press, 2003.

McKinley, Jesse. "Calaveras County Still Celebrates the Frog, but a Quarrel Has Dampened Spirits." *New York Times*, 20 May 2007, 16.

McLuhan, Marshall. *Understanding Media: The Extensions of Man*. Reprinted with an introduction by Lewis H. Lapham. 1964. Cambridge: MIT Press, 1994.

Mead, George Herbert. *Mind, Self, and Society; from the Standpoint of a Social Behaviorist*. Edited by Charles William Morris. 1934. Chicago: University of Chicago Press, 1967.

Michelson, Bruce. *Printer's Devil: Mark Twain and the American Publishing Revolution*. Berkeley: University of California Press, 2006.

Milligan, Andy. *Brand It Like Beckham: The Story of How Brand Beckham Was Built*. Great Brand Stories. London: Cyan Books, 2004.

Mintz, Lawrence E. "Standup Comedy as Social and Cultural Mediation." *American Quarterly* 37, no. 1 (Spring 1985): 71–80.

———. "Stand-up Comedy." In *Comedy: A Geographic and Historical Guide*, edited by Maurice Charney, 575–86. Westport, CT: Praeger, 2005.

Mitchell, Sean. "Homespun Radio's Cozy 'Companion.'" *Dallas Times Herald*, 22 February 1981, 7.

Mittell, Jason. "Cartoon Realism: Genre Mixing and the Cultural Life of *The Simpsons*." *Velvet Light Trap: A Critical Journal of Film & Television*, no. 47 (Spring 2001): 15–28.

Mobbs, Dean, Cindy C. Hagan, Eiman Azim, Vinod Menon, and Allan L. Reiss. "Personality Predicts Activity in Reward and Emotional Regions Associated with Humor." *Proceedings of the National Academy of Sciences of the United States of America* 102, no. 45 (2005): 16502–6.

Morris, Roy, Jr. *Lighting Out for the Territory: How Samuel Clemens Headed West and Became Mark Twain*. Simon & Schuster, 2010.

Myers, Lee Roy, director. *Seinfeld: A XXX Parody*. DVD.

Nash Information Services. "Top-Grossing Genres 1995 to 2011." *The Numbers: Box Office Data, Movie Stars, Idle Speculation*. Http://www.the-numbers.com/market/Genres/.

Navarro, Mirey. "Returning in Her Favorite Role, Herself [Margaret Cho]." *New York Times*, 10 August 2008, 19.

Newman, James L. *Imperial Footprints: Henry Morton Stanley's African Journeys.* Washington, DC: Brassey's, 2004.
Nimura, Janice P. "My So-Called Life from Hell [rev. of *Cruddy* by Lynda Barry]." *San Francisco Chronicle,* 5 September 1999, RV 2.
Ohmann, Richard. *Selling Culture: Magazines, Markets, and Class at the Turn of the Century.* New York: Verso, 1996.
Oliver, Nancy S. "New Manifest Destiny in *A Connecticut Yankee in King Arthur's Court.*" *Mark Twain Journal* 21, no. 4 (Fall 1983): 28–32.
Olson, Stephanie Koziski. "Standup Comedy." In *Humor in America: A Research Guide to Genres and Topics,* edited by Lawrence E. Mintz, 109–36. New York: Greenwood Press, 1988.
O'Neill, Jennifer A. "Twain's *A Connecticut Yankee in King Arthur's Court* and U.S. Imperialism." *CLCWeb: Comparative Literature and Culture: A WWWeb Journal* 9, no. 3 (September 2007): 1–7. Http://docs.lib.purdue.edu/clcweb/vol9/iss3/3.
Ong, Walter J. *Orality and Literacy: The Technologizing of the Word.* London: Methuen, 1982.
Oppenheimer, Jerry. *Seinfeld: The Making of an American Icon.* New York, NY: HarperCollins, 2002.
Oring, Elliott. *Engaging Humor.* Urbana: University of Illinois Press, 2003.
———. *Jokes and Their Relations.* Lexington: University Press of Kentucky, 1992.
Owen, David. "Taking Humor Seriously: George Meyer, the Funniest Man Behind the Funniest Show on TV." *New Yorker,* 13 March 2000, 64–75.
Paine, Albert Bigelow. *Mark Twain, a Biography; the Personal and Literary Life of Samuel Langhorne Clemens.* 3 vols. New York: Harper & Brothers, 1912.
Patinkin, Sheldon. *The Second City: Backstage at the World's Greatest Comedy Theater.* Naperville, IL: Sourcebooks, 2000.
Pew Internet and American Life Project. *Perceptions of Partisan Bias Seen as Growing—Especially by Democrats.* Pew Research Center, 2004. Http://www.pewinternet.org/pdfs/PIP_Political_Info_Jan04.pdf.
Pierleoni, Allen. "A Bit Off Course: Great Ambience, Casual Fare at Haggin Oaks Eatery." *Sacramento (CA) Bee,* 27 January 2006, TK41.
Pinsker, Sanford. "Tradition and the Individual Late Night Humorist: The Trouble Begins After Your Local News." *Studies in American Humor* n.s. 3, no. 3 (1996): 82–101.
Pinsky, Mark I. *The Gospel According to the Simpsons: The Spiritual Life of the World's Most Animated Family.* Louisville: Westminster John Knox Press, 2001.
Pollock, Sheldon. "Cosmopolitan and Vernacular in History." *Public Culture* 12, no. 3 (2000): 591–625.
Pornpitakpan, Chanthika. "The Persuasiveness of Source Credibility: A Critical Review of Five Decades' Evidence." *Journal of Applied Social Psychology* 34, no. 2 (2004): 243–81.
Posnock, Ross. *Philip Roth's Rude Truth: The Art of Immaturity.* Princeton: Princeton University Press, 2006.
Powers, Ron. *Mark Twain: A Life.* New York: Free Press, 2005.
Pozner, Jennifer L. "On My Bookshelf." *Women's Review of Books* 23, no. 1 (January/February 2006): 21.
Pratkanis, Anthony R., and Melissa D. Gliner. "And When Shall a Little Child Lead Them? Evidence for an Altercasting Theory of Source Credibility." *Current Psychology* 23, no. 4 (Winter 2004–2005): 279–304.

Price, Darby Li Po. "Humorous Hapas, Performing Identities." *Amerasia Journal* 23, no. 1 (1997): 99–111.

Pryor, Richard, producer and writer. *Richard Pryor—Live on the Sunset Strip*. Columbia Pictures Home Entertainment, 1982. Videocassette.

Pullen, John J. *Comic Relief: The Life and Laughter of Artemus Ward, 1834–1867*. Hamden, CT: Archon Books, 1983.

"Purchasing Power of Money in the United States," 2011. Http://www.measuringworth.com/ppowerus/.

Quirk, Tom. *Coming to Grips with* Huckleberry Finn: *Essays on a Book, a Boy, and a Man*. Columbia, MO: University of Missouri Press, 1993.

Rambsy, Howard, II. "Shine 2.0: Aaron McGruder's Huey Freeman as Contemporary Folk Hero." In *The Funk Era and Beyond: New Perspectives on Black Popular Culture*, edited by Tony Bolden, with a preface by Mark Anthony Neal, 143–58. New York: Palgrave Macmillan, 2008.

———. "The Vengeance of Black Boys: How Richard Wright, Paul Beatty, and Aaron McGruder Strike Back." *Mississippi Quarterly: The Journal of Southern Cultures* 61, no. 4 (Fall 2008): 643–57.

Raskin, Victor. *Semantic Mechanisms of Humor*. Synthese Language Library. Dordrecht: D. Reidel Publishing Co., 1985.

"Remarkable: Henry M. Stanley; London; Provided." *Springfield Republican* (MA), 29 November 1886, 4.

Rexrode, Christina. "UF Theater Troupe Adds Drama to the Workplace." *St. Petersburg (FL) Times*, 27 September 2006, 1D.

Roback, Diane. "*PW* Interviews Garrison Keillor." *Publishers Weekly*, 13 September 1985, 138–39.

Rodgers, Bernard F., Jr. "*The Great American Novel* and 'the Great American Joke.'" *Critique* 16, no. 2 (1974): 12–29.

Rosten, Leo Calvin. *The Education of H*y*m*a*n K*a*p*l*a*n*. By Leonard Q. Ross [pseud.]. New York: Harcourt, Brace, 1937.

Roth, Philip. *The Dying Animal*. Boston: Houghton Mifflin, 2001.

———. *The Facts: A Novelist's Autobiography*. New York: Farrar, Straus & Giroux, 1988.

———. *The Great American Novel*. New York: Holt, Rinehart and Winston, 1973.

———. "On *The Great American Novel*." 1973. In *Reading Myself and Others*, 75–92. New York: Farrar, Straus and Giroux, 1976.

———. *The Plot Against America*. Boston: Houghton Mifflin, 2004.

———. *Reading Myself and Others*. New York: Farrar, Straus and Giroux, 1975.

———. "Writing American Fiction." *Commentary* 31 (1961): 223–33.

Roth, Philip, et al. "Second Dialogue in Israel." *Congress Bi-Weekly*, 16 September 1963, 4–85.

Rothberg, Michael. "Roth and the Holocaust." In *The Cambridge Companion to Philip Roth*, edited by Timothy Parrish, 52–67. Cambridge, UK: Cambridge University Press, 2007.

Rothenbuhler, Eric W. "The Church of the Cult of the Individual." In *Media Anthropology*, edited by Eric W. Rothenbuhler and Mihai Coman, 91–100. Thousand Oaks, CA: Sage, 2005.

Rowe, John Carlos. "How the Boss Played the Game: Twain's Critique of Imperialism in *A Connecticut Yankee in King Arthur's Court*." In *The Cambridge Companion to Mark Twain*, 175–92. Cambridge, UK: Cambridge University Press, 1995.

Royal, Derek Parker. "Fouling Out the American Pastoral: Rereading Philip Roth's *The Great American Novel*." In *Upon Further Review: Sports in American Literature*, edited by Michael Cocchiarale and Scott D. Emmert, 157–68. Westport, CT: Praeger, 2004.

Said, Edward W. *Culture and Imperialism*. 1993. New York: Alfred A. Knopf, 1994.

Samanci, Özge. "Lynda Barry's Humor: At the Juncture of Private and Public, Invitation and Dissemination, Childish and Professional." *International Journal of Comic Art* 8, no. 2 (Fall 2006): 181–99.

Santayana, George. "The Genteel Tradition in American Philosophy." 1911. In *The Genteel Tradition: Nine Essays by George Santayana*, edited byDouglas L. Wilson, 37–64. Cambridge, MA: Harvard University Press, 1967.

Schmidt, Barbara. "Chronology of Known Mark Twain Speeches, Public Readings, and Lectures." In *Mark Twain Quotations, Newspaper Collections, & Related Resources*. 2006. Http://www.twainquotes.com/SpeechIndex.html.

———, ed. "Special Feature: *Samuel L. Clemens Vs. Belford, Clarke & Company*." In *Mark Twain Quotations, Newspaper Collections, & Related Resources*, edited by Barbara Schmidt. Http://www.twainquotes.com/ClemensVsBelford.html

Schmitz, Neil. "Twain, *Huckleberry Finn*, and the Reconstruction." *American Studies* 12, no. 1 (1971): 59–67.

Schulman, Norma. "The House That Black Built: Television Stand-up Comedy as Minor Discourse." *Journal of Popular Film and Television* 22, no. 3 (Fall 1994): 108–15.

Scott, A. O. "We'll Always Have Springfield." *New York Times*, 27 July 2007, B1, 15.

Second City Communications. "Who We Are." Http://www.secondcitycommunications.com/whoweare.

Second City Network. "About Us." Http://www.secondcitynetwork.com.

Seinfeld, Jerry, and Larry David. *Seinfeld: Seasons 1 & 2*. Directed by Tom Cherones. Culver City, CA: Castle Rock Entertainment; Columbia TriStar Home Entertainment, 2004. Four DVDs.

Seinfeld, Jerry. "Playboy Interview: Jerry Seinfeld." *Playboy* 40, no. 10 (October 1993): 47–64.

Shales, Tom. "The Groening of America: Once a Doodler on the Fringe, Bart's Bad Boy Is Now a Millionaire Slob." *Washington Post*, 13 May 1993, C1.

Shelden, Michael. *Mark Twain: Man in White: The Grand Adventure of His Final Years*. New York: Random House, 2010.

Shields, Mike. "Comedy Central Rolls Out Motherload Broadband Net." *MediaWeek* 15, no. 39 (31 October 2005): 6.

Sloane, David E. E. *Mark Twain as a Literary Comedian*. Southern Literary Studies. Baton Rouge: Louisiana State University Press, 1979.

Smith, David L. "Huck, Jim, and American Racial Discourse." In *Satire or Evasion? Black Perspectives on* Huckleberry Finn, edited by James S. Leonard, Thomas A. Tenney, and Thadious M. Davis, 103–20. Durham: Duke University Press, 1992.

Smith, Henry Nash. *Mark Twain: The Development of a Writer*. Cambridge, MA: Harvard University Press, Belknap, 1962.

———. *Mark Twain's Fable of Progress*. New Brunswick, NJ: Rutgers University Press, 1964.

———. *Virgin Land: The American West as Symbol and Myth*. New York: Random House, Vintage, 1950.

Smith, Seba. *My Thirty Years Out of the Senate by Major Jack Downing.* New York: Oaksmith & Company, 1859.

Smuts, Aaron. "Humor." In *Internet Encyclopedia of Philosophy: A Peer-Reviewed Academic Resource,* edited by James Fieser and Bradley Dowden. 2006, 2009. Http://www.iep.utm.edu/humor/.

Soper, Kerry. "From Rowdy, Urban Carnival to Contained, Middle-Class Pastime: Reading Richard Outcault's Yellow Kid and Buster Brown." *Columbia Journal of American Studies* 4, no. 1 (2000): 143–81.

Spiegelman, Art. *Breakdowns: Portrait of the Artist as a Young %@&*!* London: Penguin Books, Viking, 2008.

Spurr, David. *The Rhetoric of Empire: Colonial Discourse in Journalism, Travel Writing, and Imperial Administration.* Post-Contemporary Interventions. Durham: Duke University Press, 1993.

Stahl, Sandra Dolby. *Literary Folkloristics and the Personal Narrative.* Bloomington: Indiana University Press, 1989.

Stahl, Sandra K. "The Personal Narrative as Folklore." *Journal of the Folklore Institute* 14 (1977): 9–30.

Stanley, David H. "The Personal Narrative and the Personal Novel: Folklore as Frame and Structure for Literature." *Southern Folklore Quarterly* 43, no. 1–2 (1979): 107–20.

Stanley, Henry M. "Mark Twain at the Mercantile Library Hall Tuesday Night." *Daily Missouri Democrat,* 28 March 1867. *Mark Twain in His Times,* edited by Stephen Railton. Http://etext.virginia.edu/railton/onstage/stldemo.html.

"Stanley in New York: The African Explorer Will Lecture Upon the Dark Continent." *Springfield (MA) Republican,* 28 November 1886, 4.

Stanley, John. "'The Simpsons': Cartoon Clan of the Grotesque." *San Francisco Chronicle,* 21 January 1990, Sunday datebook, 47.

Stanley, T. L. "The Simpsons and BK: Just Because They Can." *Brandweek* 49, no. 40 (11 October 2008): 12.

"Stanley's Exploits Told: The Explorer Talks of the Great Dark Land." *New York Times,* 30 November 1886, 2.

Steinberg, Brian. "Simon Who? 'Idol' Spots Still Pricier in Prime Time." *Advertising Age* 81 (18 October 2010): 1.

Steinem, Gloria. "If Men Could Menstruate: A Political Fantasy." *Ms. Magazine* 7 (October 1978): 110.

Steptoe, Sonja. "Building a Better Mouse: Bob Iger Takes Disney's Legendary Brands Into the Digital Age." *Time* 169 (25 June 2007): Global 1–2.

Stewart, Jon, Ben Karlin, and David Javerbaum. *America (The Book): A Citizen's Guide to Democracy Inaction.* Edited by Ben Karlin. New York: Warner Books, 2004.

Stewart, Jon, David Javerbaum, Rory Albanese, and Steve Bodow. *The Daily Show with Jon Stewart Presents Earth (The Book): A Visitor's Guide to the Human Race.* New York: Grand Central Publishing, 2010.

Stewart, Jon, Stephen Colbert, Rob Corddry, Ed Helms, and Samantha Bee. *The Daily Show with Jon Stewart: Indecision 2004.* Hollywood, CA: Paramount Pictures Comedy Central Home Video, 2005. Three DVDs.

Sumida, Stephen H. "Reevaluating Mark Twain's Novel of Hawaii." *American Literature* 61, no. 4 (December 1989): 586–609.

Tennenhouse, Leonard. *The Importance of Feeling English: American Literature and the British Diaspora, 1750–1850*. Princeton: Princeton University Press, 2007.
Test, George A. *Satire: Spirit and Art*. Tampa: University of South Florida Press, 1991.
"Through the Dark Continent. Lecture by Stanley, the Famous Explorer—a Humorous Introduction by Mark Twain." *Boston Evening Transcript*, 10 December 1886, 2.
"Top Media & Marketing Innovations of 2008." *Adweek*, 15 December 2008.
Trombley, Laura Skandera. *Mark Twain's Other Woman: The Hidden Story of His Final Years*. New York: Alfred A. Knopf, 2010.
Tucker, Neely. "Like It or Not, 'Boondocks' Will Finally Hit the Airwaves." *Washington Post*, 26 October 2005, C 1.
Turner, Chris. *Planet Simpson: How a Cartoon Masterpiece Documented an Era and Defined a Generation*. London: Ebury, 2004.
Twain, Mark. *Adventures of Huckleberry Finn*. 1884. Edited by Victor Fischer and Lin Salamo. With Harriet Elinor Smith and Walter Blair. Illustrators E. W. Kemble and John Harley. The Works of Mark Twain. Berkeley: University of California Press, 2001.
———. *Adventures of Huckleberry Finn: (Tom Sawyer's Comrade)*. Edited by John H. Wallace. Falls Church, VA: John H. Wallace and Sons Co, 1983.
———. *A Connecticut Yankee in King Arthur's Court*. 1889. Edited by Bernard L. Stein. With an introduction by Henry Nash Smith. The Works of Mark Twain, vol. 9. Berkeley: University of California Press, 1979.
———. *Interviews with Samuel L. Clemens, 1874–1910*. Edited by Louis J. Budd. Arlington, TX: American Literary Realism and the University of Texas at Arlington, 1977.
———. *Letters from the Earth*. Edited by Bernard DeVoto. With a preface by Henry Nash Smith. New York: Harper & Row, 1962.
———. *Mark Twain at the* Buffalo Express: *Articles and Sketches by America's Favorite Humorist*. Edited by Joseph B. McCullough and Janice McIntire-Strasburg. DeKalb: Northern Illinois University Press, 1999.
———. *Mark Twain: The Complete Interviews*. Edited by Gary Scharnhorst. Tuscaloosa: University of Alabama Press, 2006.
———. *Mark Twain to Mrs. Fairbanks*. Edited by Dixon Wecter. Huntington Library Publications. San Marino, CA: Huntington Library, 1949.
———. *Mark Twain in Eruption: Hitherto Unpublished Pages About Men and Events*. Edited by Bernard DeVoto. New York and London: Harper & Brothers, 1940.
———. "Mark Twain in Washington." *Alta California*, 5 February 1868. *Mark Twain Quotations, Newspaper Collections, & Related Resources*, edited by Barbara Schmidt. Http://www.twainquotes.com/18680205.html.
———. *Mark Twain of the Enterprise: Newspaper Articles & Other Documents, 1862–1864*. Berkeley: University of California Press, 1957.
———. *Mark Twain Speaking*. Edited by Paul Fatout. Iowa City: University of Iowa Press, 1976.
———. *Mark Twain's Letters, Volume 2: 1867–1868*. Edited by Harriet Elinor Smith and Richard Bucci. Mark Twain Papers. Berkeley: University of California Press, 1990.
———. *Mark Twain's Letters, Volume 4: 1870–1871*. Edited by Victor Fischer and Michael B. Frank. Mark Twain Papers. Berkeley: University of California Press, 1995.
———. *Mark Twain's Letters, Volume 5: 1872–1873*. Edited by Lin Salamo and Harriet Elinor Smith. Mark Twain Papers. Berkeley: University of California Press, 1997.

———. *Mark Twain's Notebooks & Journals, Volume III, 1883–1891*. Edited by Robert Pack Browning, Michael B. Frank, and Lin Salamo. Mark Twain Papers. Berkeley: University of California Press, 1979.

———. "My Ancient Friends, the Police." *Alta California (San Francisco)*, 30 March 1867. *Mark Twain Quotations, Newspaper Collections, & Related Resources*, edited by Barbara Schmidt. Http://www.twainquotes.com/18670330.html.

———. Pudd'nhead Wilson *and* Those Extraordinary Twins*: Authoritative Texts, Textual Introduction and Tables of Variants Criticism*. 1894. Edited by Sidney E. Berger. A Norton Critical Edition. New York: Norton, 1980.

———. *1601, and Is Shakespeare Dead?* With a foreword by Shelley Fisher Fishkin, an introduction by Erica Jong, and an afterword by Leslie A. Fiedler. The Oxford Mark Twain. New York: Oxford University Press, 1996.

"Twain's Fancy Suit: Noted Humorist at Capitol in Cream-Colored Costume." *Washington Post*, 8 December 1906, 1.

Twitchell, James B. *Branded Nation: The Marketing of Megachurch, College, Inc., and Museumworld*. New York: Simon & Schuster, 2004.

U. S. Census Bureau. *Table 4. Population: 1790 to 1990*. Population and Housing Unit Counts, 2011. Http://www.census.gov/population/censusdata/table-4.pdf.

———. "Census Bureau Reports Steady Growth in Internet Publishing and Broadcasting Revenues," 2011. Http://www.census.gov/newsroom/releases/archives/economic_census/cb11-17.html.

Vaidhyanathan, Siva. *Copyrights and Copywrongs: The Rise of Intellectual Property and How It Threatens Creativity*. New York: New York University Press, 2001.

Viacom. "2nd Quarter '06." *Pulse*, 9 August 2006. Investor newsletter.

W., H. "Slick, Crockett, Downing, Etc." *The London and Westminster Review* 32, no. 1 (December 1838): 137–45.

Walker, Nancy A. *A Very Serious Thing: Women's Humor and American Culture*. Minneapolis: University of Minnesota Press, 1988.

Wallace, John H. "The Case Against *Huck Finn*." In *Satire or Evasion? Black Perspectives on* Huckleberry Finn, edited by James S. Leonard, Thomas A. Tenney, and Thadious M. Davis, 16–24. Durham: Duke University Press, 1992.

Walster, Elaine, Elliot Aronson, and Darcy Abrahams. "On Increasing the Persuasiveness of a Low Prestige Communicator." *Journal of Experimental Social Psychology* 2, no. 4 (October 1966): 325–42.

Waters, H. F., and L. Buckley. "Family Feuds." *Newsweek* 115, no. 17 (23 April 1990): 58+.

Watkins, Mel. *On the Real Side: A History of African-American Comedy from Slavery to Chris Rock*. Rev. ed. 1994. Chicago: Lawrence Hill Books, 1999.

Webster, Noah. *Dissertations on the English Language, 1789*. English Linguistics, 1500–1800. A collection of facsimile reprints. Menston, England: Scolar Press, 1968.

Wells, Paul. *Understanding Animation*. New York: Routledge, 1998.

Wheeler, Douglas L. "Henry M. Stanley's Letters to the *Missouri Democrat*." *The Bulletin of the Missouri Historical Society* 17 (April 1961): 269–86.

"Where Two Rivers Converge and Two Histories Divide." *New York Times*, 20 May 2007, 15.

Wickberg, Daniel. *The Senses of Humor: Self and Laughter in Modern America*. Ithaca: Cornell University Press, 1998.

Wilensky, Dawn. "103 Leading Licensing Companies." *License! Global* 10, no. 3 (April 2007): 34–51.

Wilson, Edmund. *Patriotic Gore: Studies in the Literature of the American Civil War.* New York: Oxford University Press, 1962.

Wilt, Napier. *Some American Humorists.* New York: T. Nelson and Sons, 1929.

Wirth-Nesher, Hana. "Roth's Autobiographical Writings." In *The Cambridge Companion to Philip Roth*, edited by Timothy Parrish, 158–72. Cambridge, UK: Cambridge University Press, 2007.

Zipkin, Amy. "Stores Fade, but Names Get New Life." *New York Times*, 14 April 2009, B1, 8.

Zwick, Jim. *Confronting Imperialism: Essays on Mark Twain and the Anti-Imperialist League.* West Conshohocken, PA: Infinity Pub., 2007.

Index

Page numbers in **boldface** indicate illustrations.

abject, 32–33, 58–59, 68
"Adult Swim" (Cartoon Network), 170
advertising, 6–8, 15, 161, 166, 168–70, 172, 193
Africa, 80, 83–90, 98, 118
African American English, 152–53. *See also* dialect, African American
African Americans, 61, 103, 107, 120, 122, 142, 150, 152–53
Air America, 3, 178
Aldrich, Thomas Bailey, 21, 111
Alger, Horatio, Jr., 34; *Ragged Dick*, 21
All-American Girl (Cho), 46
Allen, Gracie, 66
Allen, Woody, 20
amateur aesthetic, 142, 150, **154**, 156–58. *See also* vernacular humor: visual techniques
Amazing Adventures of Kavalier and Clay, The (Chabon), 92
America (The Book): A Citizens' Guide to Democracy Inaction (Stewart), 27
American culture, 3–6, 8, 21, 23, 26, 35, 104, 108, 112, 129, 157, 162, 165, 175, 192
American exceptionalism, 74, 82, 92–94, 101, 103, 105
American humor: Anglo-American context, 11–15, 71–73, 87; cultural significance, 3–6, 22–26, 71–73, 87, 91, 163, 178–79; ideology, 20, 24, 71–76, 82–83, 91–93, 105, 110–13, 123–24, 159–60; traditions, 20–22, 31, 42–43, 73, 91, 112, 120, 124, 191; Twain as symbol, **11**, 12, 20. *See also* humor
American Pastoral (Roth), 103
American Revolution, 7, 24, 38, 107
Anderson, Benedict, 4, 112
Anglo-American contrast. *See* British-American contrast
animation, 127–40, 170; compared to live action, 129, 133–35, 138; by Disney, 131–32, 165; fantasy in, 131, 136; as oppositional rhetoric, 130, 136–38; and realism, 129, 132, 134–36; and satire, 129–31, 136, 138; similarity gestalt, 138–40; Twain and, 125; vernacular humor and, 125, 128–32, 135–40; visual jokes, 135–37. *See also Simpsons, The*
Aristotle, 5, 181
Arnold, Matthew, **14**, 14–15, 86–87, 189
Assassin, 58, 61–62, 64
"At the Circus in Hogan's Alley," (Outcault), 126
Atlantic, 16–17, 78
authenticity, 29–31, 33–34, 40–42, 47, 49, 53, 56, 60, 62–63, 66–67, 124, 127
autobiography: of Barry, 127, 140–41; in branding, 16, 34–35; of Cho, 59, 62; of Keillor, 51–52, 68; of Roth, 74, 94, 103; in stand-up comedy, 30, 33–35, 40, 46–47, 49, 52, 59, 62, 66, 68–69; of Stanley, 86; of Twain, 12, 16, 22, 33, 35, 40, 84

215

Avery, Tex, 125
Awful Truth, The (Moore), 177

Baby Blues (Scott and Kirkland), 155
Bakhtin, Mikhail, 5, 30–31, 123–24, 184; *Rabelais and His World*, 31, 58, 123, 130
Barnum, P. T., 11, 38
Barry, Lynda, 25, 109, 127, 140–49, 152, 156, 158; career, 192; comic technique, 142–43, 148–49; and Twain, 140–41, 146
  Works: *Cruddy*, 140–41; *Ernie Pook's Comeek*, 141, 192; *The Freddie Stories*, 141; *The Greatest of Marlys*, 141; *One Hundred Demons*, 109, 127, 140–42, 145, 148–49, 157
Batman, 138, 170
Beard, Daniel, 18
Beautiful (Cho), 58
Begala, Paul, 27–28
belle lettres, 3
Benjamin, Walter, 107
Bennett, William, 129
black vernacular intellectuals. *See* vernacular intellectuals
Blair, Walter, 20–21, 92–93, 182, 187, 190
Boondocks, The (McGruder), 25, 109, 127, 150–53, **154**, 156–58, 192
Bowling for Columbine (Moore), 177
Bradstreet, Ann, 20
brands: definition of, 29; equity, 10, 162, 165, 170; extension, 171; identity, 13, 31, 166, 171; names, 9, 25, 46, 176. *See also* comic brands; information economy; trademarks; Twain, Mark
Breast, The (Roth), 75, 103
Breitmann, Hans, **15**
Brief Wondrous Life of Oscar Wao, The (Díaz), 71
British-American contrast, 24, 71–77, 79, 81, 86–88, 91, 93, 112
Browne, Charles Farrar. *See* Ward, Artemus
Bruce, Lenny, 31, 58–59, 68
Buffalo Express, 122
Burke, Kenneth, 5

burlesque, 7, 11, 41, 48, 65; by Cho, 61; by Roth, 75, 94–95, 99, 104; in *The Simpsons*, 128; by Twain, 38–39, 81–82, 91, 108, 117–19, 121, 123, 184
Burns, George, 66
Burns and Allen Show, The, 46
Bush, George H. W., 129, 171
Bush, George W., 75, 102, 150, 154
Bush v. Gore, 147, 149, 157
Butler, Judith, 45

Cable, George Washington, 17, 35
Calvin and Hobbes, 127, 154
capitalism, 6–7, 10, 128, 137–38, 147, 163, 176–77, 179
Capitalism: A Love Story (Moore), 177
capitalist culture, 20
Car Talk, 175–76
Carlson, Tucker, 27–28
Carlyle, Thomas, 86
Cartoon Network, 155, 170
cartoons: in branding, 3, **12**, **160**, 167–70; copyrights on, 129, 165, 167–68, 194; as medium, 6, 125–26, 150, 179; realism in, 125, 129–31, 192; status of, 126, 140; vernacular style in, 25, 108, 125–27, 142, 144, 150, 155, 158, 179. *See also* animation; graphic humor; print comics
celebrity, 8, 12, 16–17, 19, 22, 46–47, 57, 65–66, 137, 159, 161, 163
censorship, 129, 140, 157
Chabon, Michael, 92
Chappelle's Show, 170
Chicago *Defender*, 153
Cho, Margaret, 24, 58–65, 68; abject and carnivalesque themes, 58–59; brand extensions, 65; compared to Twain, 28, 36, 46–47, 58; identity shifts, 59–64; personal experience narratives, 59, 62–64
  Works: *All-American Girl*, 46; *Beautiful*, 58; *The Cho Show*, 62–63, 65; *I'm the One That I Want*, 36, 58, 60–61, 64–65; *Notorious C.H.O.*, 58, 61–64; *Revolution*, 58, 61, 64

Cho Show, The (Cho), 62–63, 65
Civil War, 6, 21, 34, 82, 118, 162
Clemens, Olivia (Livy), 37, 84, 88, 185
Clemens, Orion, 16, 40
Clemens, Samuel. *See* Twain, Mark
Clemens v. Belford, Clarke Company, 10, 182
Clinton, Bill, 138, 171
Colbert, Stephen, 4, 38, 68, 163, 172; as Perfect Fool, 68
Colbert Report (Comedy Central), 38, 172
comedians, 23–24, 27–33, 35–39, 48, 66, 68, 184; as commodities, 65; contemporary, 179; modern, 59; personas of, 29, 32, 66; stand-up, 3, 27–29, 31, 36–37, 39, 41–42, 46, 49, 59–60, 63, 65–66, 69, 171; women, 58
"comedification," 159
comedy, 5–6, 64, 67, 134, 163–64, 170, 172, 174, 181, 184, 187; film, 167; franchised, 31; late night, 175; lunatic, 102; sketch, 164–65, 170; theatrical, 23; TV, 47; uncensored, 171; venues, 29. *See also* American humor; humor; situation comedy; stand-up comedy
Comedy Central, 4, 27–28, 31, 170–72; as brand, 170–72; *Colbert Report*, 38, 172; *The Daily Show*, 4, 27–28, 171–75; *InDecision* specials, 171–72
comedy clubs, 3, 29, 31, 67, 164, 172
comic brands, 6, 20, 29, 35, 40, 45, 65, 67, 159, 162–63, 165, 167, 170, 179
comic commodity, 11, 35, 46, 66, 169
comic cross-cultural contrast, 13–14, 24. *See also* Anglo-American contrast
comic identity, 29, 69
comic mask, 28
comics. *See* cartoons; comedians; graphic humor; print comics
communication: artful, 29; audience, 28, 37, 184; authentic, 30; digital, 6; direct, 56; electronic, 7; interpersonal, 6; social, 29. *See also* oral communication
communication technology, 9. *See also* mass media

Congo and the Founding of Its Free State, The (Stanley), 85
Contrast, The (Tyler), 75, 110
copyrights, 25, 90, 106, 126, 162, 165; piracy, 12–13, 16; subsidiary rights, 165–70; Twain's, 8, 10, 12–13, 19, 22. *See also* intellectual property
Cosby Show, The, 46, 128
Count of Monte Cristo, The (Dumas), 118
Counterlife, The (Roth), 93, 103
Critchley, Simon, 5
Crockett, Davy, 4, 76
Crossfire, 27–28
Cruddy (Barry), 140–41
Csupo, Gabor, 130
culture. *See* American culture

Daily Show, The, 4, 27–28, 171–75
Danny Thomas Show, The, **133**, 133–34
Darwin, Charles, 9
DeGeneres, Ellen, 46
Democrats, 27, 102, 147, 172
DeQuille, Dan, 36
Derby, George Horation. *See* Phoenix, John
DeVoto, Bernard, 38, 68, 181, 184
dialect: African American, 61–62, 153, 191; Arthurian, 77; Elisabethan, 107; eye, 108, 142, 151, 158; immigrant, 24, 71, 96, 103, 127, 157; inferior, 150; Korean, 60–61; racist, 120–25; regional, 72, 110; slang, 22, 77, 127, 153; white, 119–20, 128, 191. *See also* vernacular humor; vernacular language theory
dialect writing, 3, 14, 83, 92, 105, 110–11, 120–25
Díaz, Junot, 105; *The Brief Wondrous Life of Oscar Wao*, 71
Dickens, Charles, 38
Direct from Broadway (Goldberg), 62
Disney, 169; animation style, 131–32; brand, 165–66
Doonesbury (Trudeau), 155
Downing, Jack, 4, 76, 111, 152, 175
dozens, the, 153

Dumas, Alexandre, 118; *The Count of Monte Cristo*, 118
Dunbar, Paul Laurence, 153
Dying Animal, The (Roth), 103

*Education of H*Y*M*A*N K*A*P*L*A*N, The* (Rosten), 92
Einstein, Albert, 9
eiron, 75, 110, 117–18, 126, 148–49, 152, 156
Ellen [DeGeneres], 46
Ellison, Ralph, 120
empire, 71–75, 77–78, 82–83, 86–87, 90–95, 98–99, 101–6, 118, 158–59, 179, 188
entertainment, 6, 8, 22–24, 35, 40, 118, 122, 153, 164–65, 175, 178
entrepreneurship, 10, 29
epistolary novel, 49, 111
Ernie Pook's Comeek (Barry), 141, 192
ethnic identity, 61
Everybody Hates Chris (Rock), 46
Everything Is Illuminated (Foer), 92, 105

fabrications: in fiction, 93, 95–97, 102; in hoaxes, 43–44; in situation comedy, 46–47, 59, 65; in stand-up comedy, 24, 32–33, 39–40, 46–49, 51–54, 62; Twain on, 42, 183
Fahrenheit 9/11 (Moore), 177
Fairbanks, Mary Mason, 34
Family Guy, 170
Father Knows Best, 128, 134
fiction: American ideology in, 71–74, 94, 178; autobiographical, 33–34, 49–51, 54–57, 74–75, 141; branding and, 11–13, 23–26, 168; fact and, 39–40, 43, 93–97, 103–4, 113; information economy and, 6–13; local color, 72; Twain Prize and, 23; Twain's influence on, 21–22, 108, 141; unreliable narrator in, 120–21
Flight to Canada (Reed), 71
Flintstones, The, 128, 131
Foer, Jonathan Safran, 92, 105
folklore, 20, 30–31, 75, 110, 183
frame tale, 83
Franken, Al, 3, 171, 178,

Franklin, Benjamin, 110
Freddie Stories, The (Barry), 141
Freud, Sigmund, 5, 9, 58, 185; *Interpretation of Dreams*, 9; *Jokes and Their Relation to the Unconscious*, 32
"Friendly Neighbor" (Keillor), 49, 56
Friends, 10, 65

gays, 58, 61–62, 64
gender, 18, 34, 45, 58, 61–62
"Georgia Theatrics" (Longstreet), 42
Ghost Writer, The (Roth), 93
Gilded Age, The (Twain), 20
Gleason, Jackie, 131
Goffman, Erving, 45, 54, 179, 185
Goldberg, Whoopi, 23; *Direct from Broadway*, 62
Goldbergs, The, 92
Grant, Ulysses S., 9. 83, 86, 162, 188
graphic humor, 21, 25–26, 108–9, 125–26, 137, 179. See also animation; Barry, Lynda; cartoons; McGruder, Aaron; Outcault, Richard Felton; print comics; *Simpsons, The*
Gravity's Rainbow (Pynchon), 92
Great American Novel, The (Roth), 75, 93–96, 98–99, 101–4
Greatest Marlys, The (Barry), 141
Groening, Matt, 127–31, 166, 192
grotesque, 123, 125, 143

Hanna-Barbera, 131; *The Flintstones*, 128, 131
Harper's Magazine, 16
Harper's Weekly, 17
Harris, George Washington, 128
Hawaii, 13, 21, 33, 35, 37, 39, 47, 73, 83, 184, 187
Hawthorne, Nathaniel, 95; "My Kinsman, Major Molineux," 111, 190
hegemony, 61, 63, 73, 83, 91–92, 111, 126
hoaxes, 3, 11, 29, 39, 41–44, 48, 72, 112
Hogan's Alley (Outcault), 22, 109, 126–27, 157
Hollander, Robert, 20
Hopper, Edward, 136

Hotten, John Camden, 12–13, 16
How I Found Livingstone (Stanley), 89
Howells, William Dean, 7, 16, 78, 82, 187
Hughes, Langston, 153
Huizinga, Johan, 5, 30, 164
Human Stain, The (Roth), 103
humor: African, 71; African American, 71, 153, 187, 193; carnivalesque, 58, 123, 125–27, 130, 140; crackerbarrel, 54, 72, 91–92, 110; deadpan, 16, 27, 33, 36–38, 48–49, 55, 114, 121, 158, 173–74, 184; intellectual, 163; Jewish-American, 92, 105; Literary Comedian, 20, 33, 38–39; lowbrow, 35, 128, 140, 156; midwestern, 20, 186; national, 4, 20, 40; newspaper, 11; Old Southwestern, 42, 75, 112, 128; oral, 34, 43, 45, 57–58, 71, 157; political, 171, 175, 177–78; popular, 5, 71, 123; postcolonial, 20, 24, 72–74, 79, 82–83, 87, 91–92, 105, 112, 123, 159–60; as rhetoric, 4–6, 24, 31; Sagebrush, 20, 43, 185; sexual, 4, 31–32, 58, 64, 68, 103; stage, 20, 24, 29, 46–47; theory, 5, 9, 30–31, 91, 123; transgressive, 172; verbal, 131, 156; written, 44, 123. *See also* American humor; animation; comedy; graphic humor; literary humor; print comics; radio humor; stand-up comedy; television; vernacular humor
Hurston, Zora Neale, 153; *Jonah's Gourd Vine*, 71
hypermediacy, 158

"I Always Wanted You to Admire My Fasting" (Roth), 75, 93
I Married a Communist (Roth), 103
identity. *See* self
identity politics. *See* politics: identity
ideological contradictions, 78, 81
ideology, 4–5, 10, 21, 47, 71, 73, 76, 81–82, 132, 137, 156, 163, 179; American, 76, 78, 93, 105, 109, 123, 158; democratic, 72, 75, 78, 105; nationalist, 95, 106, 110, 120, 182; patriotic, 92; political,

76; racial, 122; vernacular, 82, 92, 105, 123
I'm the One That I Want (Cho), 36, 58, 60–61, 64–65
Imagined Communities (Anderson), 4, 112
Imperfect Philosopher, 68
imperialism, 7, 73–74, 78–84, 86, 89–93, 97–99, 101, 105–6, 160, 179, 187
InDecision (Freud), 171–72
individualism, 29, 47
industrialization, 7
information economy, 6–10, 12, 19, 25, 46, 69, 106, 162–63, 165, 170, 179
information technology, 9
intellectual property, 6, 13, 16, 19, 165. *See also* copyrights; trademarks
internal colonization, 73, 99–100
interpersonal communication. *See* communication: interpersonal
Interpretation of Dreams (Freud), 9
irony, 5, 24, 43, 49, 89, 99, 114, 120–21, 129, 141, 144, 148–49, 157–58, 173–74
Irving, Washington, 20
It's a Wonderful Life, 147
Ivins, Molly, 20

Jack Benny Program, 46
James, William, 179; *Principles of Psychology*, 9, 44–45, 185
Jameson, Frederic, 176, 179
joke books, 31
jokes: Americanization of British, 77; by Cho, 58, 60–63, 65; conventional, 40; in daily life, 3; dialect, 61; by Keillor, 48, 50–51, 53, 55–56; by McGruder, 151–53; one-line, 30; by Roth, 95, 97; shaggy dog type, 95; stage, 34, 36–37, 40–41, 84, 136; in stand-up comedy, 24, 28, 31–32; theory of, 5–6, 31–32, 68; by Twain, 13, 17–18, **18**, 160, 162; on Twain, 39; visual, 131, 134–36, 144, 172–73; by Ward, 38–39
jokework, 32
Jonah's Gourd Vine (Hurston), 71
Jones, Chuck, 125

Katzenjammer Kids, 127
Keillor, Garrison, 20, 24, 28, 46–59;
    as brand, 57–58; career, 48, 50,
    54–55, 185–86; monologues,
    50–53, 55; persona, 24, 28–29,
    53, 54; pseudonym, 48; rhetorical
    techniques, 48–50, 54–57, 68; and
    Twain, 46–47, 54, 56–58, 68
  Works: "Aprille," 50–51; "Farewell
    Performance," 55; "Friendly
    Neighbor," 49, 56; "Guys on Ice," 52;
    Lake Wobegon Days, 57; *Leaving
    Home*, 50; *Pilgrims: A Wobegon
    Romance*, 56; *Stories from Lake
    Wobegon*, 53–54
Kirkland, Rick, 155

Lake Wobegon, 46–49, 50–57, 185–86.
    See also Keillor, Garrison
Lecky, W. E. H., 86
*Lectures on Mental Science According
    to the Philosophy of Phrenology*
    (Weaver), 44
lesbians, 61–62, 64
Lewis, Jerry, 20
lies. *See* fabrications; hoaxes
Literary Comedians. *See* humor: Literary
    Comedian
literary humor, 21, 24, 71, 74, 168, 193. *See
    also* Roth, Philip; Twain, Mark
Live on the Sunset Strip (Pryor), 36
Livingstone, Dr. David, 84–85
Locke, David Ross. *See* Nasby, Petroleum
    Vesuvius
London *Spectator*, 12, 16
Longstreet, Agustus Baldwin, 42
Lowell, James Russell, 71

MAD magazine, 130, 165, 169, 175
magazines, 4, 8–9, 11, 14, 16–17, 22, 25–
    26, 64, 83, 130, 167–69, 175, 177
Magliozzi, Tom and Ray, 175; *Car Talk*,
    175–76
Maher, Bill, 171
Make Room for Daddy. See *Danny
    Thomas Show, The*
Manifest Destiny, 73, 82, 91–92, 100, 187

Mark Twain Prize for American Humor,
    23, 31
"Mark Twain's Patent Scrap Book." *See*
    Twain, Mark: Works
Maron, Mark, 3
Marx, Leo, 72, 92, 107, 109, 111, 149–50
mass media: and American culture,
    4–6, 151, 156–57, 175; and branding,
    11, 29, 35, 65, 69, 163, 165, 169,
    172; electronic, 6–7, 9, 175, 177;
    environment of, 8, 126–68, 175; and
    humor, 4–6, 21, 92, 178–79; and
    information economy, 6, 10, 19–20,
    170, 178–79; narrative, 25; new, 168,
    172, 175; representations, 48, 56,
    64, 152; theories of, 158, 176–77;
    Twain and, 2, 6–18. *See also* fiction;
    magazines; newspapers; print;
    radio; television humor
Maus (Spiegelman), 4, 140
Maxwell, James Clerk, 9
McGruder, Aaron, 25, 109, 127, 150–57;
    The Boondocks, 25, 109, 127, 150–53,
    154, 156–57, 192; career, 150; comic
    technique, 151–54, 156
Mead, George Herbert, 5, 45, 185
media. *See* mass media
Melville, Herman, 95, 97
Meyer, George, 130
minstrelsy, 31–32, 35, 92, 113, 120
Moby Dick (Melville), 95, 97
mock-oral text, 21, 94–95, 108, 111, 124–
    25, 127–28, 142–52, 153, 158. *See also*
    dialect writing; vernacular humor
modernism, 7, 9, 43–44, 110, 115
monologues, 21–22, 24, 31, 47, 62, 91, 143,
    184; by Barry, 143; by Cho, 62; by
    Keillor, 47, 49–53, 56–57, 186–87;
    on *Seinfeld*, 66–67; in stand-up
    comedy, 28, 32, 47, 66; theatrical, 31,
    184; by Twain, 22, 29, 68, 91
Moore, Mary Tyler, 47
Moore, Michael, 171, 175, 177–79
"My Kinsman, Major Molineux,"
    (Hawthorne), 111, 190
My Thirty Years Out of the Senate
    (Smith), 111

myth, 7, 34, 68–69, 75, 92, 94, 96–97, 99, 103, 105

Nasby, Petroleum Vesuvius, 33, 37
national culture, 4, 100
nationalism, 20, 76, 91
nation-state, 4, 112
Native Americans, 81, 83
New Yorker, The, 49, 168–69
newspaper comics. *See* print comics
newspapers, 5, 8–11, 173, 175; and Barry, 141; and *The Boondocks*, 25, 209, 250, 254, 255; humor in, 5, 22, 37, 72, 76, 126–27, 155, 166; and Keillor, 57, 185; and Twain, 8–11, 16, 22, 30, 42, 76–77, 89, 161–62, 181–82
Nighthawks (Hopper), 136
Notorious C.H.O. (Cho), 58, 61–64

objectivity, 174–77
On the Origin of Species (Darwin), 9
Once a Week, 11–15, 85
One Hundred Demons (Barry), 109, 127, 140–42, 145, 148–49, 157
Onion, The, 177
Operation Shylock (Roth), 93, 103
oral communication, 6, 28–30, 37, 56, 112, 124, 184; vs. writing and electronic communication, 176–78
Oring, Elliot, 5
Our Gang (Roth), 93, 101
Outcault, Richard Felton, 22, 126–27; "At the Circus in Hogan's Alley," 126; *Hogan's Alley*, 22, 109, 126–27, 157; Yellow Kid, 22, 125–27
Ozzie and Harriet, 134

Pamela (Richardson), 111
parody: in branding, 68, 163; copyright and, 163, 165; graphic, 126; by Keillor, 48–49, 56; in *MAD*, 130; in *The Simpsons*, 109, 130, **133**, 134, 140; of news, 172, 175, 177; by Roth, 94, 97–98, 101–2; by Stewart, 27, 173–74
Peanuts (Schulz), 127, 154, 166
Peck, George W., 111
Peck's Bad Boy and His Pa (Peck), 111

People's History of English Aristocracy, The (Standring), 86
Perfect Fool, 38, 68. *See also eiron*
performance humor, solo. *See* stand-up comedy
performed self, 24. *See also* persona; self
persona: in branding, 10, 29, 176; of Cho, 60, 62–63; feigned, 29, 69, 47; ironic, 38; of Keillor, 48–49, 54, 58; of Literary Comedians, 33; of Nasby, 37; on-stage vs. off-stage, 28–29, 33, 34, 40, 56, 63, 65–66, 68–69; as socially constructed, 29, 38, 45; stable vs. unstable, 24, 32, 38, 69; of Stewart, 28; of Twain, 30, 33, 37–42, 44; of Ward, 38
personal experience narratives, 30, 32, 40, 57, 59, 62–64, 103, 149
Personal Memoirs (Grant), 9, 83, 86, 162
Phoenix, John, 33
Pilgrims: A Wobegon Romance (Keillor), 56
piracy (copyright), 12–13, 16
Plot Against America, The (Roth), 75, 94, 99, 101–4, 189
Politically Incorrect (Maher), 7, 171
politics, 4, 6, 27, 43, 65, 69, 72–73, 77, 107, 109, 111, 117, 126–27, 131, 140, 150–51, 157, 171, 175, 178, 191; American, 95, 104, 111, 156, 163; anti-imperialist, 73; class, 110; congressional, 174; contemporary, 101; conventional, 156; cultural, 4, 68; democratic, 152; domestic, 94–95, 102; English, 76; federal, 5; highbrow, 156; identity, 151; language, 72, 110, 158; left-wing, 150; national, 4, 111; postcolonial, 112, 123; post-9/11, 94; racial, 156; republican, 75; right-wing, 68; twentieth-century, 91; vernacular, 87; Vietnam-era, 75
Poor Richard's Almanac (Franklin), 110
popular culture, 3–6, 30–31, 92, 109–10, 150, 179
Portnoy's Complaint (Roth), 4, 21, 74, 93, 103
post–Civil War period, 8, 16

postcolonial values, 73, 79
postindustrial capitalism, 10
postindustrial economy, 6, 23
postindustrialism, 9
postmodernism, 45, 56, 110, 176, 179
Prairie Home Companion, A (Keillor), 46–49, 54–57, 185–86
Presentation of Self in Everyday Life, The (Goffman), 45
Principles of Psychology (James), 9, 44–45, 185
print (medium), 4, 6, 21
print comics, 4–5, 22–23, 25, 108–9, 125–27, 140, 143, 149, 155, 157–58, 169–70, 179, 190. *See also* Barry, Lynda; McGruder, Aaron
protomodernism, 9, 115
Pryor, Richard, 23, 32; *Live on the Sunset Strip*, 36
psychology, 34, 44–45, 52, 59, 120, 185
public culture, 4
public relations, 6
punchlines, 27, 30, 36, 41, 51, 59–60, 64, 67, 69, 98, 114, 136, 151, 173
Pynchon, Thomas, 20; *Gravity's Rainbow*, 92

race, 3, 7, 34, 58, 61, 64, 109, 111, 113, 117, 178
racism, 7, 47, 63, 83, 116–17, 119, 122–23, 145, 151
radio (medium), 3, 9, 29, 46, 50, 55–56, 68, 128, 157, 175–78, 185; public, 48–49, 57, 186
radio humor, 3, 46, 54, 175–76, 178; Brice, 157; *Car Talk*, 175–76. *See also* Keillor, Garrison
Ragged Dick (Alger), 21
Raskin, Victor, 5, 63
realism, 53–54, 66–67, 82, 103, 111, 125–26, 129, 131, 135–37, 158, 169; autobiographical, 94; comic, 49; Disney, 132; graphic, 132; narrative, 131–32; photographic, 136; TV, 133
reality, 39, 42–45, 47, 50, 56, 59, 61–62, 65–67, 79, 94–95, 104–5, 125, 136, 158

Reed, Ishmael, 71
Republicans, 4, 58, 64, 102–3, 147, 150, 171–72
Revolution (Cho), 58, 61, 64
rhetoric: African American, 150, 153; anti-intellectual, 151–52; in branding, 10, 46, 160, 176–77; of Brice, 157; of Cho, 61–64; classical, 41, 55; comic, 4–5, 43–45, 53, 64, 69, 71, 82, 92, 94, 107, 153, 185; egalitarian, 74; exceptionalist, 71–72, 93–94; extravagant, 99, 152; imperial, 77, 98; of inferiority, 41–42, 54, 121, 124; ironic, 107, 120–21; of Keillor, 53–56; literary, 150; marketing, 17–18, **18**, 46, 160–61; of McGruder, 150–56; of Moore, 178; nineteenth-century, 32–33, 37, 41, 78; oppositional, 98, 126, 150–52, 156; oral, 124–25; political, 4, 24, 71–72, 98, 101–2, 126, 175–78; postcolonial, 24, 71–72, 82, 87; process of, 4–5, 43–45, 59; racist, 120; sixth-century, 77; in stand-up comedy, 41–42, 67–69; of Stanley, 84, 86, 88–90; of Twain, 7, 32–44, 46, 187; vernacular, 25, 74–75, 107, 117–21, 126–27, 142, 157–58, 187; visual, 25, 125–26, 140–42. *See also* authenticity; irony; parody; satire; vernacular humor
Richardson, Samuel, 111
Rock, Chris, 32, 155; *Everybody Hates Chris*, 46
Rocky and Bullwinkle, 130
Roger and Me (Moore), 177
Rogers, Will, 175
romanticism, 7
Rosten, Leo, 92; *The Education of H*Y*M*A*N K*A*P*L*A*N*, 92
Roth, Philip, 4, 21, 92–105, 189; and American exceptionalism, 24, 74–75, 92, 94, 99–100, 103, 105; and imperialism, 98, 100–101, 103, 179; and parody, 97–98, 101–2; play with fact vs. fiction, 93, 95–97, 99, 103–4; and Twain, 92–93; and vernacular humor, 94–95, 99

Works: *American Pastoral*, 103; *The Breast*, 75, 103; *The Counterlife*, 93, 103; *The Dying Animal*, 103; *The Ghost Writer*, 93; *The Great American Novel*, 75, 93–96, 98–99, 101–4; *The Human Stain*, 103; "I Always Wanted You to Admire My Fasting," 75, 93; *I Married a Communist*, 103; *Operation Shylock*, 93, 103; *Our Gang*, 93, 101; *The Plot Against America*, 75, 94, 99, 101–4, 189; *Portnoy's Complaint*, 4, 21, 74, 93, 103
Rourke, Constance, 91

Sahl, Mort, 31
Said, Edward, 4, 98
Samanci, Özge, 142, 191, 192; amateur aesthetic, 125
Sandwich Islands. *See* Hawaii
Sarah Silverman Show, The (Silverman), 46
sarcasm, 7, 91, 173
satire: of American exceptionalism, 73–76, 91–93, 99–106; by Barry, 141–50; brand identity and, 164, 170–71; of class, 144–45; in corporate context, 164; in graphic humor, 109–11, 126–27; by McGruder, 152, 154, 156–58; by Moore, 177; political, 3–4, 37, 147–48, 171, 177; of news, 174–75; nineteenth-century, 37; by Roth, 74–75, 94, 101–5; in *The Simpsons*, 129–30, 132–38; by Twain, 23, 32, 73–74, 77–78, 83, 91–92, 105–6, 113–23, 178–79, 187; vernacular humor, 25, 91–92, 107–12, 118–20, 143–45, 179
Schulz, Charles M., *Peanuts*, 127, 154, 166
Scott, Jerry, 155
Second City, 163–65
sectionalism, 7
Seinfeld, 47, 65–67
Seinfeld, Jerry, 24, 27–28, 36, 47, 65–68
SeinLanguage (Seinfeld), 67
self: American ideology of, 8, 29, 69, 124; authentic vs. performed, 24, 28–29, 31–32, 35–37, 40, 45, 66; as brand, 29, 34, 46, 58, 66, 69, 182; invented, 34–35, 42; modern conception of, 3, 24, 33, 35, 37, 62, 179; on-stage vs. off-stage, 39, 59; performance of, 24, 28–29, 42, 54, 56–57, 59, 61–66, 68–69; theories of, 37, 45, 54, 179, 185
self-deprecation, 20, 32, 37–38, 47, 51, 53–54, 121, 143
self-made American, 34, 69
self-made man, 29, 34
self-mockery, 36, 43, 49, 54, 56, 147
self-reflexivity, 16, 56, 182
Sicko (Moore), 177
signifying, 153
Silverman, Sarah, 46
similarity gestalt, 138–40, 149
Simpsons, The, 25, 109, 127–32, **133**, 134–40, 157, 166–67, 171, 192
Simpson's Movie, The, 139
sitcoms. *See* situation comedy
situation comedy, 46–47, 62, 65–67, 92, 109, 123, 128–29, 133–34, 138, 140, 155, 163, 169–70, 172, 192
"Slim Graves Show, The" (Keillor), 56
Smith, Seba, 76, 111; *My Thirty Years Out of the Senate*, 111. *See also* Downing, Jack
social construction of reality, 44
social relationships, 31
Society for Psychical Research (SPR), 44
Some American Humorists (Wilt), 93
South Park, 109, 170, 172
Spanish-American War, 7, 73, 105
Spiegelman, Art, 4, 140, 149
Spunkiad, The (Woodworth), 71
Standring, George, 86
stand-up comedy, 23–24, 28–29, 31–32, 34–35, 37, 39, 42, 44–48, 53, 58–59, 62–63, 65–69, 159, 171–72, 179
Stanley, Henry Morton, 78, 83–84, **85**, 86–90; and composition of *Connecticut Yankee*, 83–90; relationship with Twain, 83–84, 86–88, 188
Works: *The Congo and the Founding of Its Free State*, 85; *How I Found Livingstone*, 89

state. *See* nation-state
Stewart, Jon, 24, 27–28, 68, 172–75; *America (The Book)*, 27; *The Daily Show*, 4, 27–28, 171–75
Story of a Bad Boy, The (Aldrich), 21, 111
Superman, 125, 169–70

tall tales, 21, 74–75, 78, 95–97, 102, 112
Tandy, Jessica, 91
television humor: American culture and, 3, 5, 23, 109, 129, 147, 151, 153, 155, 157; branding and, 22, 25, 29, 67, 163, 165, 170, 177; on broadcast networks, 60, 129, 167, 192; on cable TV, 65, 155; and comic news, 4, 27, 174–75, 177; and Hulu, 166; stand-up comedy on, 6, 28, 50; syndication of, 166; techniques of, 173–75. *See also* Comedy Central; *Simpsons, The*; situation comedy
Theory of the Leisure Class, The (Veblen), 8
Thomas, Clarence, 147
Thurber, James, 96–97, 130
Tonight Show, The, 175
Tracey Ullman Show, 127, 130
trademarks, 9–10, 176. *See also* copyrights; intellectual property
Trudeau, Garry, 155
Trump, Donald, 176
TV Nation (Moore), 171, 175, 177–79
Twain, Mark (Samuel L. Clemens): anti-imperialist politics, 73–74, 83, 91–92; birthplace, 7; as brand, 23–24, 32, 45–46; as celebrity, **11**, 11–12, 15–17, 19, 22, 33, 159–61, 181–82; childhood, 7, 21, 112; as commodity, 8, 46; Company, 10, 22; copyright actions, 10, 12–13, 19; estate, 8; Foundation, 22; on humor, 87, 189; illustrations of, **11**, **15**; influence of, 6–7, 108, 125, 141; information economy pioneer, 6, 8–10, 12, 23, 35, 106, 159–63; in international context, 6, 12–16, 22–26, 76–77, 91, 106, 159–60, 162–63, 181–82, 188; marketing efforts, 11, 17–18, 29, 44; and modern trends, 3, 6–7, 23, 26, 35, 179; patents, 19, 26, 159, **160**, **161**, 162; performance style, 24, 30, 32–33, 36; reviews of scrapbook, 159, 161–62; reviews of writings, 22, 76–78; travels, 12, 19, 21; Ward's influence on, 3–39, 44, 184
Twain's brand: and American culture, 3, 8, 23, 26, 162, 179; development, 10–12, 35, 40, 159, 162; identity, **11**, 22, 182–83; hallmark, brand-name humor business, 159–63, 165, 179; hallmark, cross-cultural contrast of American exceptionalism, 24, 73, 93–95, 105–6; hallmark, performance of unstable self, 24, 29, 46–48, 59, 62, 65–69; hallmark, satire through ironic vernacular vision, 24–25, 108–9, 113, 125, 128–29, 138, 140–41, 149–50, 152, 154, 157–58; management, 13, 16–17, 19, 46, 160–63; recognition, 16, 19, 22, 171

Works: *1601*, 107; "The $30,000 Bequest," 8; *Adventures of Huckleberry Finn*, 7–9, 14, 16–18, 20, 22, 24–26, 34–35, 42, 73, 91, 107, 111, 113–24, 126, 129, 140, 153, 157, 179, 182–83, 187; *The Adventures of Tom Sawyer*, 8, 21, 26, 108, 111, 113–16, 118, 140; "The American Vandal Abroad," 35, 37, 39, 43; "The Celebrated Jumping Frog of Calaveras County," 12, 26, 34, 73, 184–85; "The Chronicle of Young Satan," 178; *Colonel Sellers*, 17; "Concerning the American Language," 72; *A Connecticut Yankee in King Arthur's Court*, 8, 14, 17–18, **18**, 43, 73–75, 77–78, 82–84, 86–91, 94–95, 97, 102, 105, 107, 148, 179, 187–89; "Edward Mills and George Benton: A Tale," 8; "An Encounter with an Interviewer," 16; *Extracts from Adam's Diary and Eve's Diary*, 18; "The Facts Concerning the Recent Carnival of Crime in

Connecticut," 34; *Following the Equator*, 11, 14, 16, 35, 73, 110, 159, 178; "How to Tell a Story," 124; *The Gilded Age*, 20; *Huckleberry Finn* (*see* Twain, Mark: Works: *Adventures of Huckleberry Finn*); *Innocents Abroad*, 11–12, 14, 26, 35, 43, 73, 76, 107; "Introducing Henry M. Stanley," 87–88; "Jim Smiley and His Jumping Frog" (*see* Twain, Mark: Works: "The Celebrated Jumping Frog of Calaveras County"); *King Leopold's Soliloquy*, 9, 85, 89, 91, 122, 188; "Mark Twain's Patent Scrap Book," 19, 26, 159, **160**, 160–61, **161**; *The Mysterious Stranger*, 8, 18, 178; "Only a Nigger," 122; "Our Fellow Savages of the Sandwich Islands," 30, 33, 35–37, 39, 42–43, 47, 68, 73, 83–84, 162; "Personal Habits of the Siamese Twins," 34; *Personal Recollections of Joan of Arc*, 16; *The Prince and the Pauper*, 14, 19, 34, 73; *Roughing It*, 11–12, 14, 35, 37, 39–40, 42, 73, 76; "Roughing It on the Silver Frontier," 11–12, 35, 37, 39–40, 42, 73, 76; *Sketches New and Old*, 10; "Some Thoughts on the Science of Onamism," 35; *Those Extraordinary Twins*, 34; *The Tragedy of Pudd'nhead Wilson*, 8, 14, 18, 34, 48, 73, 110, 178, 183; *A Tramp Abroad*, 9, 72; "To the Person Sitting in Darkness," 73; "A True Story, Repeated Word for Word as I Heard It," 17, 26, 73, 107, 116, 122; "Wapping Alice," 18; "What Is Man?," 8; "Whittier Birthday Speech," 40–41
Twichell, Joseph, 16
Tyler, Royall, 75, 110

U.S. culture. *See* American culture

vaudeville, 31–32, 35, 92
Veblen, Thorstein, 8

verbal vernacular. *See* vernacular humor: verbal techniques
vernacular humor: aesthetic, 25, 125, 127, 130–31, 142, 148, 150, **154**, 156–58, 179; comparison of verbal and visual styles, 25, 108–10, 124–26, 142; as deviant or artless style, 24, 117, 123–25, 131, 151, 155; epistemology, 24–25, 108, 110, 115, 128, 158, 179; ideology, 72, 78, 82, 90–92, 105, 111–12, 120, 123, 147, 179; and naïve ironies, 24–25, 96, 113–17, 121, 144, 153, 157, 175; as oppositional rhetoric, 25, 72, 107, 126, 128, 149–50, 157–58; protagonists, 22, 82, 99, 102–3, 110–11, 113, 140, 149–52; as satire, 108, 114–16, 123, 125, 137, 140, 142, 156; traditions, 21, 73–74, 88, 105, 111–12, 134, 138, 146, 151–52, 193; Twain's brand of, defined, 75–76, 90, 140; verbal techniques, 42, 83, 92, 107–10, 113–18, 120, 123–24, 152–53; visual techniques, 125–27, 130–33, **133**, 134, 136, 138, 140, 142, 149, **154**, 156–58. *See also* Barry, Lynda; *Boondocks, The*; ideology: vernacular; politics: vernacular; rhetoric: vernacular; *Simpsons, The*; Twain, Mark: Works: *Adventures of Huckleberry Finn*; vernacular language theory; vernacular vision; Yellow Kid
vernacular intellectuals, 150–51
vernacular language theory, 72, 76, 111–12, 123–24, 190–91
vernacular values, 81, 87, 95, 107, 109, 112, 123, 126, 140, 147, 157, 178, 187
vernacular vision, 24, 107–10, 115–17, 123, 125, 129, 141–42, 144, 149–50, 156–58, 179
victimization, 79–81, 84, 87
Vietnam War, 75, 101, 103–4
vision vernacular. *See* vernacular vision
visual vernacular. *See* vernacular humor: visual techniques

Wait Wait!...Don't Tell Me, 175
Walker, Nancy, 5

Wallace, David Foster, 20, 71, 120
Ward, Artemus, 33, 44, 68; "Babes in the Wood," 38–39; influence on Twain, 38–39
Watergate, 75, 95
Weaver, George Sumner, 44
Webster, Charles, 9, 83, 86, 162, 188
Webster & Co., 9, 82–83, 86, 159, 162, 188, 190
Welty, Eudora, 20
Whad'ya Know, 175
Wilt, Napier, 21, 93
Winters, Jonathan, 49
Woodworth, John, 71
Wright, William. *See* DeQuille, Dan

"Yankee Doodle," 75, 110, 187, 190
Yellow Kid (Outcault), 22, 125–27

www.ingramcontent.com/pod-product-compliance
Lightning Source LLC
Chambersburg PA
CBHW070315240426
43661CB00057B/2644